THE
TEACHING OF LANGUAGE
TO DEAF CHILDREN

BASED ON

THE NATURAL DEVELOPMENT

OF THE CHILD

BY

AGNES LACK

OXFORD UNIVERSITY PRESS

LONDON · GEOFFREY CUMBERLEGE

1955

Oxford University Press, Amen House, London E.C. 4

GLASGOW NEW YORK TORONTO MELBOURNE WELLINGTON
BOMBAY CALCUTTA MADRAS KARACHI CAPE TOWN IBADAN

Geoffrey Cumberlege, Publisher to the University

PRINTED IN GREAT BRITAIN

ACKNOWLEDGEMENTS

THIS book is written for all teachers of the deaf and deaf children with love and thanks for all the encouragement, help, and inspiration I have received from them on both sides of the Atlantic and at all times.

I should like to acknowledge in particular the debt I owe to the staff (both past and present) of the Moseley Road School for the Deaf for their practical aid and friendly encouragement; to the former Headmistress of this school, Miss I. B. Longwill, for her fostering of the adventurous in oral language; to my first Headmaster, Mr. J. O. White, formerly of the Margate School for the Deaf, for his grounding in language teaching many years ago; to Miss M. Gullen for first introducing me to the 'Rhythmic Approach to Spoken Poetry' and her interest in its adaptation; to Mr. Barrow Cadbury for his helpful encouragement, and to the late Mr. John Spalding, O.B.E., M.A., for his reading of the text and for his kindly comments.

My thanks are due to the following for permission to reprint copyright material: to Edwin Ashdown, Ltd., for 'Drift down, drift down', by Harold Simpson; to the Children's Encyclopedia for poems from 'The Children's Treasure House'; to Miss Eleanor Farjeon and Messrs. Gerald Duckworth, Ltd., for 'A Marble Arch for Heroes'; to Miss Farjeon for 'The Tide in the River'; to Mrs. Lorna Hill for 'A Child's Grace', by Edith Rutter Leatham; to the Holiday Fellowship; to Alfred Lengnick and Co., Ltd., for 'The Sandman'. I have made every effort to trace the sources of all the rhymes included, but the origins of some are obscure. If, therefore, I have omitted any from these acknowledgements, I apologize to the holders of the copyright, and assure them that no discourtesy was intended.

A. L.

LITTLEBROOK
EAST THE WATER
BIDEFORD, DEVON

CONTENTS

INTRODUCTION

SOME ASPECTS OF LANGUAGE TEACHING

T HE aim of this book is to give, as concisely and clearly as I can, an outline of teaching the English language, showing how the structure can be built up one step at a time and giving some suggestions as to method of presentation. It also suggests some ways of correlating this to other aspects of language teaching with special attention to both impression and expression by means of speech (spoken language) and composition (written language).

All who are connected with the education of the deaf child are convinced of the pre-eminent importance of spoken and written language. Indeed, it is the chief concern of the schools, for it comprises the whole field of teaching the child to understand, and to be understood, to receive language impressions from others and to express himself in spoken and written language. The task is indeed a great one, and must be approached with thought, realizing its magnitude but analysing the problem and planning the approach, so that on a firm foundation of simple things a good language structure is built up. It has often been said how difficult it is to teach language to the deaf child, but it would be well to turn round this sentence and think for a moment how difficult it is for the deaf child to learn language. We cannot take away the difficulties but we can give the child confidence in his ability to overcome them. We can make the upward steps of the ascent towards the goal of normal language within the child's capacity to take, and we can give him the exhilaration of an ascent and the joy of accomplishment; what is more, we can make him want to ascend.

I am convinced that both the daily happenings, the

experiences and the natural desires of the child must be used to teach language, whenever and wherever possible and also that a language plan must be made to lead the child happily and easily from a simple structure to a more difficult one. It must be ensured that the child has many experiences for which he requires language, and also that the experiences are really the source of language and that this language is taught, applied, and fitted into the whole language structure.

The language taught must be used and practised again and again and in as many ways as possible. Only so will it really be apprehended and retained by the child.

I think it will clarify our ideas if the various aspects of language teaching (how it is taught, used, and practised) are enumerated.

(*A*) The English lessons, teaching the language principles or framework.

The method may be either incidental or planned language teaching, or a combination of both, both spoken and written.

(*B*) The use and practice of the above.

These definite language lessons are a small part of the wider subject of language teaching.

1. How the child receives language impressions.
   (*a*) Conversation, news giving and talk on expeditions and daily or unusual happenings by:
      i. Teacher.
      ii. Other staff.
      iii. Head teacher (assembly, news, praise, reprimand).
      iv. People at home and met in child's environment.
      v. Other pupils.
   (*b*) Story telling or reading of stories or poems by teacher to child.

(c) Dictation and lip-reading lessons.

(d) Assembly—taking of prayers and hymns by head teacher or teacher in charge.

(e) Reading.

(f) Written form of (a) above given by the people enumerated.

(g) Use of an English book (older pupils only).

(h) Written notices at school and outside.

(i) The captions of cinema and film-strip pictures.

(j) Receiving letters from home.

2. How the child expresses himself.

(a) Oral exercises and conversation by the child to:
   i. Teacher.
   ii. Other staff.
   iii. Head teacher.
   iv. People at home and met in child's environment.
   v. Other pupils.

(b) Dramatization interpretation in mime, &c.—

(c) Speech in action.

(d) Rhythmic and choral speech.

(e) Stories given by teacher with interpolations by child.

(f) Saying prayers and hymns at assembly.

(g) Games involving language forms both written and spoken.

(h) Written exercises to any of the above.

(i) Composition including diary writing.

(j) Interpretation in drawing, &c.

All these things must dovetail into each other and help each other.

So often these parts of one whole seem to be divorced from each other. Conversation, speech training, stories, and reading matter are often too difficult with relation to the language development of the child, and the composition often requires language forms which have never been taught. We jump too many steps and too often, and the result is that the child is unsure. He becomes diffident and later despondent. He will not attempt new things and he has no joy or confidence in his ability.

We cannot expect a child to love reading if the matter is always too difficult for him, nor to speak if too much is expected, nor to use language if we insist on stilted sentences no normal child would ever use.

The work should be so planned so that all these things practise both what the child already knows and the new work that is being taught. In this way the pupils gain amazingly in poise, confidence, and attainments.

It is essential then to have clearly in mind not only language correlation but also the language outline. It is of great importance that every teacher of the deaf whether of primary, intermediate, or senior children should have a clear idea of the whole scheme in use in the school. It is not enough to be able to teach one level. He should know how the children have been taught before they reach his class, and not only what he should teach, but why, and what is to follow. There should be no isolationism in a school for the deaf. It is not fair to the deaf child who has so much to learn in such a little time. For the child's sake each teacher should pool his resources and discipline himself to fit in with the whole. The teacher should be able to spot not only the child's weaknesses in language but just where he has gone wrong. Only in this way will he be able to correct and cure these weaknesses.

Having then studied the language outline, and found where his pupils fit in the scheme, the teacher should not be afraid to experiment in different ways of teaching the same thing, of using the plan of correlation, and using the natural instincts of the age of the pupil. The work should be thought out and activity directed to the end at which the teacher is aiming. It must be remembered that the pupils must practise. The teacher who can think up the happiest and most enjoyable ways of practising the same thing, who has many different ways of presenting the same lesson, is the one who will get results in all subjects and whose class will be alive, happy, and progressing—i.e. the teacher who can find the happiest and most enjoyable ways not of filling in the time but of practising and learning a definite thing.

In each part of this book I am including suggestions of different ways of practising the language taught. These suggestions are by no means exhaustive. There are many more ways, and the ones invented by the teacher himself or the adaptation of those given may be of greater value to his own teaching than ways suggested by other people.

Let us experiment, vary, improvise, plan, and use anything which we think may help, not for the sake of the methods themselves but for the realization of our goal, the acquisition of language by the pupil.

WRITTEN AND SPOKEN LANGUAGE

Throughout the introductory talk on the teaching of language you will note that the matter is presented and the practice is given in two ways—by spoken language, by written language.

If you will examine the aspects of language teaching enumerated in the Introduction you will note this very clearly. Taking impressions first, we find that (B) (i), (a) to (d) are spoken forms of language, while (e) to (j) are written forms. Again, in the list of language expression,

(*B*) (ii), (*a*) to (*f*) are spoken forms, (*g*) comprises both spoken and written forms, and (*h*) to (*j*) are written forms. The language lessons themselves comprise both spoken and written language.

It is essential that both these parts of a whole should be present in the teaching of language. Writing for and by the pupil to make definite and sure the impression made by lip-reading alone or by lip-reading and partial hearing, and speech to and by the pupil to make the whole thing come alive. To teach language while neglecting the understanding of spoken language by lip-reading and its expression and practice by the use of speech, is a one-sided and lifeless thing. To speak language gives it life and purpose.

At the end of each language section in this book, you will find a subsection on composition and another on speech which focus attention on these two aspects, written and spoken language.

It follows that the media for receiving impressions of spoken language, i.e. lip-reading and hearing, should be as easily used, as efficient, as definite, and as clear as we can possibly make them; just as the reading of written language by the child should be as efficient as we can make it, and the writing and printing used should be clear and easy to read.

It also follows that the media for expression by the pupil of written language, i.e. writing and printing, should be clear, easy to read, speedy, legible, and pleasing as possible; just as the medium for the expression of spoken language, speech, should be clear, easy to produce, speedy, intelligible, and pleasant as possible.

The teaching of the actual mechanics of speech to deaf children is of such difficulty that it has tended to obscure the scope and size of the problem—that of teaching the child first to understand spoken language and second to express himself in spoken language. The first part of the problem comprises learning the names of things and sentence construction as it is lip-read only or partially heard and lip-read by the deaf pupil, and the second part comprises learning what to say (spoken language) and how to say it (the mechanics of speech).

This book does not deal with the teaching of the mechanics of speech, a wide, difficult, and fascinating subject. It presupposes that the pupil has been through this stage and can say and lip-read simple words. All teachers of the deaf know that this is but entering the wicket-gate on the child's progress to the goal of normal spoken language. There is a long road ahead, both as regards what to say, and how to say it, and there is a great need for practice in speech in as many ways as possible and as often as possible. This speech practice should be graded in difficulty from the simple to the complex, both as regards its utterance and its meaning. The purpose of the speech sections in this book is to show how a dual purpose can be achieved; how language teaching can help speech and speech-teaching language.

It first suggests material for speech practice which would

1. be suitable to the language development of the pupil;
2. be suitable to the average age of the pupil and at the same time to his interests and natural impulses;
3. definitely help the pupil in the practice of language principles by means of spoken language;
4. give practice in speech of graded difficulty;
5. present, practice, and preserve correct speech and so prevent the rise of incorrect speech;
6. foster facility and naturalness of speech.

It presupposes that each lesson is given to the pupil both

orally and by writing and that it is clinched by expecting reproduction of the lesson from the pupil both orally and by him writing.

A child with normal hearing begins to speak by saying one-word sentences; he goes on to phrases, and later to very simple sentences. He acquires mastery of speech during this development, slowly and happily. A deaf child is older when he begins this process, but he should go through the same stages as the normal child, with a great deal of practice in each stage. In this way his speech development will be a happy and natural thing.

What I said as regards language progress, i.e. that we can give the child the joy of accomplishing a difficult task, is true also of speech teaching. It should be so graded, that although the pupil has to put forth effort, too much is not required of him too soon, that, instead of despondency and self-consciousness in speech, we shall find self-confidence and spontaneity. It is most unwise to make haste too quickly and to try to skip stages in a deaf child's speech development. Over-anxiety on the part of teachers of the deaf has sometimes spoilt good speech taught in the nursery. Let us forget the age of the children from this point of view and concentrate on their language development. The speech sections of this work are an attempt to solve the problem and at the same time to make of the speech lessons a happy, jolly thing by catering for the interests of its age group.

I am not minimizing the work to the teacher, but I am suggesting that the practice which brings facility and naturalness can be a happy thing for the child.

Throughout I am presupposing that every child has a hearing aid and that even the very severely deaf child uses one. The effect on the naturalness of speech and the awareness of sound to such a child is incalculable. Its use will not solve speech problems but will help the skilled teacher to do so.

Let me emphasize that with speech teaching as with language teaching a fostering of a feeling of self-confidence is of the utmost importance. The child must feel that he can cope with the situation. Here the teacher must combine encouragement of any real effort with an insistence that the child works towards the goal of correct speech.

Under the section for the backward deaf pupil I have included some suggestions on the correction of common faults of speech. These can be adapted by the teacher to difficulties experienced by children of any age. My chief purpose, however, is to show how systematic and graded teaching can avoid these mistakes. I hope so much that it will help to do so.

JUNIOR AND INTERMEDIATE STAGES

INTRODUCTION

WHEN considering where to begin and how to progress in teaching the English language to deaf children there are two factors to be considered—the natural instincts of the child and the range of his interest.

The young child has, at first, a limited area of interest. He is interested in himself and the things which concern his bodily needs, food, clothing, hygiene, washing, &c., and his social needs, security, love, and trust. The people in his orbit are interesting as they supply these needs. The young child likes doing things, running, skipping, jumping, and making things move by pushing, pulling, building, knocking down, throwing, sorting, &c. He begins to play with, other children and to like doing things with them.

Therefore teaching of these little ones should start from themselves—to the names of people around them who attend to their needs, to things around them, things they play with, and actions they do.

This is the nursery stage where vocabulary and actions should be taught, where the bodily and social needs of the child should be catered for, and where plenty of space and apparatus should be provided to satisfy their desires to move and cause other things to move.

Second, the interests expand to embrace other people, beginning with their own immediate circle of family and class. They are interested in their own possessions, their

B

family's possessions, and those of the other children in the class.

They are interested in how these people behave, what they do, and what they like or dislike.

They are interested in things out of doors, flowers, grass, colour, animals, and especially all young or small animals.

They are very active and want to try and to handle all the things they see. They like to imitate everything they see other people do and be. They want to draw attention to what people are doing or to tell what they did.

Therefore we must give them the language to express their interests and desires and their language teaching should include: the past tense (what they and their circle did), to have (possessions) some qualities of kind and colour in relation to people, animals, and objects in and out of doors, the present participle (what they saw someone doing), an easy version of the present progressive tense (what someone else is doing), and 'to like' with relation to food and activities.

Their desire to do all that other children do, to copy their parents and older children's actions in their play, their love of movement, of trying things out, and of handling things must be utilized to the full in teaching these language forms.

These two development phases are included in Stage 1 of this book. Although it is presumed that the preliminary work of the nursery should have been taught before this, it revises these interests before going on to the second step.

These interests widen to include what they and other people have seen and done, in other places at other times at first confined to their own circle. They are interested in where other people and animals live, in what things are made of, and in what they and other people can or cannot do.

They love to look forward to events which are going to happen as well as to re-enact those which have happened. They love to go and see things and places (the farm-animals at the zoo, &c.). They are interested in their class-mates and want to know why they are absent, what is the matter with them, or where they have gone. They are interested in their physical powers and what they can do. They want to do things, to see things, to know about things, to imitate, to re-enact, to use their physical powers to play with other children.

The language of Stage 2 of this book tries to cater for these interests and includes:

1. more work on the past tense and the present pro-gressive tense—acting specific events. Telling about events and expectations;
2. the beginning of the present perfect tense (telling where they have been and what they have seen);
3. the use of the verb 'to live' in the habitual tense;
4. what things are made of;
5. what they and other people can or cannot do;
6. the use of the future tense in looking forward to events.

The teaching throughout this stage should use the natural instincts and desires of the child in its manner of presentation of the language structures.

By the end of the junior stage normal children are interested in everything. They want to know what . . ., how . . ., why . . ., when . . ., where . . ., what for. . .? How to do things, what they are made of, how they work. It is the collecting age, the experimenting age, the age when all the world and all its wonders are opening out and when they are ready for anything. They are very active, throwing themselves into all physical movements, games, dramatizing, dancing, working with joyful abandon. They have none of the shyness and diffidence of adolescence and you can make them like anything, learn anything, and work them as hard as possible and they will still tire you out and be ready for mischief at the end. This is when we should pour in as much language, oral and written, as possible. We must use all these natural bents and take this wonderful opportunity.

Stage 3 should then cater for the child's inquiring mind, giving him facts about the world around and of how things and people work. It should, in method of presentation, cater also for the child's love of physical activity and dramatization. We should teach him the question forms which will help him find out for himself, and we should practice these things in dramatic interludes, rhythmic movement, and games.

You will notice that most of these facts and questions are couched in the habitual tense, so this is the concentration at the beginning of this period and there are many examples of its use, e.g. where things come from, where they grow, what people do, what shopkeepers sell, what things cost, where animals live (at home and abroad), what natural things do (the river flows, &c.), what you do things with, how you do things (first I do this, then I do that), at what time you do things daily, how you spell.

In this stage should also be included the consequences of certain actions (if you do that . . . this will happen) and the purpose of certain actions using the infinitive (I went to town to buy a new suit).

There should be much practice in phrase work; in answer to the question Where . . .? the pupil should say the whole phrase—'to the sea' never 'the sea' or 'to'.

Contrasts and opposites and superlatives begin (*a*) the

comparison of one thing with another and (*b*) compound sentences with 'and' and 'but'.

The adverbial clause is introduced with 'when', using the tenses already taught with the addition of the past continuous tense.

We are trying to teach the children to think, to wonder, and to be aware of the wonderful world around them and to ask questions about all these things. The speech composition and reading should illustrate and practise this.

Arising out of this is the next stage—the intermediate (Stage 4 of this book), where the foundation of the complex and compound language of books is laid, where the boy or girl is beginning to wonder not only how but why, and not only about things but actions. Seize on this imaginative stage and use it. Drama, stories, games, poetry, and rhythmic movement have a very great appeal here.

The language given should include the expression of thoughts about:

A. *The Future*

1. He states what he would like to do, to see, to be, at a certain time in the future (using adverbial phrase or clause).

2. He is concerned with wondering, knowing, feeling sure, feeling doubtful, hoping, wishing about things which are going to or may happen (using noun clauses).

3. He speculates what he would do in certain circumstances (if something happened I should do . . .), conditional clause.

B. *The past*

1. What he used to do when . . . (adverbial clause of time).

What he remembers doing when ... (adverbial clause of time).

What he thought when ... (adverbial clause of time).

What he was doing when or while . . . (adverbial clause of time).

2. What someone told him or asked him (noun clause).
3. What he read, saw or heard (noun clause or participle).

C. *The present*

1. What he enjoys doing, dislikes doing.
2. What he may or may not do, what he is made to do, what he has to do.
3. What it is right to do, wrong to do.
4. What one person is doing while another is doing.
5. He apologizes for and explains his actions.
6. He finds out what things are used for, and how they compare in weight, height, and age.

You will see that the work of this stage lays the foundation of noun, adverbial, and adjectival clause usages, and points out the interdependence of the tense in the subordinate clause on the tense on the main clause.

The aim throughout should be the stimulation of thought and the expression of thought in language. Considered and imaginative replies to questions are expected.

Here imaginative and adventure stories come into their own, told in simple language, whether of witches, giants, princes or princesses, or of journeys in space-ships to the moon.

It is possible here to use an English book (as one of the methods of gaining impressions and of expressions of which I have spoken). During the work of this stage you would find the *Oxford Reader for Africa*, Book III (a combined reading and study book) very useful. I shall say a little more about this series when dealing with the senior work (Stages 5, 6, and 7 of this book).

This is a most important section of the work for, as I have said, it lays the foundation of the complex and complicated language of books.

If you get this framework of language laid before the child is adolescent, you need not fear for the future development of language in your pupils.

LANGUAGE

IN this first stage the work has necessarily been divided into 'lessons' for the sake of convenience and clarity in setting out the vocabulary and language forms to be taught. Most of the simple language necessary for the child to express his wants, his doings, and his feelings have been included.

It is good for the teacher of young children to have this plan in mind, but this does not mean that all of one lesson should be taught before going on to the next. She will probably need to use the language of several lessons simultaneously. She must study the natural instincts of the age of child she is teaching and the special interests of the individual child, and use these in her teaching. This will affect both *when* and *how* she teaches. I have tried to bear this in mind in these suggestions as to *what* you should teach first, but do not hesitate to teach more or less than this as the occasion and the child warrant.

Remember that the prime necessity of the young deaf child—as distinct from the child with normal hearing, is to learn to communicate freely with the people around him, first to express his own feelings and wants, and secondly to understand what others want of him. It is this lack of communication, more than anything else, which causes the frustrations and the tragedies of the deaf child's emotional life. It is the duty of every teacher of the deaf to teach the children in her charge the normal means of communication with the world around (i.e. words and sentences, lip-read, spoken, read, and written) as quickly as possible. Do get a sense of urgency here, and teach, teach, teach language.

This means that you should always be on the alert to teach new words and language forms as occasion arises. You must create happenings where suitable language is needed. You must promote activity both of mind and body. You must encourage self-confidence, self-reliance, and an inquiring mind. Remember that the deaf child has learnt to accept much that he only half understands and therein lies a danger for his future intellectual life. Teach him to understand what goes on around him and he will want to understand more.

Teach him also with thoroughness. Insist on the child's putting forth an effort to remember correctly what he is taught. Give plenty of practice in as many ways as possible. Have fun, laughter, and games which teach language. I have suggested a few in my notes on the lessons. From the beginning try to get both the written and the spoken form of sounds, words, phrases, and sentences correct and clearly classified in the child's mind.

You cannot expect clear thinking and expression from a child if your teaching and blackboard work is muddled and haphazard. Practise your blackboard writing so that it is clear and well formed and plan the position of your blackboard work. New verbs should go in a particular place—new nouns, new names of people, all under headings. At the end of each session these should be transferred to their appropriate box or compartment. (See details of lessons for more about this.)

One of the chief causes of backwardness is lack of clarity in teaching. If the child is sure of what he knows, and can classify his vocabulary, you have laid a good language foundation. On it both the brighter and slower child can build to the best of their ability.

When you start the scheme your children will probably have learnt to lip-read, say, and read some words. Begin with these first, adding one or two new ones, and see that these are thoroughly learnt.

It is very important in teaching to give the child a feeling of confidence—not by smoothing away or avoiding difficulties—but by presenting them in easy stages so that the child gets confidence in his ability to learn and to conquer difficulties.

A great deal of the earlier language is taught either incidentally or by means of diary or calendar work. This is most important and should be taken without fail every day. It should comprise greetings—calendar work—changing the name of the day—changing the weather picture. The names of the treasures the children have brought into school should be given. This should not occupy all told more than a quarter of an hour. Do *not* have the whole class either standing or sitting round you for more time than this. It is better for them to concentrate well for ten minutes even than to learn to fritter away time waiting for the attention of the teacher while he or she is attending to one child only. Let them disperse to various activities and let the teacher take groups of children, three or four at most, whose attainments are on a level as far as possible. Then can be given to each child his own particular language and that of his group if desired. 'I have a ball, . . . has a train'. Each group will disperse in turn to draw, build up with cards, or write the language concerned.

Try to work quickly and thoroughly. You will do so if you have small groups and if you teach the children to come and go promptly.

Later in the day should come the varied activities and games by which you mean to clinch the individual language given. Correlate the work as much as possible. If the children have brought eatables to school or if a birthday party is imminent, then is the time for 'I like'—and an addition of more eatables to the vocabulary. Then is the time too for a jingle in Rhythm Speech 'I like' (see Speech section) and the time for revision of (3), (4), and (5) in the speech lesson (See Lesson 8). And so partly led by the children's natural wishes and partly by the teacher's forethought, toys, animals, people, food, feelings, actions, colours, and numbers are talked about and the appropriate language learnt. 'I have, he has', 'I like, he likes', 'I am, he is'.

The incidental language of the classroom is very important:

> Tell . . . to come to me. Go to Miss . . . . I'm sorry.
> May I have . . .? I have no chalk. Where have you
>   been?
> I've been to . . . . Get the . . . book from the cup-
>   board, &c.

There is a list of probable and suitable language of this kind at the end of this chapter.

You will notice that almost every lesson may be divided into two parts, one of greater difficulty than the other. In almost all classes for deaf children there are pupils of varying degrees of intelligence and language backgrounds. I have advocated previously the breaking up of the classes into groups. If the brighter group is given the more difficult section in addition to the easier one, both groups will be able to go on to the new work together. At the end of the period the slower children should revise by taking the more difficult section of the known work and the brighter ones go on to the higher section. In this way, as far as is humanly possible, the teacher will be giving the best possible opportunity for learning to both the bright and the slower children. They will all (even the slow children) have a chance to succeed, which is most important, and yet the brighter child will be given the material for his full development, which is just as important.

Note on the definite and indefinite article

There should be no attempt to differentiate to the children between the use of a . . . and the . . ., but preparation for correct usage can be made by the teacher's care to use 'a' or 'the' correctly herself from the beginning, e.g. 'run to a window [if there is more than one], show me the doll's house, go to the slide, go to the playground, bring me a pencil, have you a pencil? John has a ball, &c.' The children will naturally do as the teacher does and the beginnings of correct usage will be laid. This is all that can be attempted in Stage I.

Exclamations and colloquial language likely to be needed at this stage

Oh!	I'm sorry	Hullo!
Oh dear!	Please move	Goodbye
How lovely!	May I have . . .?	Good morning
Please	May I go . . .?	Good night
Thank you	May I look . . .?	Good afternoon
Yes. No	Excuse me	How are you?
Yes, please	More, please	How do you do?
No, thank you	(May I have	Very well, thank
It is time for	more, please?)	you
It is playtime	No more, thank	I have no . . . .
It is time to stop	you	
The sun is shining	Go to	
It is warm	Come to me	
It is cold	Tell A to come to	
It is raining	me	

The days of the week should be recognized

Where?	to school	upstairs	to town
	at home	downstairs	to Grandma's
	away	outside	
How?	by bus	on the bus	in the car
With whom?		with Daddy	with Mummy, &c.

A SUMMARY OF THE LESSONS IN STAGE I

Lesson 1. Simple commands and vocabulary of things in the room.

2. The verbs 'to have' with vocabulary of toys, clothes, and possessions. Pronouns 'I', 'you', 'we', 'they'.

3. The verb 'to have' with vocabulary of parts of body, tools. Names of children and numbers one to ten. Pronouns 'he', 'she', 'it'.

4. More verbs and vocabulary of things used in classroom. Past indefinite and present continuous tenses (one word only). Possessive pronouns 'my', 'your', 'our'.

5. More verbs and vocabulary of parts of body, clothes, and things used in washing and dressing. Past indefinite and present continuous tenses. Possessive pronouns 'his', 'her'.

6. The verb 'to be' with vocabulary of people, animals, and adjectives.

7. Past tense and present continuous tense (participle only) with vocabulary of more verbs, and common objects. Series of actions.

8. The verb 'to like' with vocabulary of food and meals.

9. The verb 'to like' with vocabulary of lessons and games.

10. Colours with vocabulary of things seen out of doors.

ADDITIONAL QUESTIONS

Key words to questions

What?	Who?	How many?
What colour?	What kind of?	What did . . . do?
		What . . . doing?

Preparatory and incidental only

Where . . .?	When . . .?	
What . . .?	**Who?**	
What have you?	Who did that?	
What is that?	Who has . . .?	
or	Who likes . . .?	
What's that?	Who is . . .?	
Have you . . .?	Are you . . .?	Do you like . . .?
Has he . . .?	Is she . . .?	Does . . . like . . .?

Incidental work

How do you come to school?	What is your name?
How old are you?	Where is . . .?
How are you?	When did we go . . .?
	When shall we go . . .?

Which $\begin{cases} \text{colour} \\ \text{lesson} \\ \text{food} \end{cases}$ do you like best?   May I?

LESSON 1

Simple commands and vocabulary of things in the room

Actions

Do

run	come	lie	point
walk	go	fall down	open
hop	stand	skip	shut
jump	sit	play	look

Vocabulary of nouns

Show me—What?

door	table	desk	barrow
chair	window	doll's house	pram
wall	cupboard	slide	rocking-horse
floor	blackboard	sand-tray	

Names of children in class

Who? I and you.

Combinations of the above

John run to the rocking horse.
Mary hop to the slide, &c.
Open the door, &c.

Incidental language as needed by the child

I fell down, &c.
Look! . . . jumping.
      . . . walking.

Questions

What's that? the door, a chair.
Who's that? John, &c.

Notes

Commands and nouns

These commands and words may appear hackneyed to
you, but remember that they are not so to the child. They
express the thing he can do and enjoys doing and names
the thing he can see, touch, or move. He enjoys the actions
as a class activity, and as an activity in the playground.
Teach the children to be alert and quick to respond. In
teaching the nouns give plenty of movement too. Do not
worry if not all the children are lip-reading at first. Those
who are not sure will gain confidence from following the
others for a time. Notice, however, those who are really
lip-reading and put them in a group together. Teach them
to take the teacher's place with their own group. You will
find that others in the second group emerge as leaders.

Give flash-cards of the same actions and nouns and in the case of the children who are ready for this, let them copy the words and draw the objects or actions on black-boards or with thick coloured pencils. Use pictures and models of these things too, for lip-reading and matching with flash-cards. Be sure that your pictures are bright, clear, and obviously pictures of the objects or actions. It is worth while being exact and careful over these things from the beginning. You are laying the foundation stone of accuracy and clear thinking and, what is essential for a deaf child, self-confidence. Even when you think the children are sure, keep on running through these things every day. Always give the children something they *can* do every day. Then the new work will not loom so large or sap the confidence you are so carefully building up. Try to make the work happy and jolly, but expect effort.

The combination of the actions and nouns in 'run to the doll's house', &c., is also greatly enjoyed and can be taken by the first group, first of all by lip-reading, and then by flash-cards. The children will soon read them if your early work has been well and truly done, and they will prob-ably play games spontaneously, taking the place of the teacher, both with lip-reading and with the flash-cards. If this is not spontaneous, lend the idea a helping hand and play with the children.

Many will try to put in 'to the' as two short unaccented syllables just as you say it. Clinch this in the speech lesson (see special section).

You will notice that the lip-reading of 'show me the door, the doll's house, &c.' comes first. This should be the first impression. Follow this with teaching the children to say it correctly. This gives them also a tactile impression. At the same time link it with the written form so that the child can read it both in speech and by sight silently. Here are two more impressions. These impressions are at all times given with the object itself or a good picture definitely linked. The next step is to visualize the object from the lip-reading and the written form, and after this to say 'What's that?' And for the child to answer, 'The door' and find the written form. Last of all to write the written form from memory correctly. Practise all of these steps and teach the child early to ask, 'What's that?' You are beginning to cultivate an inquiring mind.

It is well always to bear in mind that children are different. A commonplace, you say, but do we really believe this? I believe strongly that as a general rule lip-reading should come first. But I taught one child to whom lip-reading was nothing until he had been taught to say and read the word phonetically. I mention this case to emphasize my point that lip-reading should be reinforced by the spoken word and the written form as *impressions*. The speech as expression comes later—but the very fact of saying the word is a valuable impression. Do not discourage the child by using speech only as expression, i.e. in expecting the final stage, 'What's that?', too soon. Give much practice in speaking as an impression also, and make this speaking a happy thing.

The incidental language suggested should not be forced. If an opportunity or a desire arises, teach it. The children must all too soon be introduced to the problem of tenses. Which shall we take first? How can we present this difficulty in easy stages and yet give them what they need for self-expression?

I suggest that the flash-cards should have the simple command written on one side in one colour and on the back in a different colour should be the past tense written as needed in the child's work, e.g. on one side, 'fall down': on the other, 'I fell down' or 'Who? fell down'. Or one side, 'open the door': on the other, 'I opened the door', or 'Who? opened the door'. If you are meticulous about the use of these cards, the children will soon realize that when the teacher or the child is giving a command, the first side is used and that when anyone wants to indicate what was done then the other side is used. The calendar work calls for this second side and so does the incidental work from day to day.

Again, if the children are pointing out an action as they sometimes do, give them the present participle without hesitation and keep a separate box and colour for this. Of course, do not use 'am', 'is', or 'are', but gradually introduce 'I'm', 'John's'. (See note under Lessons 4 and 5, also 7.)

From the beginning keep separate boxes, compartments, or folders labelled conspicuously 'Who?', 'Do', 'What?'

Let the children sort them into appropriate headings. Play games with them, at first asking for a card from each heading and later play without the cards. You can extend this to 'doing' and 'did' later.

LESSON 2

The verb 'to have' and vocabulary of toys, clothes, and possessions. Pronouns 'I', 'you', 'we', 'they'

Vocabulary

What?

1. **Toys**	2. **Clothes**	3. **Verbs** (Do)
train	cap	play with
boat	hat	fetch
bag	jersey	bring

aeroplane	coat	get
car	frock	
bus, &c.		
horse		

(Children's own possessions and those provided in school)

Pronouns

I, you, we, they—Who?

Language

I have	I have not	I haven't
You have	You have not	You haven't
We have	We have not	We haven't
They have	They have not	They haven't

What have you? *or* What have you got?

Have you . . .?   (Yes, I have)
                          (No, I have not/haven't)

or

Have you got . . .?

The verb 'to have', or 'to have got'.
'To have got' is in almost universal use and it is well to take it as an alternative here.

LESSON 3

The verb 'to have' with vocabulary of parts of body, tools, names of children, and numbers one to ten. Pronouns 'he', 'she', 'it'

Vocabulary

1. **Parts of body**	2. **Tools**	3. **Names**
eye	pencil	Who?
ear	pen	Children in classroom

arm	chalk	Some teachers
nose	book	Mother *or* Mummy
mouth	ruler	Daddy
foot	rubber	

Pronouns

He, she, it.

Numbers to 10

Names and figures

Language

1. He has   John has . . .
   She has
   It has
2. What has . . .?   Who has got . . .? *or*
   Has he . . .?   Who has . . .?
   Has she . . .?   How many . . . have you? *or*
                                     have you got?
3. Addition of 's' for plural.
4. What is your name?
   How old are you?
5. One book or a book.
   Two books, &c.
   A foot—two feet.
   A tooth—teeth.

Notes on Lessons 2 and 3

The children always enjoy these lessons, concerned as they
are with their own possessions, their family's possessions,
toys, and things to do things with and play with. There is
no particular difficulty in teaching. It is good to take 'I'and
'you' first. Seize opportunities of teaching 'we' and 'they'
when identical things are brought to school by two or

more children. The calendar work should provide many examples of their use and the teacher should manufacture more. Dramatization helps here. Be sure that the children do not confuse 'you' and 'they'. The child should turn towards the person addressed as 'you' and away from those referred to as 'they'. The use of 'has' is best begun with the name of the child or teacher concerned. 'He' or 'she' should follow this. Take one difficulty at a time and introduce not only dramatization, but games, and speech jingles to help.

A game the children enjoy in the first stage is for the teacher to bring forward a tray of known objects. The teacher closes her eyes while each child takes one and puts it behind her back. Before opening her eyes the teacher says, 'Are you ready?' The children soon learn what this means and answer 'Yes' or 'No' correctly. The teacher says to one child, 'Have you the . . .?' The child (in the first stage) answers, 'Yes' or 'No'. If 'Yes', he produces it from behind his back. If 'No', the teacher goes on to the next child. In the later stage the answers should be 'Yes, I have', 'No, I haven't'. When she has found out where all the objects are she says, 'Tell me what you have' (or 'have got' if you prefer it). In the first stage the child says 'the ball', &c., later, 'I have the ball', &c.

The children will soon want to play this game themselves. It is good then to split up into groups, say four in each, and let them take the part of the teacher in turn. Insist on correct speech here, practice in the special speech lesson. Take the easy stage first. While this group work is taking place, the teacher has a chance to help the shyer or duller group. Insist that all have equal chances of taking the leading part. Do not, as a rule, play this with the children's own belongings. It might lead to a confusion as to ownership.

A variation of this game brings in the word 'Who?' As before each child takes an object while the teacher's eyes are closed. When they are ready she opens them and says, 'Who has the *ball*?' The one who has holds up the article, saying, 'I have'. This is the first stage. Later, after going all round in this way the teacher says to the class, 'Who has the ball?' They answer, 'John has'. (John answers again, 'I have'.)

A similar game can be played with numbers. Be sure to think out carefully the stages, first answering in the name of the number only. '*How many* balls have you?' 'Three', *not* 'Three balls'. (Would you answer in this way to an inquirer?) Think out the normal way a child answers and do not expect more from a little deaf child. Play this again using 'Who?' 'Who has five counters?' 'Who has four counters?' 'I have', 'John has'.

Later, *much* later, 'Tell me about John, what has he?' 'He has three balls.'

Devise as many ways as possible of practising the use of each new language form you teach. Use it in their calendar work, incidental work, games, dramatizations, speech work, drawings; as I have said before, the teacher who can invent the greatest number of ways of practising the same thing will get results. Practise is necessary, only by practice and constant repetitions will the child gain confidence in his knowledge. But the only practice worth while is that where the interest is aroused, for then the mind is concentrated and the memory stimulated.

LESSON 4

More verbs and vocabulary of things used in classroom. Past indefinite and present con-

tinuous tenses (one word only). Possessive pronouns, 'my', 'your', 'our'

Vocabulary

1. Verbs

write	show	bring
read	fetch	thread
draw	sew	look at
cook	cry	laugh

2. Things in classroom

beads	comic	letter
box	picture	puzzle
doll's bed	paper	clock

Possessive pronouns

my, your, our.

Language

1. What did he do? ran, wrote, drew.
2. What are you doing? . . . ing.
   Leading to I'm, he's . . . ing (not at first).
3. Look at . . . writing.
   Look at . . . reading.

LESSON 5

More verbs and vocabulary of parts of body,
clothes, and things used in washing and dressing. Past indefinite and present continuous
tenses (one word only). Possessive pronouns,
'his', 'her'

Vocabulary

1. Verbs connected with hygiene, washing, dressing, and household duties.

    e.g. wash, put on, do up, clean, sweep, mop, &c.
2. Parts of body connected with 1.

    e.g. hair, neck, teeth, &c.
3. Clothes connected with 1.

    e.g. shoes, buttons, gloves, &c.
4. Things used in washing and dressing.

    e.g. soap, towel, &c.

Language: continue present continuous and past indefinite

What are you doing? Washing my hands.
Introduce 'What did ... do? Washed my hands, &c.'

Possessive pronouns

his, her.

Further work

Lessons in personal hygiene and in social behaviour, dressing oneself, helping mother should be given.

Speech. Refrain of 'What shall we do for mother?'

       ,,   ,, 'Here we go round the Mulberry Bush'.

Note on the use of the modified form of the present continuous tense

I have been struck by the great number of times in a day the normal-hearing little child says 'What's that?, What's he/she/it doing?' It comes before 'Why?', at least in my observation.

Therefore, although the present progressive has difficulties for the deaf child I have included it in this early

work in a modified form, i.e. the present participle given
in answer to the question, 'What is . . . doing?' Later the
child can be taught, as the hearing one does, to say, 'The
man's running. I'm jumping.' How often does the mother
say, 'Look at the . . . ing'. So should the teacher of deaf
children say, 'Look at . . . running. Look at . . . laughing.
I saw you playing. I saw you jumping in the playground.'
Do not work at this laboriously but treat it lightly, introducing it orally and with descriptions of pictures. 'I can
see a tree, the sun, flowers. I can see a boy running. I can
see a cow eating, &c.'

This makes for the use of more normal language than a
slavish sticking to the past tense. In this form it can be
introduced very early.

Encourage the use of the participle in diary work.

Notes on Lessons 4 and 5

Think of these lessons, not as difficult lessons on verbs, but
as action lessons, as opportunities for the child to use his
desire to act and mime. The first stage in these lessons on
verbs is, as I have pointed out in Lesson 1, learning to lip-
read, say, read, and do the action.

The children love these action lessons if they take an
active part in them. The children by this time should,
through their calendar work and class lessons together, be
getting an idea of tense, i.e. that when they are telling you
about a happening they use the past tense, when they are
pointing out an action or doing an action they use the
present participle (beginning now to couple 'I'm' and
'he's' with this) and that when they are giving a command
they use the simple form of the verb. If you are logical and
consistent in your own use of these, although they will
make mistakes, they will have some idea of what their

mistakes are, and by using the labelled boxes, be able to correct them. The present perfect should be given in individual work in such sentences as 'I have brought some flowers, Where have you been?, I've been to . . ., John has gone to the Clinic.' These sentences prepare for its use at a later date. You are not dealing with this at the moment.

To give an example of a class lesson at this stage, have a chart ready with slots into which can be fitted the cards with the present participles written on. Head it with the card 'Doing'. Let each child choose a card, then the articles she needs for the dramatization. These should be readily available in the apparatus cupboard and should be simple, e.g. a book, some paper, a box, a ball, a pencil, a pastry board and bowl, some patty pans, a puzzle, beads, a doll for Lesson 5, things used in washing, brushing up, sweeping and dusting, and outdoor clothes. Let each child occupy the centre of the stage for one minute, after putting his card on the chart. He acts, looks up and says, 'I'm . . . ing'. The class say, 'He's . . . ing'. Give him time to feel important, then insist that he goes quickly with his apparatus to his seat. Another comes forward and repeats the process, and so on round the class.

Then each child in turn collects his card. On the back should be written the past tense of the verb. The heading should be changed to 'Did', 'What did you do?' Then each in turn puts up his card showing the past tense now, shows the apparatus he used or the drawing or writing he did and says 'I drew this, &c.', and the class says, 'He drew that'.

There are many variations of this. This is the easiest stage, for the correct form of the verb is always before the children.

The verb 'to be' with vocabulary of people, animals, and adjectives

Vocabulary

1. People

Boy, girl, mother, father, &c.

2. Animals and birds

Twelve of the most usual.

3. Adjectives

pretty	good	tall	tired
kind	bad	short	sleepy
fat	naughty	big	
happy	round	little	

Questions

1. What does a sheep say? &c.
2. What's that? A mouse, a sheep, &c.
3. Are you sleepy? No, I'm not.
                       Yes, I am.
   What are you? I'm a boy.
   Who is happy? I am.
4. Point out exceptional plurals.

man	men	baby	babies
woman	women	lady	ladies
sheep	sheep	puppy	puppies

Notes

Adjectives should, of course, be taught incidentally as early as they are required. Here, some of them are gathered together for practice. I have grouped them with talks on people and animals as it is concerning these subjects that adjectives will probably be volunteered by the children, e.g. 'Daddy is tall. Baby is small. A lamb or kitten is pretty. My puppy is naughty.'

Visits to see animals are indicated, and visits from kittens, puppies, and rabbits encouraged. Lessons upon how to handle animals should be given here. You may be overwhelmed in a day school with a variety of pets, but you will be amazed how much the children learn, when their vivid interest is aroused, much more than is listed here as a minimum. Most children love young animals, so try to arrange for these.

The possessive 'my', 'your', 'his', 'her', will easily be practised here.

Keep up the separate compartments or boxes, clearly labelled, for each classification, e.g. 'What?' and under it, 'Animals and Birds'. 'What kind?' or 'What sort? Who?'

At a later stage of this work on adjectives the child's love of acting should be used. Give a card with an adjective such as 'tired, sleepy, happy, unhappy, naughty, kind, &c.', to each child and keeping the word on the card concealed, each in turn acts his adjective. I saw this done in a school in America, to the staff of whom I am indebted for the idea. There, the child who got the card 'generous' was very popular. He was allowed to go to the cupboard and get a box of biscuits to hand round. 'You are generous', they said, as they munched the biscuits.

LESSON 7

Past tense and present continuous tense (participle only) with vocabulary of more verbs, and common objects. Series of actions

Tenses

1. Present continuous tense in a modified form.

2. Past tense with yesterday, today, and days as needed in diary.

Vocabulary

1. **Additional verbs**

give	see	cook	drink	lay (the table)
buy	hear	think	break	hang up
make	speak	try	catch	
say	drop	eat	throw	

2. **Common objects**

cup	saucer	plate	spoon	tablecloth
dish	glass	mug	knife	fork, &c.

Language

Answer required to:

1. What are you doing? Writing, leading to, I'm writing.
2. What is . . . doing? &c. Reading, leading to, He's reading.
3. Are you running? Yes, I am. No, I am not, *or* No I'm not.
4. Is . . . writing? No, he is not. No, he's not.
5. Who is walking? He is. She is.
6. What did he do? He dropped the cup.
7. Did he break it? No, he didn't. Yes, he did.

Series of actions

1. Series of pictures showing one action each. Language added by child. Vice versa.

2. Reading lesson involving a series of actions may here be given:

    (*a*) Laying the table—for dinner, for tea.
    (*b*) Pouring out tea.
    (*c*) Going to the shop.
    (*d*) Getting ready for a walk and coming in.
    (*e*) Going for a walk.
    (*f*) Visiting.
    (*g*) Short stories involving past tense are now possible.

Notes. (*See also Lessons 4 and 5*)

This is an important section. Although (with the exception of the new verbs) most of the work has been taken incidentally already, yet a thorough grounding in the two tenses will lay a firm foundation for clear and well-used language. Much activity, dramatization, and opportunities for combining enjoyable speech and language are now possible. The daily news should now become more interesting. For instance the following forms should be used now:

We went to . . . on Monday. We saw . . . . We played . . . . We looked at . . . . He . . . fell down. He cried. She ran. She dropped . . . . She broke . . . . He brought . . . to school. Mother gave him/me . . . . He went to a shop. He bought . . . . He has a new coat on. He didn't come to school yesterday. He was ill. . . . has not come to school today. Mother made . . . . It was . . . birthday yesterday. We had a party. We had . . . . J's Mother made the cake. I like . . . . We went to the park yesterday/on Wednesday. We saw . . . . We saw a boy running. We saw a bird flying. I went to tea with Grandma. I have brought . . . to school. I have . . . at home. I shall go to tea with Grandma tomorrow.

I have included the notes for the teaching of this lesson

with Lessons 4 and 5. There is a further advance here in the reading lessons suggested in the fourth section. The first one, under (1), should have an action in the past tense for each picture. They can be used as reading lessons or for adding the language as a class exercise, or for dramatization. There are many variations of this, e.g. given the language, adding a drawing of each action. The reading lessons under (2) should involve a series of actions in the past tense without pictures. Each action should be dramatized by the children from the written form. During the dramatization teach the children to change the tense to the progressive, e.g.

John laid the table for dinner yesterday.

First he put the cloth on the table.	He's putting the cloth on.
Then he put the knives on.	He's putting the knives on.
Then he put the forks on.	He's putting the forks on, &c.

Then he put the spoons on.

Then he put the salt on.

Then he put the $\begin{cases} \text{tumblers on.} \\ \text{mugs} \end{cases}$

Then he put the chairs round.

There is much repetition here and it is an easy one to begin with. Try to use normal language. Notice above after the first 'on the table', 'on' only is used for the subsequent sentences. In pouring out the tea remember the same point.

Jane poured the tea out yesterday at tea-time.
She put the sugar in the cups.
Then she poured the milk in.

Then she poured the tea in.
She passed the cups of tea round.

Note that these are reading lessons first.

After much practice of this kind the child could be asked to write a series of two or three actions. Do not expect more though you may perhaps get it.

LESSON 8

The verb 'to like' with vocabulary of food and meals

Vocabulary

1. **Food and drink.** What?

   About twenty of the most usual.

2. **Meals.** What?

   Tea, supper, breakfast, lunch, dinner.

3. **Verbs.** Do.

   Eat, drink, like.

Sentences and questions

1. What do you like to eat?
   What do you like to drink?   I like . . . to eat, drink.
   Do you like . . .?   Yes, I do.
                                 No, I don't.
2. What does . . . like to eat? . . . likes . . . to eat.
   Does . . . like . . .?   Yes, . . . does.
                                 No, . . . doesn't.

   Revise animals and birds here.
3. What do you like for dinner?
   What do you like for tea?

4. What did you have for dinner yesterday?
Did you like it? Yes, I did. No, I didn't.

5. **Incidental**

Yes, please. No, thank you.
May I have some more, please?
No more, thank you.

Notes

This lesson is much enjoyed by the children, especially when active participation is involved. Even in retrospect and anticipation it is pleasurable. Remember to teach also the incidental language involved, e.g. 'May I have some more, please?' (earliest stage, 'More, please'), 'Please pass . . . '.

In answer to 'Would you like some more . . .?' 'Yes, please; No, thank you.' 'What would you like?' 'Some . . ., please.' This normal polite behaviour will help them very much in their social relations.

There is one difficulty, that of quantity and number, in this lesson which cannot be explained to these young children. You can, however, prepare for the correct usage by teaching them from the beginning in this lesson on 'like' to say apples, pears, oranges, &c. 'I like apples', &c. Only with 'I have' or 'had' should 'an apple', 'two apples' be used. Teach them to use 'cake', 'jam', 'butter', 'tea', without an article; and use 'some more' or 'some' (as I have pointed out in the incidental language) with both 'jam' and 'potatoes', &c.

Avoid 'a piece of' or 'a slice of' at first unless the children ask for it. They may do so in telling you how many slices they have had. Then, do not hesitate to teach it at once. Try to get these things right from the start.

LESSON 9

The verb 'to like' with vocabulary of lessons and games

What? Lessons and games

drawing	writing	rhythm	speech	football
dancing	sums or	playing	the band	rounders
reading	arithmetic	skipping	P.T.	swimming

Language

1. What lessons do you like?
   Which lesson do you like best?
   What do you like playing?
   Do you like reading? Yes, I do.
   Do you like Arithmetic? No, I don't.

2. **Incidental language**

   I love . . . .
   I like . . . very much.
   I like . . . best.

Notes

There is no particular difficulty in this lesson except that the lessons and games are on the whole rather hard to say. If you have built up your speech work, as I have suggested, however, you will not find this difficulty insurmountable. Apply the verb 'to like' to animals, flowers; use also with the verbal noun. 'I love going for a walk with Daddy. I love going in the car with Daddy. I like writing on the blackboard. I like writing with a pencil. I like writing with a pencil best. I like writing with a pen.'

The bright children will find much of interest to talk about here. They will suggest many things. Give them the phrases needed, but do not expect the slower child to want to branch out so much. Let him consolidate and gain self-confidence, and stick if he wants to do so to the simpler forms.

LESSON 10

Colours with vocabulary of things seen out of doors

Colours

Twelve to sixteen of the most usual.

Vocabulary of out of doors

1. **Natural objects**   2. **Things in the park or road**
   Cloud, wind, &c.   Grass, trees, &c.

   3. **Flowers**   4. **Vehicles**
      Daisy, rose, &c.   Lorry, bus, &c.

Questions

1. (*a*) What colour is . . .?
         Is . . . blue?
         Sentences.
   (*b*) Tell me some blue things, &c.
         The sky is blue.

2. Compare 'to be' and 'to have' and combine with Sections 2 and 4.

   I have a blue jumper on.
   I have blue eyes.
   I have not a brown jumper on.

3. **Incidental language**

   (*a*) How do you come to school?
   (*b*) How do you go to the playing fields? By tram, &c.

(*c*) I went to the park.

I saw . . . .

I have brought some flowers.

We shall go to the playing fields. I have . . . at home.

Notes

Throughout these first sections the way should be being prepared for more tenses of the verbs by giving the children the past, perfect, or future in their incidental work.

It is presupposed that the children will already have received sense training, colour matching, sorting of objects, training in observation, &c.

The lesson then in colours should be a happy and an easy one.

Group under the heading 'What colour?' Be sure that the colour is associated with many objects and various shades of the same colour.

Take the children for walks to discover colours. The blue sky, the white clouds, the green grass, the red and brown robin.

Teach them from an early age to see beauty and colour around them. Make their classroom as bright, cheerful, and happy as you can. Deafness is a limiting, cramping handicap. If you can help them to delight in outdoor things, in beauty of any kind, you have helped them to happiness not only at the moment but later in their lives.

COMPOSITION

WE are dealing here with the very beginnings of things. Encourage drawing by the child to tell you what he wants you to know. Add to it the vocabulary or language. Even when the child can write, an illustrated diary is of much more use than one with writing only. It can be used to encourage reading, to revise happenings, to help with letters.

It is good to have a separate book for the diary. Work for neat, accurate writing and drawing. Have a special place for the drawings. Do not allow slipshod, muddled, or untidy work. When the child begins (it may be on blackboards, or on large sheets of drawing paper with coloured pencils), however large or unformed his effort is, it should follow a plan which allows for no ambiguity as to which writing belongs to which drawing. It is worth while insisting on this from the beginning for it helps towards clear and definite knowledge.

1. *Daily diary*

(*a*) First built up with cards and drawings, then written with drawings. This daily diary can be used in boarding schools for letters home. At first the children will copy from the diaries and, later, refer to them but remember the language for themselves. The diary is a thing which is gradually built up from words to very simple sentences, e.g. 'I have a . . .' to a record of happenings. Be sure that they are copiously illustrated by drawings and paintings. Remember that drawing is the child's first way of writing.

(*b*) The diary leads up to accounts of happenings with

two or three sentences in sequence. No more than this should be expected.

2. *Series of pictures showing actions.* The language is added by the child.

The language of a series of actions can be given and the drawings or pictures supplied by the child.

Begin this very simply and gradually build up to four or five sentences.

3. *Descriptions of themselves and people around them*

    e.g. About Myself.   About Daddy.

First a drawing or photograph of the person concerned, underneath:

This is	
My name is	His name is . . . .
I am 7.	He is grown up.
I am a boy.	He is a man.
I have blue eyes, &c.	He has blue eyes, &c.
I have a blue jersey on.	He has a $\begin{cases} \text{car.} \\ \text{motor-bike.} \end{cases}$
I like	He likes . . . .
I don't like	

Children usually love this.

4. *Descriptions of a picture*

    'I can see some trees—I can see two girls playing—I can see a boy running, &c.'

In all these begin very simply. In this as in all other aspects of language teaching it is essential that the children are given work within their capacity which they really enjoy. Be sure that each child is putting forth effort, but expect more of the bright child. Here is a great field for more advanced work individually, but be sure that the ability of the more intelligent child does not lead you to disparage or belittle the effort of the slower child who has painstakingly produced what you have taught him and nothing else. Give as much praise and encouragement to one as to the other.

SPEECH

I N the introduction to this book it has been suggested that the first two principles governing the choice of material for speech practice should be:

1. That it should be suitable to the language development of the pupil.
2. That it should be suitable to the average age of the pupil and to his interests and natural impulses.

Let us consider these first two factors with regard to the child taking Stage 1 in this language scheme.

First his language development is very limited. It begins with the one-word sentence stage, passes on to phrases, and finishes with simple sentences. Therefore his first speech lessons must be very simple, practising sounds, phrases, and later simple sentences. He is also young and his interests are in the things around him, in his familiar world, in the happenings of every day. He is at the active stage, he wants to move, to participate in what is going on. He has a strong sense of rhythm, although his lack of hearing may not have developed it as strongly as it may be developed in his hearing brothers and sisters. We should therefore use his desire to move and his love of rhythm, in this subject as in any other. Rhythmic movement to sounds, words, phrases, and jingles all concerning the things which are familiar and loved takes account of these desires and natural impulses of the child.

The other principles enumerated in the introduction are:

3. That the material should definitely help the pupil in the practice of language principles.

4. That it should give practice in speech of graded difficulty.
5. That it should present, practice, and preserve correct speech, and prevent the rise of incorrect speech.
6. That it should foster facility and naturalness of speech.

If we have our material correct as regards the first two principles, (3) is also taken care of; (4) also requires that we should examine the material as regards difficulty of articulation. The last two principles have to do with the skill with which the matter given is presented. On them depend whether the spoken language we are practising is of real use as an instrument of expression by the child. In the detail of material which follows, I have tried to take into account all the factors governing choice and have also suggested methods whereby correct speech, spoken with ease and naturalness, can be obtained and preserved.

Before we begin our choice let us think of an individual lesson, in outline. The Speech Lesson with young children should always comprise:

(*a*) handkerchief drill and breathing. Deep breathing should be encouraged rather through activity than through conscious exercises, blowing helps to empty lungs, and so encourage deep breaths, and pretending to smell flowers will encourage intake through the nose and deep breaths without tension.

(*b*) Practice in sounds that you know they can say correctly.

(*c*) A difficulty or the chief sound you are revising. There will, of course, be individual speech correction lessons as well as these. If possible, these should be taken in private. If you find the children cannot do this, leave out (*d*) and go on to (*e*).

(*d*) A rhyme or refrain with movement, practising this sound.

(*e*) Enjoyable rhymes and movements which the child already knows and can do well.

Always end with something the child knows well and enjoys.

Detail of material

The simplest form of spoken poetry to movement is the rhyme with a refrain, and a good deal of the work with this section is of this type.

Having told the story of the poem with pictorial illustration and dramatization beforehand, the teacher should say the rhyme, marking time by quietly clapping her hands together (and allowing the children to do so too), and inviting the children to say the words of the refrain with her. She should then definitely teach the words of the refrain both in their spoken and written form, with special attention to the main sound she is emphasizing.

The teacher returns now to the poem, speaking the main verses while the children either clap hands (quietly) or make some other movement in time to the rhythmic beat, coming in with the refrain when it is time for it, on the correct beat. Remember to leave time for the silent beat when there is one.

For further work from which this is adapted see *The Rhythmic Approach to Spoken Poetry* by Marjorie Gullan.

In the pages that follow there is some detail as to movements and procedure.

1. **The Naughty Boy (or The Naughty Girl if desired)**

This is an example of a rhyme with refrain which can be taken very early. Its refrain is simply 'Oh' and 'No' repeated in each case three times.

There was once a little boy and a naughty boy was he,
> Oh, oh, oh,

When his mother said 'Come here' his answer used to be
> 'No, no, no.'

His Aunties and his Grandma talked to him with pain,
> Oh, oh, oh,

But after they had finished he just would say again
> 'No, no, no.'

When Daddy heard this story which you have heard from me,
> Oh, oh, oh.

Can you guess the thing that happened when he had had his tea?
> No, no, no.

> (*Pause for pantomime of chastisement, counting* 4)

Then did that bad boy scream and cry aloud in pain,
> 'Oh, oh, oh!

Oh mother please forgive me, I'll never say again,
> No, no, no.'

And now my little children please hearken unto me,
> Oh, oh, oh,

Like that naughty little boy, I'm sure you'll never be.
> No, no, no.

One child stands with his back to the class (but able to see the teacher's mouth movements), hands clasped behind, head bent in attitude of dejection.

The teacher should tell the story of this graphically and with illustrations by sketches and dramatization. It is within the comprehension of all the children although they will not understand every word. Let them make appropriate gestures for Oh, oh, oh, sometimes of disapproval and sometimes of pain. Remember the silent beat at the end of the refrain. Allow time for it and do not hurry.

Insist on good round 'oh's and correct 'n's. Take these under heading (c) in the outline of a lesson.

2. **All together**

	Verses	*Refrain*
1. We'll all shake hands together		Shake
,, ,, ,, ,, ,,		,,
,, ,, ,, ,, ,,		,,
As children ought to do.		,,
2. We'll all clap hands together.		clap
,, ,, ,, ,, ,,		,,
,, ,, ,, ,, ,,		,,
As children ought to do.		,,
3. We'll all be quiet together		Sh!
,, ,, ,, ,, ,,		,,
,, ,, ,, ,, ,,		,,
As children ought to be.		,,

The teacher again speaks the lines and the children the refrain. Repeat with appropriate action for as many verses as you like, being sure to make the verb into two syllables by the addition of another word, e.g. 'sit down (refrain "sit") stand up, jump high, &c.' For the first two verses I have suggested, the children and teacher could form a ring, all clapping or shaking hands. At the end of the third verse they could turn and follow the teacher on tiptoe with raised finger saying 'Sh!' on the beat, and wind their way to their seats. There is quite a lot of practice in sounds here. 'Sh', 'k', 'p', should be taken under (c) in the lesson outline. Be sure that they are correct.

3. **Walking is fun**

Walking is fun for everyone,
Walk, walk, walk,

So come let us walk, let us all walk,
Walk, walk, walk.

Repeat for 'run', 'jump', 'hop', 'skip', 'play', 'laugh'.

As before, the teacher speaks the line and the children the refrain. This might be taken in a ring, children holding hands and marking time with teacher. After the silent beat at the end of the last refrain let the children walk round still holding hands for eight beats, then stand ready for the next action. This gives extensive lip-reading as well as speech practice.

Do not allow slipshod speech here. The words should be practised first and the teacher should listen particularly for the final consonants. 'Walk', 'jump', 'hop', 'skip', and 'play' all have plosive unvoiced consonants, practice these by letting the children hold up the forefinger and feel the breath on it—p p p p t t t k k k, then the continuous 'h', 's', 'f', 'th'. Be sure that they are entirely unvoiced. One of the causes of unintelligible speech is the vocalization of unvoiced consonants. It is worth while taking time to see that the children understand when they are vocalizing and when not. Hearing-aids help a big percentage of the children here, but there are still those to whom it must be demonstrated and who must learn to feel for themselves when they are vocalizing and when not. Practice in the correct way when the children are young will make all the difference to their speech when they are older. So, listen for those final consonants in 'walk', 'hop', 'jump', 'skip', and 'laugh', and the initial ones in 'play' and 'skip'. Work for the 'j' in 'jump' (but leave out 'jump' rather than confuse the issue) and contrast 'run' which has both con- ·
sonants voiced.

4. **The Farm**

> We went one day to see a farm
> > Away, away, away,
> There to run all free from harm
> > And play, play, play.
>
> We saw the big cows in the field,
> > Moo, moo, moo,
> And doves flew up and o'er us wheeled,
> > Coo, coo, coo.
>
> We saw the sheep and big horned rams,
> > Baa, baa, baa,
> And laughed to see the funny lambs,
> > Ha, ha, ha.
>
> Two big dogs came and barked at us,
> > Bow, wow, wow
> And a little kitten followed us,
> > Miow, miow, miow.
>
> At last 'twas time towards home to get.
> > Oh, dear oh,
> Such a day we never would forget,
> > No, no, no.
>
> We said 'Goodbye, we'll come again',
> > Ta ta, ta ta, ta ta.
> And we cheered them all with might and main,
> > Hurrah, hurrah, hurrah.

There are appropriate actions here, e.g. pointing to the distance far away, clapping hands for play, leaning forward to say 'moo' and 'baa', imitating flying for 'coo'; most of them are self-evident. There is a little more speech practice than usual here. It might be well to take two or three verses only for each of the preliminary lessons.

5. **'Hee Haw Hum',** to be found in many poetry books for children, is much enjoyed. This is an excellent voice exercise, as the continuous sound 'h' helps to bring the voice forward. Practice also a good 'm'.

Many nursery rhymes can be used in part or adapted. Do not try to teach little deaf children the whole rhyme. Wait until they are ready. Have patience at this stage and you will be rewarded by the children's desire to learn more and their ability to do so later on.

6. **The band**

Here is a jingle for the young children which can be adapted for practice in 'ng' when you are taking it. *Do* try to perfect this sound early. It makes such a difference when teaching the tenses. Remember it is easier from the 'A' position. 'Bang' is the best to start with, so change the 'Bom' of the drum to 'Bang', then follow with the cymbals 'Tang', and later, with the triangle 'Ting'. You might add a chorus with the refrain 'Sing, sing, sing, sing'.

1. Listen to the drum
     Here we come,
   Bom, Bom, Bom, Bom.

2. Listen to the trombone
     Loud and true tone
   Boo, Boo, Boo, Boo.

3. Here is the fiddle
     Hey, Hey, diddle
   Wee, Wee, Wee, Wee.

4. Here's the cymbal
     Light and nimble
   Tang, Tang, Tang, Tang.

5. The triangles sweet
     Mark the beat,
   Ting, Ting, Ting, Ting.

6. All together
     As we march along,
   (The various refrains).

Each section should march round alone first while the teacher says the first two lines and they respond with the refrain. Then all together.

7. Ding, dong, bell

You might follow this with a variation of the nursery rhyme, 'Ding, dong, bell', making this a refrain.

Preparatory chorus.   Ding dong, ding dong,
                            Ding dong bell.

(a) *Children.*   Ding dong bell
    Teacher.   Pussy's in the well.

    Children.   Ding dong bell
    Teacher.   Pussy's in the well.

(b)   Who put her in?
                        Ding dong bell
                  Little Tommy Flynn
                        Ding dong bell.

    2nd chorus. Ding dong, ding dong,
                        Ding dong bell.

(c)   Who pulled her out?
                        Ding dong bell.
                  Little Tommy Stout
                        Ding dong bell
                        Ding dong, ding dong,
                        Ding dong bell.

The teacher speaks the lines, the children the refrain. Throughout they are pretending to pull a bell. Be very careful of the silent beat here. Some dramatization by the two boys concerned might be used here; Tommy Flynn's before the first verse during the preparatory 'Ding Dong's, Tommy Stout's at the appropriate time, i.e. at a pause for 'Ding dong, ding dong, Ding dong bell' after the second verse. The teacher might finish with the admonition with raised finger, 'What a naughty boy'.

8. **Hush-a-by**

Here is a rhyme which can be used either with the
children saying 'Sh!' only or a little later with the children
saying some of the words, e.g. the first and fourth lines,
or the first word of these lines:

> Hush-a-by baby, go to sleep,
> Mother is watching near;
> While the stars above you peep,
> Hush-a-by baby dear.

In the easiest version the teacher says the verse while the
children say 'Sh!' and sway from side to side, hushing baby
to sleep in time to the rhythm of the words.

9. **Tiptoe**

Another rhyme which can be used as an exercise for
'sh' or with the children saying a few words of the verse
is this:

> Tiptoe sh! baby's asleep.
> Tiptoe sh! creep, creep.
> Sh, sh, sh.

The action is obvious.

Practice 't' and 'p' as well as 'sh'. Be sure the final 'p's are
crisp.

10. **Housework**

Here is another rhyme with a refrain:

> What shall we do for mother
> Upon this busy day?
> What shall we do for mother?
> Wash, wash away.

Repeat with 'sweep', 'dust', 'iron', 'mop', 'cook', &c.,
with appropriate action.

Use this first as a refrain, the children answering the teacher, then use older children or better speakers for the questions.

Practise a good attack of the initial and finish of the final consonants.

11. **The sewing party**

Here is one for the girls, towards the end of Stage 1.

> We are as busy as busy can be,
>> Sew, sew, sew.
> Making new clothes for our dollies you see,
>> Sew, sew, sew.
>
> Up very straight like Mother we sit,
>> Sew, sew, sew.
> We don't want to go to play a bit,
>> Sew, sew, sew.
>
> As soon as our children are fit to see,
>> Sew, sew, sew.
> Perhaps we'll invite you all to tea,
>> Sew, sew, sew.
>
> So don't stop us now, we must hem and run,
>> Sew, sew, sew.
> And try on the dresses. Oh! isn't it fun?
>> Sew, sew, sew.

A good exercise in 's' and 'oa'.

12. **How shall we go?**

Here is another nursery game which we can use:

> When we play at horses,
> How shall we go?
> Trot away, trot away,
> Trot away so.
>> (8 *trots round room*)

When we play at aeroplanes
How shall we go?
Fly away, fly away,
Fly away so.
> (*Run round room saying 'm, m, m'*)

When we play at engines,
How shall we go?
Puff away, puff away,
Puff away so.
> (*Dramatize engines saying 'ch, ch, ch', &c.*)

This can be used very early for practise of sounds only, e.g. 'm' and 'ch'. Later it can be used as a refrain, using the last two lines of each verse in this way. Later still it might be used for group work, one group taking the questions and the other the answers.

Phrasing

Most of the refrains I have given bring in only sounds or single words. Here are some suggestions for teaching the beginning of phrasing.

The very first lesson in phrasing is learning to treat both the definite and indefinite article lightly, joining them to the following word. Do not teach 'ah ball' for 'a ball'. Teach the short indefinite unaccented neutral vowel ə 'aball'. Similarly with thedoor, thewindow.

Make up jingles to practise this:

Teacher	*Child*	*Teacher*	*Child*
Whát's thát?	Thewíndow.	What's thát?	Adóll.
Whát's thát?	Thedóor.	Whát's thát?	Ahát.
Whát's thát?	Thecúpboard.	Whát's thát?	Abáll.
Whát's thát?	Theflóor.	Whát's thát?	Abát.

Let the children clap these. They will see that neither 'a' nor 'the' has a clap of its own. Be careful again of the silent beat. I am sure you can think of many more rhymes of this kind if you find they help. The above can be transposed to form a jingle with easy sentences such as the child can say.

Thát's the wíndow.	Í've a báll.
Thát's the dóor.	Hé has a bát.
Thát's the cúpboard.	Shé has a dóll.
Thát's the flóor, &c.	The dóll has a hát.

The same thing can be practised when playing the game I suggested in the lessons on 'I have': 'What have you? Thebáll'. (Lessons 2 and 3.)

Here is another jingle of which the children could probably say every word, starting with the last words of the lines in 1 and the first in 2, 'the sky, the sea, the grass', and 'we'.

1 Blúe is the ský.	2 The gráss is gréen.
Blúe is the séa.	The ský is blúe.
Gréen is the gráss.	Wé are glád.
Háppy are wé.	And só are yóu.
	(Lesson 10)

The well-known rhyme 'I see the moon' can also be used here. Be very sure that you have a good 'm' when accelerating the pace here, 'themoon'. Teach the children to touch lightly on 'the' but to accentuate 'm'.

A little more advanced one of the same kind is:

> God made the sun, the moon, the stars,
> He made the sky so blue;
> He made the birds, the trees, the flowers,
> He made both me and you.

If you taught no more phrasing than this in Stage 1
you would have done much. Until the child is ready, do
not worry about the next stage. If they are ready, the next
stage is the whole phrase. Introduce them to it in this way:

rún tothewindow

'to' is the easiest preposition, I think, to start with.

If you have taught the unaccented 'the' well you will
not find this a great difficulty. Be sure to clap or move to it.
Here are some rhymes

Úp in the ský.	Rún to the wíndow.
Úp so hígh.	Sít on the flóor.
Hére we flý.	Júmp to the bláckboard.
Yóu and Í.	Ópen the dóor.

Do not teach this if you find the children are not ready for
it. Facility comes with happy practice, with movement,
dramatization, and fun.

Here are some more useful rhymes for this stage:

Í líke jám.
Móther líkes téa.
Dáddy líkes hám.
Só dó wé.

Yés, I dó.
Nó, I dón't.   } Two groups of
Yés, I wíll.   }   children.
Nó, I wón't.

Hulló, hulló.
Hów are yóu?   } Shaking hands either in
Véry well, thánk you. }   a ring or in pairs.
Hów are yóu?

Óne, twó, thrée four fíve,
Ónce I caúght a físh alíve,   } Lines 1 and 3 spoken by
Síx, séven, eíght nine tén,   }   the children at first, and
Í lét it gó agaín.   }   lines 2 and 4 dramatized.

Ráin, ráin, gó awáy,
Cóme agáin anóther dáy.

Óne, twó, tíe up my shóe,
Thrée, fóur, sít on the flóor.

'Here we go round the mulberry bush' can be used. Expect the children to say either the verb only, e.g. 'This is the way we *wash* our hands' or the phrase 'wash our hands'. 'Round and round the village, In and out the windows', &c., can also be adapted.

'Thank you for the world so sweet' by Enid Rutter Leatham:

> Thank you for the world so sweet,
> Thank you for the food we eat,
> Thank you for the birds that sing,
> Thank you, God, for everything.

There are many more rhymes you can adapt or, better still, make up to fit the happenings and events of the children's lives. 'The Farm' quoted in this chapter is an example of this and was for that reason especially liked by the children. If you can make up rhymes bringing in exclamations, verbs, actions, and comments, concerning something in which the children have participated, you will tap an inexhaustible source of joyous speech practice. The same thing can be done with simple stories bringing in appropriate comment. The difficult part from the teacher's point of view is that you must tell it exactly as before, and this is not so easy in prose as in rhyme. You will notice that I did not say 'poetry'—as long as you have rhythm the children will love it and that is what matters.

Here is a suggestion for a story:

Last Thursday I said to you, 'Shall we go to the Park?' You said, '*Yes. Yes, please*, we're going *to the park*'. I said, '*Hurry up, get ready*'. So you hurried up and got ready and we walked *to the park*. We walked *along the paths* to the children's playground. We said '*Hurrah! Hurrah!*' We saw *the swings, the roundabout, the see-saws,* and *the chute.* You said, '*May we go on?*' I said, '*Yes, you may*'. So John, Dick, and George went *on the roundabout.* They went *round and round and round* (repeat).

Josie, Sally, and Mark went *on the swings.*
> They went *up in a swing, up in a swing.*
> > *up in the air, and down.*

Jim and Maurice went *on the chute.*
> They went *up the steps* and *down the chute* (repeat).

Stella and Joan went on the see-saw.
> They went *up and down, up and down.*
> > *See-saw, See-saw.*

Then we *changed over.*

Repeat, changing the names of the children as many times as you like. They will probably insist on three times bringing in each child for each action.

Then I said, 'It is *time to go back* to school for dinner.' We walked *along the paths.* We went *back to school for dinner.*

I have underlined the words and phrases I suggest should be repeated by the children. Of course you can use a story like this very simply with the children at the beginning of this section. At that stage the repetition should be only 'yes', 'the park', 'the paths', 'round, round, round', 'up', 'down', 'see-saw'.

Have a number of these story happenings that the children know by heart. Normal children have many of them and can correct one word alteration in the repetition. Try to give deaf children a part in this valuable and loved method of language impression and spoken language expression.

LANGUAGE

READ again the summary in the introduction of the interests and natural desires of the child who has reached Stage 2 and the suggestions for teaching language which tries to satisfy these instincts and cater for these interests.

As we have seen, the section is concerned with the idea of time and the tenses. The tenses included are the past, the future, the present continuous, and the present perfect. The present participle is used in '. . ., I saw . . . ing'. Phrases of time and place are begun, and the child's horizon is widening from the home and classroom to the school and beyond to places where people and animals live, and where people have been.

The language of telling the time, health and ailments, simple reasons, ability, what things are made of, and to whom things belong is used. The vocabulary includes prepositions, adverbs, places, materials, adjectives from materials, games and sports, ailments, relationships, young of animals, parts of things, numbers, pets and possessions, and, of course, more verbs.

The use of spontaneous questions by the children is encouraged, especially with the perfect tense.

There are two hurdles to cross here: first, the giving of the correct tense with the appropriate phrase and adverb; second, using the phrase, not single words, where applicable, e.g. in answering the questions 'When?' and 'Where?'

A SUMMARY OF THE LESSONS IN STAGE 2

Lesson 11. Future tense with practice in the past. Vocabulary of days and months. Phrases and adverbs of time. 'When?'

12. Prepositions with vocabulary of rooms, furniture, and utensils. Phrases of place. 'Where?'
13. Perfect tense with prepositions and vocabulary of names of places and animals at the zoo. More adverbs.
14. Tenses already introduced revised with additional verbs, adverbs, and adverbial phrases of time. 'Going to' introduced.
15. Materials with vocabulary of clothes and common articles. Possessive pronouns and colours extended and revised. Apostrophe 's'.
16. 'Can' and 'can't' with vocabulary of verbs, games, and sports.
17. Adverbs of manner 'How?' This lesson combined with previous one.
18. Language and vocabulary connected with animals. Homes, parts, and young.
19. Present participle with the verbs 'saw', 'watched', 'heard', and 'can see'. Vocabulary of more verbs and prepositions.
20. Adjectives formed from materials. Order of adjectives. Vocabulary of materials, colour, and adjectives.
21. Relationships with numbers 10 to 20 and parts of things, furniture, clothes, buildings, books, and boxes, vehicles, cars, aeroplanes, parts of body. 'There is, there are'.
22. Telling the time. Appropriate vocabulary, adverbs, and roman numerals.
23. Reason, with health and ailments and appropriate vocabulary. Revision of weather.
24. 'Belongs to'. Child's personal possessions. Family possessions. Possessive pronouns revised.

ADDITIONAL QUESTIONS

1. **Key words**

When?	Why?	Where?
What?	What can . . . do?	At what time?
What . . . made of?	What is the matter . . .?	What . . . called?

How many ... are there? To whom ... belong?	Whom . . . go with?	What . . . covered with?
2. When did . . .?	Where is . . .?	What have . . . done?
When will he . . .?	Where was . . .? Where did . . .?	What will . . . do? What did you see . . . doing?
	Where will . . .? Where have . . .?	
3. Have you been to?	Can you . . .?	Who is . . . ing that?
Have you seen . . .?	Can he . . .?	
Did you . . .?	Have you any . . .?	
Will you . . .?	Are there any ...?	
Are you . . . ing?	Does . . . belong to . . .?	
Are you going to . . .?		

LESSON 11

Future tense with practice in the past. Vocabulary of days and months. Phrases and adverbs of time. 'Why?'

Future tense

I shall	He will	I am (not) going to
We shall (not)	She will	You are (not) going to
	It will	We are (not) going to
	They will	They are (not) going to
	You will	He is (not) going to
		She is (not) going to
		It is (not) going to

Vocabulary

Days of the week.   Heading, 'Which day . . .?'
Months of the year.   'Which month . . .?'
On which day do you have dancing? &c.—Monday.

Time adverbs and phrases

yesterday	today	tomorrow	on Monday
this morning	last night	in March	
this afternoon	next week		
soon	after dinner		

Heading, 'When?'

Questions

1. When did you go to the park? Yesterday.
   When are we going } to the playing fields? On
        shall we go } Wednesday.
   What lessons did you have yesterday?
   What did you have for dinner yesterday?
   What shall we have for dinner tomorrow?

2. **Incidental language**

   What would you like for dinner today?
   What do you want for your birthday?

Notes

This lesson is not difficult in itself if you take one step at a time.

The first, that of using the tense freely to the children, has been taken in incidental calendar work and in stories by the teacher.

The second should be taken now, that of pointing out the change of verb and showing them in stories and news what that change is. Another box or compartment should be added to those already given, labelled 'Future', where the child can look up what that change is. Three cards could be put in:

Shall	Will	Going to
I.	you, he, it.	I'm, she's.
we.	they, she.	he's, we're, they're, you're.

The full answer should not be expected of the child yet, but he should understand and be able to look it up.

This lesson aims at giving him the tools for more time work. He should learn the days of the week by heart and have preparatory work on the months. (Each child should learn his own birthday month as a beginning.)

He should learn phrases of time and begin to answer the question 'When?' in a phrase or an adverb. Concentrate on: 'On Monday', 'in March', 'last night', &c., 'last week', 'last Monday'. This answering in phrases is most important. Much of your work in this whole section will have this theme, the idea of time and tenses and the use of phrases of time and of place. So take your time and be sure that each step is understood.

Always relate the use of this tense to a definite fact and time.

Learning a new tense always helps to revise the former work on tenses, so relate the past and present to this. Do not forget the past and future forms of the verbs 'to have' and 'to be'.

It is worth while to take time over this and to relate 'When?' to past, present, and future. Play games with headings as in Stage I. You can devise one which resembles Lotto. The children have a card divided into squares containing a phrase of time, of place, or separate words of vocabulary, persons, colours, adjectives, or numbers, one in each square. They have also little piles of separate cards on which are written 'What?', 'What colour?', 'When?', 'Where?', 'What kind of?', 'How many?', 'Who?'. The teacher takes one of the cards from a box before her, reads out the heading, and places it on a chart in sight of the children. They take up a similar card and cover one of their squares with it, e.g. the teacher reads 'Who?', placing the card where the children can see it. The children take a similar card having 'Who?' on it, and place it over the name of a person on their squared card. (As in Lotto vary the position of the words and phrases to discourage copying.) A minimum of time should be allowed. Teach the children to be alert both to look at the teacher and to put on their cards.

I have mentioned phrases of place. The actual lesson on 'Where?' has not been taken, if you have not taught it incidentally do not include this until you have, but if the previous work has been taught it should have come in naturally many times, e.g. to the park, to school, at home, &c. This game can be played with vocabulary only, sorting into food, lessons, games, colours, toys, animals, clothes, parts of the body. This apparatus can, of course, be used individually or in groups, especially if you find some children are always winning and others always losing. Remove both these groups and give them either individual or group work.

There are variations of these games. The large card could contain the heading only in the squares and the children could be given assorted phrases to place in the appropriate squares.

The teaching of the future tense brings up the question of whether to teach the colloquial use of 'going to' used so often instead of 'shall' and 'will'. I have found it a good thing to do so. In any case it should be given incidentally and you will find that parents and friends will use it to the children orally or in letters. It is not too great a difficulty and children of the junior stage take it in their stride. It is all new to them and is not confusing if given as an alternative now. Give it in its easiest form first.

> I am going to Grandma's this afternoon.
> We are going to the park tomorrow.
> We are going on the swings, &c.

Then, with specific events of interest.

> . . . is going to the seaside in the holidays.
> ,, ,,   ,, ,, play on the sands.
> ,, ,,   ,, ,, dig.
> ,, ,,   ,, ,, swim.
> ,, ,,   ,, ,, bathe, &c.

The negative form of the future tense is quite easy but while teaching it remember the difficulty of the past negative tense and revise it at the same time. In fact, refer to it whenever you teach a new verb and give them the past affirmative and negative in both speech and writing.

The lesson is useful for revising former vocabulary, a good thing at the beginning of the stage. Meals, foods, names of lesson, actions can all be related to this.

LESSON 12

Prepositions with vocabulary of rooms, furniture, and utensils. Phrases of place. 'Where?'

Prepositions

in	behind	near	to
on	beside	above	
under	by		

Vocabulary

1. **Rooms in school and home**

cloakroom	kitchen	classroom	hall
bedroom	stairs	dining-room	corridor
staff room	bathroom		

2. **More furniture and utensils**

rubber	cupboard	window-sill
duster	box	ceiling
blackboard	shelf	

3. **Revision. Things seen out of doors**

(Lesson 10.) Add to them as needed, e.g. shops, field, fence, post office, gate, hedge, &c.

Language

1. Where is . . .? On the shelf, &c.
2. The book is on the shelf.
3. Where are you going? To the playground.

Notes

This is a lesson much enjoyed by the children. In your teaching concentrate on two things, first that the children should answer the question 'Where?' in a phrase, and secondly that they understand, lip-read, and recognize from writing the word 'where'.

Where. The lesson calls for plenty of activity. Do not only place books and rubbers in, on, and under a chair. Go with the children out of the classroom and make the lesson real. There are a number of hiding and finding and guessing games that can be played in teaching this language form. Again, insist on the whole phrase as answer to the question. Never allow either the preposition or the noun alone as answer, e.g. in answer to the question, 'Where is your book?' 'on' is equally wrong with 'the shelf'. 'On the shelf' is the correct answer.

Perfect tense with prepositions and vocabulary of places and animals at the zoo. More adverbs

Perfect tense

I have been to . . . . I have never been to . . . . *or* I've never been to . . . .

I have seen . . . . I have never seen . . . .

I have nearly finished this. I have almost done.

Prepositions

Across, to, over, along, up, down.

Adverbs

Never, ever, once, twice, many times.

Vocabulary

1. **Places.** London, Birmingham, &c. Hot countries, Cold countries, &c.

2. Animals at the zoo.

Questions

Where have you been?

What have you seen?

Have you ever } No, I haven't
been to . . .?

Have you ever } No, I've never { seen a . . . .
seen a . . .? { been to . . . .

Have you learnt your tables?
Have you done that? Not quite, nearly.
almost.

I've never been there, have you?

I've seen a lion, { haven't you?
{ have you?

You have seen that, haven't you?
You've not seen this, have you?

Incidental work

Go to the hall and come back. Where have you been?
I should like to go to . . . . I want to go to . . . .

Notes

This tense will have been used by the teacher to the children and given to them in their incidental work frequently before it is introduced here. It is used a great deal in conversation (apart from conversational telling of a story). It is difficult for many foreigners learning English to be quite certain when it should be used in preference to the past tense, and we should bear this in mind and be patient with our pupils, and thorough in our teaching of this tense.

I have found that the best way is to introduce it incidentally in diary work. 'I have brought . . ., . . . has not come to school. Where have you been? Have you finished?' And to follow it by the presentation suggested here, linking it up with conversation on visits to places. 'Have you ever been to the zoo? Who has been to London? I've never been to London, have you?'

It is helpful to keep a scrapbook of places to which the children have been for holidays, &c. Ask them to send picture postcards when they go away. The teacher can start the ball rolling. Each child should write a simple description of the place, e.g. 'I have been to . . . . It is by the seaside. I went there on . . . .' The change of tense with a definite date can then be pointed out. One page of the book will look something like this:

Picture post-card or other picture

Picture post-card or other picture

The sands

The illuminations

Blackpool

I have been to Blackpool.

I went with mother and father on September 20th for a week.

It is by the seaside.

It is beautiful.

I played on the sands and built castles.

I saw the illuminations.

I like Blackpool very much.

Denis Jelfs.

It is my experience that the children will read and re-read such a book as this and are eager to talk and ask questions about the places too.

Be careful of your headings here too. Head the names of towns and countries with the word 'Places' *not* 'Where?'. The word 'Where' should head the column containing phrases or adverbs, e.g. 'to London', 'in Birmingham', 'at the zoo', 'there', 'over there', 'here'.

It will be noted that the children's horizon is widening to include places and things beyond their own environment. It is still limited to include places to which they or someone they know, has been, or things which they or others have seen. They will enjoy finding these places on a map and learning about how the traveller went by car, train, bus, or plane.

Animals, too, are a never-ending source of interest to children. Of course a visit to the zoo is indicated. It is sufficient for them to learn that the animals live in hot or cold countries and to show them the areas on the globe.

When I taught children at this stage I used to play a lip-reading game with them like this:

'Tell me the name of the animal that lives far away in a hot country; it is very fierce, and has black and yellow stripes.' The children were required to answer in one word.

They had to wait until the very end to give their answer as the last sentence gave the deciding clue, for instance it might have been, 'and has a mane'. This was played with farm animals too.

I have said that this tense is used a great deal in conversational English. This lesson is a great opportunity for teaching the children to ask pertinent questions. As the name of a new place crops up ask, 'Who else has been to this place? Have your parents been to this place? Ask them tonight, tell me tomorrow', or if a boarding school, 'I wonder if Miss . . . has been to this place. Who would like to ask her? Ask her to tell you about it.' The difficult question, 'What is it like?', may be used with a bright class.

Liaison between parents and teachers is at all times important and never more so than here. The parent who will trouble to understand and answer the child's questions is invaluable to that child's mental growth. In the boarding school teach the child to ask questions in his letters, and ask the parents to answer these questions, ask similar ones and tell the children interesting items of news about themselves and the rest of the family, where they have been, and what they have seen. All this gives new life to the weekly letter.

The teaching of the affirmation followed by the shortened question adds very much to the naturalness of the deaf child's conversation. Begin it here and continue in the next lesson with the other tenses of the verb. Deaf children sometimes like this form better than the full question form.

There are two usual forms (for this stage):

1. An affirmation about oneself or a third person, followed by asking the shortened question of the person to whom one is speaking

> I *am* tired, are *you*?
> He has been there, have you?
> He went, did you?
> I don't like porridge, do you?

2. An affirmation about the person to whom you are talking or about the weather followed by the shortened question to verify it.

These are of two kinds:

(*a*) An affirmative statement, followed by a negative question:

> e.g. You've seen a lion, haven't you?
>   It's a lovely day, isn't it?

(*b*) A negative statement, followed by an affirmative question:

> You've not seen a lion, have you?
> It's not very nice, is it?

Bring this language form into your dramatic interludes, general conversation, talk on lessons, &c., both in the spoken and the written form. Do not expect them to master it all at once. As in all other work, give plenty of impression, and from now on see that it finds a place in any reading lesson, story, or play you prepare.

LESSON 14

Tenses already introduced revised, with additional verbs, adverbs, and adverbial phrases of time. 'Going to' introduced

Tenses of the verb

All verbs of previous sections.

1. Past indefinite	I . . . yesterday	
2. Future	I shall . . . . tomorrow	Alternative form, 'going to'
3. Perfect	I have	
4. Present continuous	I am . . . ing	
,, ,,	with all pronouns.	

Adverbs and adverbial phrases of time

Once upon a time. The next day. After.

this year	this month	The seasons—
next year	next month	spring, summer,

last year	last month	autumn, winter
tonight	tomorrow afternoon	
last night	yesterday afternoon	
tomorrow night	in 1952, in 1953, in 1954, &c.	

More verbs

say	smack	hit	touch
scrub	take care	wash up	feed
carry	look after	tidy	meet
kick	help	cut	pick up

Sentences and questions

1. What are you doing now?
   What did you do yesterday?
   What shall you do tomorrow?
   What are you going to do this afternoon?

2. **Full sentences**

   I . . . yesterday.
   He will . . . tomorrow.
   He is going to . . . tomorrow.
   I have been to London, &c.
   He has gone to . . . .

3. **Special attention to negative form, especially of past tenses.**

   I didn't see.

4. When did you go to London?
   In what year did you come to this school?
   How old were you when you came to this school?
   What is this year? . . . was last year?
   I went to see the Coronation, did you?
   I didn't go, did you?
   You didn't go, did you? You went, didn't you?

5. **Incidental language.** I saw you . . . when I was in the train . . . when I was coming to school, &c.

Notes

This is a revision lesson introducing new verbs. There are no special difficulties if the previous work has been well taught. It is good here to practise the colloquial future tense 'going to'.

The negative 'did not' or 'didn't' needs a good deal of practice. Try to find many ways of practising this.

Give much practice, too, in the adverbial phrases and see that they are thoroughly understood. Much work with the calendar is indicated. Give the children calendars or diaries of their own and teach them to look up what they want to know. They should learn the months by heart now, both in the spoken and written form. As I said in the last lesson, the horizon of the children is widening and they are interested in and able to comprehend short stories about other children or people. Tell stories and read stories to the children, act them and illustrate them in every way possible. After telling, acting, and illustrating, give the children the story to read.

I am not going into the difficult problem of finding reading material suitable for deaf children. I know quite well that most of it will have to be manufactured or at the best adapted by you yourselves. You all know that the National College of Teachers of the Deaf is tackling the problem but that publication is a slow job and that meantime your children depend on you. It is a fascinating work, and as you go on you will gather together a number of suitable stories. If you can draw and paint and so illustrate your books, so much the better, but if you can't, do as well as you can. Children are very kind and understanding.

Let them illustrate their own if you can get them typed or duplicated in some way. They will probably mean more to them than the most beautifully illustrated book. Take this part of your work very seriously. Remember that our deaf children lack *impressions* of language so much; the impressions that normal children get, not only from ordinary conversation but from stories and reading books in quantities. We cannot, through lip-reading, give them *as many* impressions as the normal child gets through his hearing, but we ought to give them as many suitable stories and books as the normal child has. Combine these with exclamations, repetitions, and phrases in which the child joins, as I have suggested in Stage 1 in the chapter on Speech.

Be sure that the children understand and enjoy the stories. So much depends upon it in after life.

LESSON 15

Materials with vocabulary of clothes and common articles. Possessive pronouns and colours extended and revised. Apostrophe 's'

Vocabulary

1. Materials

Twelve to sixteen of the most usual, e.g. wood, leather, silk, iron, &c.

2. More common articles

Envelope, shilling, watch, badge, &c. (about sixteen).

3. More clothes

Jumper, blouse, cardigan, slippers, &c. (about sixteen).

Possessive pronouns

Revised

Apostrophe 's', e.g. Mary's jumper is made of wool.

Put . . . in Miss . . . 's room.

Revise colours and add more

Beige, crimson, scarlet, nigger-brown, &c., as required.

Questions

What is . . . made of? Whose is this?
What things are made of wool?
Tell me . . . things made of cotton.

Sentences

My desk is made of wood, &c.

Descriptions

Two or three sentences.

I have a badge.
It is green and gold.
It is made of enamel.

Notes

This lesson is usually much enjoyed by the children. Here is a definite step from the mere naming of objects. They have learnt classification of things on a colour basis, now they apprehend it on a material basis. Do not limit yourself to the classroom here. Do not be afraid to give the name of any modern material of which things are made, nor again be afraid to say you do not know the name of some material. What an opportunity to send the children to ask if anyone else knows, to ask their parents, in fact to find out for themselves.

LESSON 16

'Can' and 'can't' with vocabulary of verbs, games, and sports

Vocabulary

1. **More verbs**

swim	run races	ski
fly	ride a horse	jump
drive a car	slide	⎧football
skate	climb	play ⎨cricket
milk a cow		⎪golf
pilot an aeroplane		⎩tennis

2. Football, tennis, cricket, golf as above.
3. A car, a horse, a length, a width, a race, 5 feet high, &c., an aeroplane.

'Can' and 'can't'

1. I can ⎫
   He can't ⎬ combined with above.
2. Can you . . .? Yes, I can. No, I can't.

Sentences

Miss . . . can drive a car.
I can't drive a car.
I can swim a length.
I can jump 5 feet, &c.

Incidental language

(*a*) I wish I could . . . . I am learning to . . . . I can nearly . . . .
(*b*) A cricketer, a footballer, a golfer, a rider, a pilot, a driver, &c.

LESSON 17

Adverbs of manner. 'How?' This lesson combined with previous one

Adverbs

quickly	carefully	untidily	a little
slowly	neatly	fast	nearly
nicely	well	better	
happily	badly	not very well	

Commands

Write neatly.
Carry that carefully to . . . .

Questions

How did you write it? Neatly.
How did you carry it? Carefully.

Sentences

1. I wrote neatly in my book. I carried it carefully to Miss . . . .

2. **Combine with Lesson 16.** I can run quickly. Miss . . . can skate well.

3. **Incidental language.** Forecast of past tense (could) and future tense (shall/will be able to). I can swim now. I could not swim when I was a little boy. John cannot swim now. Perhaps he will be able to swim soon.

Notes on Lessons 16 and 17

Lesson 16. This will also have been introduced incidentally, earlier than this. The children at this stage should be interested in sport and people's ability to do things. It is not difficult to teach this in the present tense. 'Could' should be introduced incidentally and 'shall be able to' as well with the brighter children. Here is a clear example of how you can give the same basic lesson to your whole class and then add more difficult terms for the brighter children.

For instance, you would give the whole class a lesson on 'can'. Be sure they apprehend the basic idea of ability. Give each child a possible and impossible thing to do and teach 'I can' and 'I can't'. Do not give any new verbs in the first lesson. Give practice in this. The verbs and vocabulary suggested may then be taken. Swimming 'a length' and 'a width' will, of course, be taught when the children either do these things or are learning to do them. It is wise to gather them together in one lesson now and for the children to exchange news of abilities and endeavours. I am visualizing the children receiving this lesson at the stage and age when bodily activities and powers are of great interest, i.e. 7, 8, 9 years of age.

The incidental language will probably be asked for by the 'A' (brighter) group. They have more adventurous and confident mental approaches, and will thrive on more language forms. On the other hand, do not overwhelm the duller group with too much to remember at once. They need confidence given by practice and they enjoy routine. It is a wise teacher who can bring out the best in each child and work each child to the utmost of his ability. Avoid boredom for the bright child and lack of confidence leading to a veneer of 'don't care' in the dull child.

Lesson 17. The class can go on to the next lesson together although the duller group have not learnt all the incidental work. Here again practice the 'B's on the basic idea and give the brighter ones practice to some extent in the past and future tenses. Much dramatic work is needed here, e.g. in doing a thing carefully or carelessly, slowly, quickly, &c. Keep up this dramatic activity throughout your teaching. It will give life and reality to it.

LESSON 18

Language and vocabulary connected with animals: homes, parts, and young

Vocabulary

1. **Homes of animals**

   Horse, stable, rabbit, hutch (rabbit hole), the fields, the woods, the jungle, &c.

2. **Young of animals**

   Sheep, lamb, &c. About twelve of the most usual.

3. **Miscellaneous**

feathers	hoof	fur	hide
paws	claws	whiskers	wings
webbed feet	beaks		

Language

1. What is a baby sheep called? It is called a . . . .
2. What is a sheep covered with? It is covered with . . . .
3. Where does a sheep live? It lives in . . . .

Notes

Here is an easy lesson and one which both bright and slow children enjoy. It has no special difficulties. It provides an opportunity for short descriptions such as are suggested in the chapter on composition.

LESSON 19

Present participle with the verbs 'saw', 'watched', 'heard', and 'can see'. Vocabulary of more verbs and prepositions

Present participle and prepositions

Taken simply with 'I watched', 'I saw', and 'I heard', 'I can see', with revision of verbs.

1. I saw you walking.   I heard you shouting, talking.
   I can see . . . playing.
   I saw two dogs fighting. I heard you making a noise.

2. Along, across, over.

3. **Continue with adverbial phrases**

I saw you walking along the road.
I saw you running in the playground.
I saw a little boy running across the road.
I saw a little boy walking slowly to school.
I saw a little boy walking across the road.

4. **Description of pictures**

I can see a boy riding a bicycle.
I can see a girl picking flowers.
I can see a girl walking.

5. **Incidental**

Look at John laughing.
Look at Sally frowning.
Look at the aeroplanes flying high, &c.
What can you see John doing?

Note

This is a clarification and revision of work which has been done conversationally and individually, earlier. Notice that it is taken only with the verbs 'see, watch, hear, look at'. New prepositions, 'along, across, and over' are needed. If the previous preparation has been well done, there is no special difficulty here.

LESSON 20

Adjectives formed from materials. Order of adjectives. Vocabulary of materials, colours, and adjectives

Revision

Of materials (see Lesson 15) and adjectives.

Adjectives formed from materials

Sometimes addition of 'en', e.g. wooden, woollen, golden (now usually used for the colour).

Add to materials: velvet, stone, rubber.

a wooden horse	a brass pot	a leather sole
a woollen jumper	a paper handkerchief	a brick wall
a gold mug	a stone wall	a gold ring
a rubber heel	an iron fence	
a cardboard box	a cotton dress	

More colours

golden	silver-grey	stone-grey (golden curls)
sky-blue	dark blue	pale blue

Adjectives from materials used in cooking

a fruit cake	a ham sandwich
a milk pudding	an egg sandwich
a rice pudding	an apple pie, &c.
	a plum pudding

Order of adjectives

1	2	3	4	5	6
Number	**Kind**	**Size**	**Colour**	**Material made of**	**Noun**
a	pretty	little	blue and white	cotton	frock
two	lovely		red		roses
a	delicious			rice	pudding
a	soft			woollen	jumper

Notes

Not many new words are given in this lesson, but a new use of words. The names of all kinds of materials and colours are shown in their use as adjectives. The addition of 'en' now used in a very few cases, is pointed out. Even 'golden' which used to denote 'made of gold' is now usually used for the colour only and 'gold' for the material attributed, e.g. 'golden hair' and 'a gold ring'.

It is well to point out the order of the adjectives.

Deaf children need a guide here. That the number comes first is obvious, next comes kind or sort followed by size . . ., colour . . ., material. Practise by having a group of children and giving each a card bearing the name of an adjective such as those given above, and one child a card bearing the name of a noun. On the floor have numbered squares 1–5. At the word 'Go' each child moves to his appropriate square. They all hold up their cards and the class reads the whole phrases and approves or criticizes as the case may be.

Children enjoy sorting these out in proper order. Make a chart of this. Don't over-emphasize it but let the children keep a copy of the order to which to refer and, when a mistake is made, show the child where he is wrong by referring to the chart. It is so disheartening to a child to be told he is wrong without giving him a guide to the right procedure.

Adjectival phrases

A purse made of leather.
A glass full of water.

Give questions to see that the children really understand.

What is a woollen jumper made of?
What is a stone wall made of? &c.

LESSON 21

Relationships with numbers 10 to 20 and parts of things, furniture, clothes, buildings, books, and boxes, vehicles, cars, aeroplanes, parts of body. 'There is', 'there are'

Cardinal Numbers to 20

1. Learn numbers.
2. Many, a lot of, a few, some, any.

Relationships

Family:

mother	son	aunt	nephew
father	daughter	uncle	niece
cousin	sister	grandfather	grandmother
family	brother	husband	wife

Parts of things

1. **Furniture.** Legs, arms, back, seat, &c.
2. **Clothes.** Sleeves, cuffs, bows, &c.
3. **House.** Doors, windows, rooms, &c.
4. **A book.** Leaves, cover, pages, &c.
5. **A box.** Sides, top, bottom.
6. **A car.** Door, windows, windscreen, seat, steering-wheel, wheels, &c.
7. **Aeroplanes.** Wings, propeller, &c.
8. **Ship.** Deck, cabin, funnel, &c.
9. **Parts of body.** Wrist, elbow, nails, knuckles, ankle, instep, palm, sole, shoulder.

Use of 'there are', 'there is'

There are fourteen desks in this room.

There are . . . pictures on the walls.

How many legs has a chair? Four, *or* It has four.

How many children are there in your family? Three *or* There are three.

How many doors has your father's car?

The car has four wheels.

I have two brothers, &c.

Have you any . . .? Yes, I have some. No, I haven't any. Yes, I have three, &c.

Notes

There is no particular difficulty in the understanding of 'there is' and 'there are' by the child but he does find difficulty in using it. It is combined here with numbers and connected with the description of rooms, furniture, houses, as these are good examples of its use.

How many desks are there in this room? There are . . . .

Are there any pictures in this room? Yes, there are three/some/a few.

No, there aren't any.

Practise the use of 'some' and 'any'.

Notice the chapter on Composition for this lesson.

Relationships are often difficult for the deaf child. Try to treat it as naturally as possible with concrete examples. In a boarding school ask the parents to send photographs of relatives, with the name and relationship plainly written on the back. What often confuses the deaf child is the fact that his mother, for instance, is his father's wife and his cousin's aunt, and so on. The one relationship with himself is to him the only and permanent one. Be sure that he knows the relationship with himself first, and gradually widen the circle.

Be sure that the names of the numbers to 20 can be lip-read, spoken, and written correctly here. Take time for this.

LESSON 22

Telling the time. Appropriate vocabulary, adverbs, and roman numerals.

Telling the time

1. **Roman numerals** to 12.
2. **Vocabulary.** Hands, minutes, hours, seconds.
3. Counting in fives from 5 to 30 forwards and backwards.
4. **Adverbs.** Early, late, past, nearly, fast, slow, right.

Language

1. **Questions**

What is the time?

At what time did you get up? &c.

Is this clock right?

2. **Sentences**

I came to school at . . . .

I got up at . . . .

The clock is slow, &c.

I am late because the clock was slow.

Notes

It is presupposed, of course, that a clock and/or a clock-face will have been used in the classroom throughout this section and much incidental work such as putting the hands on this clock-face to correspond with the clock's hand will have been done. The teacher will tell the children—'It is 10 o'clock, it is time to stop', or 'It is time for P.T. It is half past 12. It is time for dinner', &c. It is good to teach the time first with the ordinary numerals, but the children should, as soon as they have an understanding of the time at all, learn the roman numerals. They are usually very much interested in learning the time. Concentrate on the o'clock; half past, quarter past, and quarter to first. Go on with other lessons and come back to it for the 'five past' to 'twenty-five past', again leaving the more difficult work on 'twenty-five to' to 'five to' till much incidental work has been done on this.

The brighter children can go on, of course, and learn the adverbs suggested; 'slow', 'fast', and 'right' should be taught incidentally.

Do not expect 'It is five minutes to ten', but 'It is five to ten'. This is correct colloquial use.

The alternate form, 2.45, &c., can be left till later.

LESSON 23

Reason, with health and ailments and appropriate vocabulary. Revision of weather

Vocabulary

1. medicine
   cough sweets
   cough mixture
   ointment
   cod-liver oil
   oil

2. ill
   well
   better
   not very well
   a little better
   sick

3. a cough
   a sore throat
   measles
   a cold
   a pain
   tooth-ache
   ear-ache
   a headache

Phrases

At home, in bed, in hospital, absent, present, away
from school.

Verbs

hurt
break
sprain

cough
sneeze

feel well
feel poorly

Weather

It is
or
was

{ windy
wet
cold
sunny
fine
foggy
misty
warm
hot
raining

The sun is shining.

Language

1. **Questions**

How are you? What is the matter with you? Why is . . . absent? Why did we not go to the playing fields yesterday?

2. **Answers**

I am very well, thank you. I am not very well, thank you. John is absent because he is ill. We did not go to the playing fields because it was wet.

3. **Incidental language**

We shall go to the playing fields if it is fine tomorrow.
I want to go to the playing field.
I want to go home because I am not very well.

Notes

A great deal of this lesson will have been done incidentally but it needs clarifying and consolidating. It lends itself to much imaginative play and is enjoyed by the children in spite of the aches and pains enumerated. A number of dressing-up games with doctor and nurse can be used to give practice in this lesson.

LESSON 24

'Belongs to.' Child's personal possessions. Family possessions. Possessive pronouns revised

Language

1. Revision of 'my', 'your', 'his', 'her', 'their', 'our'.
2. Belongs to, does not belong to; belong to, do not belong to.

3. Mine, yours, his, hers, theirs, ours, . . . 's, my own (my very own).

Vocabulary of personal possessions

Family, books, pencils, &c., clothes, toys, animals, things at home, parents' possessions, school's possessions.

Chiefly revision but probably added:

1. pen-knife, purse, pochette, key, diary, bicycle, string, bag, mirror, photo, books.
2. **Pet animals.** Hedgehog, guinea-pig, white mice, puppy, kittens.
3. **Father's and mother's possessions.** Car, motor-bike, bicycle, suitcase, garage, green-house, &c.

Whose is this? It belongs to me. It is mine.

Notes

Here is an easy lesson which appeals to the children and which revises the possessive pronouns and a good deal of vocabulary. It is good also that the children should have a lesson here on what is or what is not their own property and on respecting the property of others.

Incidental language

Verbs 'to lend', 'to borrow' (contrast, 'to give').

May I borrow your pen-knife?
This pen-knife does not belong to me.
It belongs to John.
He lent it to me.
I must give it back to him.
I haven't a pen-knife of my own.
I want a pen-knife of my own, &c.
Perhaps Daddy will give me one at Christmas.

COMPOSITION

1. *Fuller diary*

IF in your language lessons you are giving the children the right tools for self-expression, then the daily diary should be getting fuller and the language more diverse.

Some idea of paragraphing should be given by grouping all matter concerning one thing together (it may be only two sentences, e.g. 'I went to the park with Daddy. We played cricket') and beginning it with a fresh line and the correct spacing from the margin. Full stops and capital letters should be insisted upon, and the apostrophe for the possessive.

2. *Fuller letters* resulting from the above. An attempt to ask and answer questions.

3. '*What I have at home.*' Several possessions required with at least two sentences about each.

e.g. I have a kitten at home.	I have a ball at home.
It is black and white.	It is grey.
It is pretty.	It is made of rubber.

4. '*Myself*', '*my family*', '*my friend*'. Limited to about five sentences.

5. '*Where I have been and what I have seen*' (see Lesson 13). Geography book.

6. A visit (to the zoo, the park, &c.), very simply, e.g.

We went to the zoo on Monday with	We went to the park on . . . .
We saw lions. They were fierce.	We saw some ducks swimming on the pond.
We saw elephants.	We fed the ducks, &c., *or*

They were very large, &c.	We watched the ducks. We saw some boys playing cricket. We watched them.

Try as in the diary to get the children to write at least one more sentence about something they saw after stating the bare fact. This will be very valuable as they progress through the language scheme and help to prevent that baldness of most deaf children's compositions. Start simply in this way, but remember to keep it simple. Let them practice this for a long time before insisting on more than this. Make haste slowly. Once again do not forget that self-confidence is more than half the battle. If you can once get deaf children to think 'Why, this is easy, I can do it', you will have accomplished much.

7. *Descriptions of animals*

This should follow the lip-reading game mentioned in Lesson 13. When they have acquired facility in this, the writing of it down will be a simple matter; for the child, after much repetition, will have memorized the outline: e.g. '. . . lives far away, . . . in a hot country, . . . is very fierce, . . . has black and yellow stripes'. This becomes:

A tiger

A tiger lives far away in a hot country (or 'where it is hot').

It is very fierce.

It has black and yellow stripes.

A polar bear

A polar bear lives far away in a very cold country (or 'where it is cold').

It is fierce.

It has a white fur coat, &c.

Always follow the same pattern.

Do *not* take this composition until the children know the lip-reading almost by heart.

They might add—'I have seen a tiger at the zoo', or 'I have never seen a tiger.'

Encourage in these and in other compositions the use of the pronoun after the first sentence.

8. *Rooms*

'My classroom, my bedroom, Miss . . . 's room, my school', &c. This practises the use of 'There are' and 'There is'.

e.g. My classroom is large (or 'small').

> There are four windows in it.
> There are ten desks in it.
> There is a teacher's table.
> There is a vase of flowers on the table.
> There are some pictures on the wall.

Take this simply first to practice 'There are'. Then later return to it and encourage two sentences about each thing as before. Let them turn up their former composition and copy the first sentence, and the first 'There are . . . .' and ask for another observation on the windows. 'They are large. They are open. They are tall. They are dirty', &c. Let each write his own observation and so continue. The children who find difficulty with this should go back to the simple cataloguing.

9. *More descriptions of pictures*

'There are' can now be used instead of 'I can see'.

> There are five children in the picture.
> There is a boy running. He is happy. There are two girls . . . ing, &c.

Short descriptions of a certain book, car, aeroplane, &c., bringing in the use of the new vocabulary of Lesson 20.

e.g. **My story book**

My story book is called . . . .
. . . gave it to me.
The cover is blue.
It is made of . . . .
There are . . . pages.
I like my story book.

Our car

Our car is grey.
It has four doors.
       two
It has a screen wiper.
The seats are grey.
My father drives the car.

My box

That is my box.
It is made of . . . .
It is brown.
It has flowers on the top.
It has my name on it.
It has cards in it.

These are more difficult. The brighter children will love them. Give the slower ones a cataloguing of the parts of things if you feel they will fail in the more difficult particular thing.

e.g. **An aeroplane**

An aeroplane has two wings.
It has a propeller, &c.

A car

A car has four wheels.
It has . . . seats.
It has a steering-wheel, &c.

SPEECH

THE aim of the speech work in this section should be ease with clarity. The phrase work of Stage 1 should be continued and extended. The children are learning many new phrases and they should learn to speak them as phrases and not in separate words. Do not, however, sacrifice clarity nor try to quicken the pace too much. Clarity with accuracy will only come with practice. Therefore practice in as many ways as you can.

Continue movement to their spoken rhymes and refrains. Keep the rhymes very short. It is better to enjoy two lines than to learn four and find them difficult. Refrains and repetitive rhymes are still the order of the day. The refrains can be a little more difficult and the theme should be suitable to the age and interests of the child. Stories such as those I suggested in Stage 1 with interpolations, repetitions, and interjections by the children are still very useful.

The children should learn to say the days of the week correctly by heart and, later, the months. They should learn to count (correctly again) quickly and easily to 20 and back to 1 again, then in twos, and so on. They should also begin to learn the twice- and three-times table, both twice one and two ones, &c., in both ways, i.e. twice one are two, and two ones are two. There are many ways of making this enjoyable, one of the chief of these is by acting it, the children themselves forming and reforming themselves into groups. Learning by heart at this stage is most valuable and the names of the numbers are an excellent speech exercise, comprising both easy and also very difficult words.

The correct stress in words of more than one syllable

should be taught from the beginning, clapping or other movement is the most obvious way and probably the best. All the new work taught should be practised in this way.

The children of this age enjoy intonation work (with the hearing-aids, of course). They enjoy trying to copy the teacher's voice who, of course, sings very high and very low in order to get a clear-cut difference in the children's minds as far as possible.

Begin very simply, try a few refrains, exclamations, and phrases first.

One word of caution. Let this be an added joy even with the very deaf ones. Do not try to find out what the child hears for your own satisfaction, but encourage him to listen and watch at the same time. If by reason of your actions (drawing the curves in the air), your diagrams, and the hearing-aid he gets some little difference in his voice, express great pleasure. It will help to get a more natural voice and give him the feeling that he *can*. It may lead to a greater perception of what he hears. Do not deprive him of lip-reading while listening. Use the hearing aid as an aid, not an end in itself. Apart from the effect on naturalness of the deaf child's voice, the teaching of intonation can be used as another method of presenting the language taught.

I have found it a great help in the practice of asking questions to teach the children the two tunes concerned and divide them into the two headings. It is approaching the problem from a different angle and that is always valuable. Use as many visible devices as possible, drawing the curve in the air, moving the whole body up or down, dropping (Tune I) and bouncing (Tune II) a ball and using different colours for the different tunes.

As you teach your language forms, begin to teach the simple intonation. Do not confuse the issue with the young children by teaching emphasis and stress unless it comes up naturally. The tune of the whole question or answer is what should be aimed at.

Beginning of intonation work

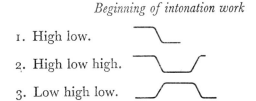

1. High low.
2. High low high.
3. Low high low.

Tune I

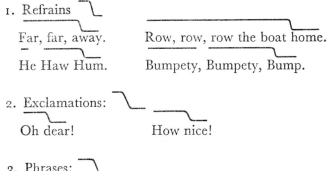

1. Refrains

Far, far, away.   Row, row, row the boat home.

He Haw Hum.   Bumpety, Bumpety, Bump.

2. Exclamations:

Oh dear!   How nice!

3. Phrases:

over the road   in the garden   to London

4. Questions beginning with 'What', 'Where', 'When', 'Why', 'Who', 'Whose', 'How'.

What is your name?

5. Answers to questions: Yes I do. No I haven't (very simply).

6. Commands.

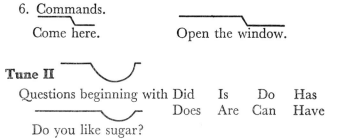

Come here.   Open the window.

Tune II

Questions beginning with Did   Is   Do   Has
                               Does Are Can   Have

Do you like sugar?

Refrains and rhymes

Here are some more refrains and rhymes suitable for this stage.

1. **'Hee Haw Hum.'** To be found in *Mother Goose* (also suggested for Stage 1).

This, apart from the enjoyment of it, is a very good voice exercise. After the sound 'h' it is very difficult to get a harsh sound, so, teach a good 'h', insist on its use, and practice this refrain for helping to soften harsh voices.

2. **'Bumpety, Bumpety, Bump.'** To be found in *Mother Goose*.

This gives good practice in 'mp'. Work for both a good 'm' and a good plosive 'p' (unvoiced, of course). Work such as this with the accent and the movement coming so definitely on the first syllable is a good basis for more work on accent. Get these things right from the start and, by clapping or moving in some way, show where the accent falls.

The action of these two rhymes with refrains is self-evident. Use them only for refrain work, i.e. spoken by teacher and refrains spoken by the children.

3. **Row the Boat Home.**

This is a good exercise for the sound 'oa'. Insist that this should be rounded, with the corners of the mouth drawn in. This refrain also practises phrasing. Notice the four

beats of the line and that 'row the boat' comes on the third
beat and 'home' on the next, i.e. 'Rów, rów, rów theboat
hóme'. Listen for a good 't', being sure that it is unvoiced,
and finish the refrain with a good 'm'.

Can you get a difference in tone and volume of sound
between the speaking of the refrains for the strong second
verse and the quiet last verse?

The children sit down in lines of four or five on the floor
and row to the beat.

> Gently we're gliding over the stream,
>> Row, row, row the boat home,
> The day's work is over and now we may dream,
>> Row, row, row the boat home.
>
> When we rowed up the river, the sunshine was bright,
>> Row, row, row the boat home,
> And we sang of the morn as we pulled with our might,
>> Row, row, row the boat home.
>
> And now falls the evening all gentle and still,
>> Row, row, row the boat home,
> The shadows are lying on meadow and hill,
>> Row, row, row the boat home.
>
> Gently we're gliding over the stream,
>> Row, row, row the boat home,
> The day's work is over and now we may dream,
>> Row, row, row the boat home.

4. Far, Far, Away

> I should like to go o'er the rolling sea
>> Away, oh, ay.
> To where monkeys, lions, and snakes you see,
>> Far, far, away.

There the sun shines bright all the happy day,
 Away, oh, ay,
And little black babies laugh and play,
 Far, far, away.

In the forest, elephants roam about,
 Away, oh, ay,
And beautiful birds fly in and out,
 Far, far, away.

Then let us go o'er the rolling sea,
 Away, oh, ay,
All these wonderful things to see,
 Far, far, away.

The children stand, hands resting on hips, feet apart, as on the deck of a ship. They sway from side to side with the rhythm.

This refrain, also, helps to correct harsh or nasal voices. If this is the trouble in your class use 'far, far, away' only, for a time, returning to the double refrain later.

Let the children feel the breath of 'f' on their fingers. Let them keep their finger in front of their mouths for the whole refrain for a time. I think you will find this simple exercise a help. (Be sure that they feel the breath coming out of their mouths.) Practice in Lessons 13 and 18.

5. Here is another 'speech without tears' exercise for bringing the voice forward into the mouth cavities. This is especially enjoyed by the boys and is an adaptation of 'I smell the blood of an Englishman'.

Heroes and Giants

Giants. Fee, Fo, Fi, Fum,   *Heroes.* Let who will come,
 Wait till I come.   Fee, Fo, Fi, Fum.

Giants. Fee, Fo, Fi, Fum,	*Heroes.* Fee, Fo, Fi, Fum,
Wait till I come,	Let who will come,
Hee, Ho, Hi, Hum,	Hee, Ho, Hi, Hum,
Fee, Fo, Fi, Fum.	Fee, Fo, Fi, Fum.

Giants move forward with heavy tread, bodies bent forward, shaking fists. Meanwhile heroes stand, arms folded, attitude of defiance. They speak the first line of their verse without movement. For the second line they pretend to draw a sword and flourish it in time to the beats in the line. For the last two lines they move slowly forward, flourishing their swords while the giants move back. On the last 'Fum' the heroes point their swords down while the giants fall on their knees.

Note

You will notice in the rhymes I have listed below that there is a certain amount of repetition. It is quite permissible to put more repetition in. Remember that your aim is the enjoyment and improvement of spoken language. Give them plenty of easy speech, and they will want to speak more.

6. Here is a way of treating **Hickory, Dickory, Dock.**

> Tíck-Tóck, Tíck-Tóck,
> Tíck-Tóck, Tíck-Tóck,
> Híckory, Díckory, Dóck.
> Tíck-Tóck, Tíck-Tóck,
> The moúse ran úp the clóck.
> Tíck-Tóck, Tíck-Tóck,
> The clóck struck óne. Tíck-Tóck,
> The moúse ran dówn. Tíck-Tóck,
> Híckory, Díckory, Dóck.
> Tíck-Tóck, Tíck-Tóck,
> Tíck-Tóck, Tíck.

There are various ways of taking this, with some children doing the Tick-Tock only, moving their arms as a pendulum of a clock throughout, others acting and others speaking the lines. This is a good exercise for the two plosive sounds 't' and 'k'. As before, feel the breath on the finger. (Lesson 22.)

7. **'Pease Pudding Hot.'** To be found in *Mother Goose*. Clapping rhythm.

8. **Oh dear! What can the Matter be?** (traditional rhyme, four lines only).

In this rhyme there are three repetitions of the first line and only one more line to negotiate.

9. **Hot Cross Buns.**

In this rhyme the more difficult

> 'If you have no daughters
> Give them to your sons'

can be said by the teacher.

Let the children walk to this rhythm, ringing the muffin bell! Be careful of the silent beat. The phrasing of 'óne apénny' is greatly helped by the rhythm.

10. **Pussy Cat, Pussy Cat, Where have You been?**

An easy rhyme and much enjoyed. Very applicable for Lesson 13.

11. **'Rice Pudding.'** From *When We were Very Young*, by A. A. Milne.

The children will find this very amusing to dramatize. The line 'What is the matter with Mary Jane?' can be taken as a refrain. The line 'It's lovely rice pudding for dinner again', should also be spoken by all. (Lesson 23.)

12. **'How Many Days shall Baby play?'** This is found in *Mother Goose*. (Lesson 11.)

Good practice for saying the days.

13. The second verse of **'I Caught a Fish Alive'** (*Mother Goose*). Added practice in the numbers 1–10. It also brings in 'Why' . . .'Because'. (Lesson 23.)

14. The first verse of **'Glad that I live am I'** is much enjoyed by the children as choral speech. No movement is necessary.

15. **'Bell Horses'** (*Mother Goose*) is another suitable rhyme.

Movement—the pawing of horses, galloping at the end of the verse. (Lesson 22.)

16. **Polly put the Kettle on.** Has much repetition and is soon learnt by the children.

17. **September**

> Golden in the garden,
> Golden in the glen;
> Golden, golden, golden,
> September's here again.
>
> Golden in the tree-tops,
> Golden in the sky;
> Golden, golden, golden,
> September's going by.

This has much repetition and is very good practice for 'g' and 'n'. (Lesson 20.)

18. **Please come to My House**

> Please come to my house,
> To my house, to my house;
> Please come to my house
> And have a cup of tea.

A good exercise on 'm' and 'ee'.

19. I have a New Umbrella

> I have a new umbrella,
> I have a silk umbrella,
> I have a new red silk umbrella,
> I wish that it would rain. (Lesson 20.)

20. 'The Rain is raining all around.' *The Child's Garden of Verse*, R. L. Stevenson.

Some of the traditional skipping rhymes can be adapted for use. Their rhythm is very marked and the pace fairly slow, two things which make them very suitable for our deaf children. Here are two:

21. All in Together

> All in together
> This fine weather.
> I saw Peter
> Hanging out of the window.
> Shoot, Bang, Fire!

Children skipping together in rope. At 'Fire!' all run out.

22. Cups, Saucers, Plates, Dishes

Cups, saucers, Plates, dishes, I have Three wishes. One, two, Three, now	Children jump over the rope as it is swung from side to side.
Right over My head.	Rope sent over the head, normal skipping resumed.

Some poems, for instance those in *When We were Very Young* and *Now We are Six*, are suitable to be read to the children as stories with interpolations. The story should be

told simply first, then read to the children in the words of
the poem, acted, read to them again and their part of it
written for them, spoken correctly, and acted with speaking. There are many from various sources which can be
used in this way, here are a few:

23. **From 'When We were Very Young'**

(a) Puppy and I.   (Lesson 13.)
(b) Market Square. (,,   )
(c) At the Zoo.   (,,   )
(d) Missing.   (,,   )
(e) Hoppity.
(f) In the Fashion.

24. **From 'Now We are Six'**

(a) The Good Little Girl. (Lesson 13.)
(b) Journey's End.

The children also enjoy,

(c) 'Pussy can sit by the Fire and sing' from *Just So
Stories*.

25. **Here are some more nursery rhymes** which
are enjoyed at this stage:

(a) Little Bo Peep.   (f) Little Miss Muffet.
(b) Jack and Jill.   (g) Little Boy Blue.
(c) To Market, to Market. (h) Hey Diddle Diddle.
(d) Cat and the Fiddle.   (i) Molly My Sister and I
(e) Little Jack Horner.   fell out.

Treat them as stories first, which the teacher tells to the
child, which they act and which she repeats often, then
let them learn lines or phrases which they say themselves.

Do not teach them the whole rhymes and expect them
to learn and say them correctly. That way discourage-
ment lies. Let them learn them happily as hearing children

do by constant repetition to them. Let the part in which they join be correctly said. Do not forget the part played by stories of things which have happened to the children, with speech interpolations.

These stories can now be added to by stories of happenings to other children apart from themselves. A series of stories about two children could be invented. (Be sure to have both a boy and a girl.) Treat them in the same way as I have suggested in Stage 1, bringing in exclamations, remarks, and repetitions by the children. I have seen this done with a class of children of this stage. The children looked forward from week to week with great eagerness to the next instalment in the very ordinary adventures of two very ordinary children. Meanwhile, a repetition of 'this week's story' was asked for again and again.

LANGUAGE

READ again the summary in the Introduction of the interests and natural desires of the child. You will see that the main theme of Stage 3 is the habitual tense with a number of examples of its use. The child's horizon is widening to include where things come from, where they are grown, what work people do, what things cost, foreign lands, and physical geography. He learns to express how to do things, what to do things with, the consequences of certain actions, and the purpose of certain actions.

We are trying to teach the children to think, to wonder, and to ask questions.

Contrasts and opposites and superlatives begin the comparison of one thing with another.

Compound sentences with 'and' and 'but', and the beginning of complex sentences with the adverbial clause introduced by 'when' are taken, using the tenses already taught with the addition of the past continuous tense.

The chief difficulties here are the habitual tense, which is difficult despite its seeming simplicity, and the use of spontaneous questions by the children.

Speech, composition, reading stories, conversation should all centre round these language principles and interests.

A SUMMARY OF THE LESSONS IN STAGE 3

Lesson 25. Past and future continuous tenses with practice in telling the time. Revision of names of lessons and verbs.

26. Opposites, contrasts, shapes, compound sentences joined by 'and', 'but', and 'so is'. Some work in 'although'. Appropriate vocabulary.

27. Irregular plurals. Names of letters with the alphabet and appropriate vocabulary.

28. Adverbial clause of time with 'when' and 'while'. Past continuous and past indefinite tenses.

29. Present indefinite (habitual tense). How often? Revision of everyday and weekly happenings, lessons, and duties. Practice in telling the time.

30. Shopping with vocabulary of coins, shops, and things bought in the shops. Practice in the habitual tense. 'How much . . . cost?'

31. Purpose (simple) with the infinitive. What . . . for? Appropriate vocabulary and verbs. Combination with Lesson 30.

32. Habitual tense (present indefinite), with new verbs, phrases, and adverbs, and combined with Lesson 30. More fruits and foods, trades and occupations, &c.

33. 'If' in the present indefinite and future tenses only, with vocabulary of weather and adverbs. 'Happen' and 'behave'.

34. Adverbial clause of time with future tense. Introduction of 'until' with 'to wait'.

35. 'With.' Means of doing things. Practice in habitual tense chiefly. Appropriate verbs and nouns.

36. Cardinal numbers to 100, the date. Superlatives and the beginning of comparison. Appropriate verbs.

37. Revision of adverbial clauses with 'when'. Past and future tenses of 'can'.

38. 'How to' with more verbs and habitual tense.

39. Habitual tense with verbs and vocabulary of natural objects. Animals and what they do.

40. Adverbs and adverbial phrases relating to Lesson 39. Questions 'How?' 'When?' and 'Where?'

41. 'How much?' and 'How many?' Revision of shopping. Appropriate vocabulary.

QUESTIONS

What were you doing at . . . o'clock yesterday?
What will you be doing . . . tomorrow?
Could you . . . when?
Will you be able to . . . when?
What will you be able to do when . . .?
What were you doing when . . .?
What could you not do when . . .?

What is the opposite of . . . ?
What is the plural of . . .?
What shape is . . .?
What is it like?
Do you know how to . . .?

How do you spell . . .?
Is it . . . or . . .?
How much is that?
How much did . . . cost?
How much does . . . cost?

What is the date?
Who won the race?
Who was first?
Who was second?
Who wrote the best of all?
Who is the tallest boy in the class?

Where do you buy . . .?
What can you buy at . . .?
Do you sell . . .?
Does a baker sell . . .?
What do you do every day?
What does a postman do?
How often do you . . .?

Were you late this morning?
Do you ever . . .?
Do you wash yourself?
Do you . . . every day?
At what time do you get up?

Where does . . . come from?
What did you . . . with?
What do you do with . . .?
What did you . . . for?
What will happen if . . .?

What grows in the garden?
Where does the sun rise?

LESSON 25

Past and future continuous tenses with practice in telling the time. Revision of names of lessons and verbs

Past and future continuous tenses

I was . . . ing.   I shall be . . . ing.

Vocabulary

1. **Phrases**

At 12 o'clock yesterday (I was . . . ing).
At 12 o'clock tomorrow (I shall be . . . ing).
It is . . . o'clock now (I am . . . ing).

2. **Revise** and add to names of lessons.

Incidental work

Alternate method of recording the time.

20 past 1 = 1.20.   a.m. and p.m.
Half past 1 = 1.30.
20 to 2 = 1.40, &c.

Colloquial expressions

to do homework.
to do arithmetic.
to have a reading lesson.
to learn geography.

I shall be doing my homework at 5 o'clock to night.
I shall be doing arithmetic at 10 a.m.
I was having a reading lesson at . . . .
I was having a reading lesson at . . . yesterday.
I shall be learning geography at . . . .
I was learning geography at . . . .
I was playing football at . . . .

Notes

It is always good to begin a new term or stage with revision, but if this revision can introduce something new so that the pupils do not know that they are revising, it is all to the good.

Here you can revise the time, introduce or rather gather up previous incidental knowledge of a new tense, and also bring in work on the tenses already known, insisting on their use with time phrases and adverbs, e.g.

Yesterday I played football.
Tomorrow I shall go to the pictures.
It is 5 past 12. I am writing now.
                    I have seen a lion at the zoo (no time phrase).
                    I was writing at 12 o'clock yesterday.
                    I shall be playing football at 12 o'clock tomorrow.

Use plenty of action in this as in earlier lessons, noting the time as well. Many of these speech and action lessons can be devised. Concentrate on the past continuous tense here. The future continuous tense is less used. It suffices if it is understood and can be used when necessary.

LESSON 26

Opposites, contrasts, shapes, compound sentences joined by 'and', 'but', and 'so is'. Some work in 'although'. Appropriate vocabulary

Revision of adjectives and adverbs and addition of more

sad	glad	sweet	sour	**Adverbs**	
right	wrong	good	bad	slowly	quickly
happy	unhappy	smooth	rough	quietly	noisily
right	left	crooked	straight	here	there
young	old	rich	poor	carefully	carelessly
pretty	ugly	this	that		
high	low	these	those		

Contrasts

sunrise	sunset	**Verbs**	
absent	present	go	come
yes	no	love	hate
black	white	like	dislike
male	female		
round	square		
day	night		
summer	winter		

Shape

round	oblong	triangular
square	oval	three-cornered

Language

1. Joining sentences with 'but' and 'and'.
2. The use of 'or'.

Questions

What is the opposite of . . .?
Is . . . smooth or rough?
Which do you want, . . . or . . .?
Which do you like, . . . or . . .?
Do you like this or that?

Sentences

1. . . . is smooth but . . . is rough. I like . . . but I dislike . . . . is absent but . . . is present. . . . is absent and so is . . . . They are both . . . .

2. What shape is . . .?

3. **Incidental language**

What is . . . like?

Comparison begun:

He is taller than Jane. This orange is sweeter than that.

Descriptions can now be amplified:

That is an apple. It is round.
It is like a ball. It is green and red.

LESSON 27

Irregular plurals. Names of letters of the alphabet and appropriate vocabulary

Plurals

1. **Regular plurals adding 's'**

Combine with verb practice, i.e. put this sentence in the plural:

The little girl is playing with her ball.
The little girls are playing with their balls.

2. **Irregular Plurals**

man	men
child	children
knife	knives
loaf	loaves
leaf	leaves
lady	ladies
baby	babies
berry	berries
mouse	mice
box	boxes
fox	foxes
sheep	sheep
woman	women
goose	geese
tooth	teeth
foot	feet

knives, loaves, leaves } Learn rule—change 'f' to 'v', add 's', &c.

ladies, babies, berries } Learn rule—change 'y' to 'i', add 'es'.

boxes, foxes } Rule—add 'es'.

Names of letters

Alphabet, spelling.

Revision of pronouns

Pointing out change for plural, e.g. I—we, he—they.

Some masculine and feminine—chiefly revision

Male	**Female**	**Male**	**Female**
man	woman	he	she
men	women	him	her
boy	girl	lad	lass
father	mother	lord	lady
daddy	mummy	king	queen
uncle	aunt	prince	princess
grandfather	grandmother		
grandpa	grandma		
	granny		

Language

1. What is the plural of . . .? What is the feminine of . . .? What is the singular of . . .? What is the masculine of . . .?

2. How do you spell . . .? (names of letters given in the answer).

3. Continue:

someone	no one	everyone
somebody	nobody	everybody
anyone	anybody	anything—with
		negative
something	nothing	everything

4. Change of verb for plural (revision of tenses, especially habitual).

Notes on Lessons 26 *and* 27

We continue this section with two more lessons of classification and revision. The first is concerned with opposites, contrasts, and shapes, and the second with plurals, feminines, and spelling. The skilful teacher will use the added interest of the new idea to consolidate and revise previous work. The pupils should gain in accuracy of thought and expression. Capital letters, full stops, question marks, commas, correct spelling, and clear and legible writing should be insisted upon. Practice the children in producing good writing at a reasonable pace, neither too slow and laboured nor hurried and badly formed. This is the same point I have tried to make in the teaching of speech. The aim should be to encourage fluency without sacrificing accuracy.

In Lesson 26 active language games can be taken. First children can choose attributes; sad, glad, young, old, some being duplicates of the others, &c. Two pupils take the part of the conjunctions 'but' and 'and'. One comes forward, holds up his card and says, 'I am glad'. The class says '. . . is glad'. The teacher asks for an opposite. The one holding 'sad' comes forward and says 'I am sad'. The class again says '. . . is sad'. The pupil holding 'but' comes to stand between them, and all say:

 '. . . is sad, but . . . is glad'.

Repeat with two similar attributes, using 'and':

 '. . . is glad and . . . is glad'.

Have another card showing 'and so is'. Let one come forward and remove 'and', substituting 'and so is'. Let the class say:

 '. . . is glad and so is . . . .'
 'They are both glad'.

This can be extended during subsequent lessons to 'although'.

In this case two opposite attributes of one person must be taken. '. . . is young. He is tall'. 'But' can be interposed as above. '. . . is young but he is tall.' Then show the transposition. The child holding 'but' moves away, 'although' goes to first place. 'Although . . . is young, he is tall.'

These should, of course, be taken *after* the incidental and anecdotal use of 'although'. The children enjoy it, and it helps to fix its use firmly in mind.

Further note on 'although' and 'though'

This conjunction should be taught incidentally in response to the child's need and experience, and this use can be clinched with stories and anecdotes.

Some examples of the anecdotal and incidental use of 'although'

1. After telling about a kitten standing up to a big dog:

   A kitten is small but it is brave.
   Although a kitten is small, it is brave.

2. After a race:

   John is short. He has short legs.
   Harry has long legs. He can run fast.
   John is short, but he can run fast.
   Although John is short, he can run fast. He ran as fast as Harry.

3. Tony is thin. He is not very strong.

   James is rather thin but he is strong.
   Although James is thin, he is strong.

4. Bill is little, but he is brave.

   Although Bill is little, he is brave.

LESSON 28

The adverbial clause of time with 'when' and 'while'. Past continuous and past indefinite tenses

Adverbial clause of time

Revise time phrases and expand, e.g.

I was writing at 12 o'clock yesterday.
I was writing when the bell rang at 12 o'clock yesterday.
I was reading when Daddy came home last night.
It was raining when I went home last night.

Combine with new and old weather phrases

1. The sun was shining when he . . . .
   The moon was shining when I . . . .
   The wind was blowing when she . . . .
   The wind was blowing hard when . . . .
   The stars were coming out when . . . .
2. I was walking home when it started to rain, &c.

Simultaneous action expressed by 'while'

He was writing while I was reading.
Last night I was reading while my brother was doing a jig-saw.

Notes

The two thoughts in this lesson are quite easy to apprehend.

1. The adverbial clause of time with 'when' has probably been used much in incidental work. It can be combined with new weather expressions and revision of others.

If the children understand this time phrase, the expansion into a clause is not difficult.

e.g. It was raining at half past three yesterday.
It was raining when I went home at half past three yesterday, &c.

Oxford English Readers for Africa, Book 3, pages 53–61, has some work on this which you may find useful.

2. **Simultaneous action with 'while'**

This is a very easy lesson. Use 'while' chiefly with the past continuous tense. It is not often used with either the present or the future continuous tenses. Use plenty of action and dramatic presentations as I have already suggested in other work on tenses. Be sure that the action is finished before the children speak.

LESSON 29

Present indefinite (habitual tense). 'How often?'
Revision of everyday and weekly happenings,
lessons, and duties. Practice in telling the time

What we do

Every morning, every day, once a week, every Monday, every summer, every evening, on Sundays. Always—never—sometimes.

Verbs

get up	dress	go home
go to bed	sleep well	go to the playing fields
wake up	go to sleep	go to church
wash	come to school	say your prayers
have **reading** (other lessons)		

have a bath	help mother	wash your hair
cook	chop sticks	go to the pictures
clean	bring in the coal	wash up

Further use of reflexive—with wash and dress—bath.

I wash myself, I dress myself, I bath myself.

Revision of time with this tense

At what time do you get up?
       ,,   ,,   ,,   come to school?
       ,,   ,,   *did* you get up this morning?
Were you late this morning?
Are you ever late?

Question forms

Do you . . . every day?

Do you wash yourself?

Do you ever {hit your sister? / hit a girl?}

Does your mother wash you?

Do boys . . .?

Does . . . every day?

Do we . . .?

Does she . . .?

How often do you go to see your grandmother?

How often do you go to the pictures?

Notes

This is a tense which the children find difficult to use and to use correctly. It has been used previously with the verbs 'to like', 'to want', 'to have', 'to be', 'to live', 'to feel well', 'to feel poorly', 'to belong to'. It has also been used in calendar work incidentally—goes home, &c., every Friday.

It is good to start simply in the way suggested here, with the happenings of every day. As soon as it is apprehended, contrast it with the more definite time tenses. 'I *shall do* it tomorrow. I *did* it yesterday. I *do* it every day. He will do it tomorrow. He did it yesterday. He does it every day'.

The 's' presents a difficulty. It seems such a small thing to the child and we adults seem to attach too much importance to it. Coming as this lesson does after one on 'Plurals' its use can be shown diagrammatically thus:

They
The boys } play football every Wednesday.
A boy   plays football every Wednesday.

One 's' only needed in each sentence.

Does he play? Yes, he does.
Do they play? Yes, they do.

The *Oxford English Readers for Africa*, Book 2, Lessons 5–10, has good exercises on this tense, which may be helpful to you.

LESSON 30

Shopping, with vocabulary of coins, shops, and things bought in the shops. Practice in the habitual tense. 'How much . . . cost?'

Vocabulary

1. Names of coins

A penny, half-crown, &c.   threepence, &c.
(about twelve)

2.   Shops   People in the shops

The grocery, the draper's,   The grocer, the draper,
&c.   &c.
(about twelve)

3. **Things you buy in the above shops**

tea	cloth	sweets	bread
bacon, &c.			
sugar	ribbon	toffee	buns
ball	wool, &c.	chocolate	cakes
whip, &c.	milk	butter, &c.	medicine

4. **Verbs :** sell, buy, cost, keep, get, spend.

Language

1. What is that? A shilling.
2. Where did you buy . . .? At the toy shop } Past
                              At Lewis's   } tense.
3. How much did it cost?
   What can you buy at the dairy?
   Where do you get cream?   } Habitual tense.
   How much does sugar cost?
   Who keeps a dairy?

4. **Sentences**

That is a . . . .
I bought it at . . . .
It cost . . . .

Shopping lessons and expeditions should be given, bringing in:

Do you sell . . .? How much is that? I want . . .,
    please.

Notes

Here is a lesson which lends itself to much activity, dramatization, expeditions, and imaginative play. There are several difficulties in it, but the interest is so great that care in teaching will solve them.

1. 'Do not over-emphasize the giving and receiving of change. Let the children do it concretely but do not worry them here to work it out mentally.

2. Differentiate carefully between the name of the shop or store and the person who owns or serves in it. Allow the colloquial 'the butcher's', 'the chemist's', but insist on its correct usage.

3. It is a great opportunity to practice the use of the past and habitual tenses. In playing at shops they will use the habitual tense, (1) 'I am a grocer. I sell . . .', (2) 'Do you sell . . .? Yes I do. How much is it?' or 'How much does it cost? It costs . . . . I want a pound of . . ., please'. In telling about this they will use the past tense. 'I went to the grocer's. I bought . . . . It cost . . . .'

In talking about shops, shopkeepers, and what they sell, the habitual tense is used.

4. In their news.

I go shopping with mother every week.
We always go to the butcher's and the grocer's.
We sometimes go to the chemist.
We buy . . . at the grocer's, &c.

contrasted with

Last Saturday I went shopping with mother.
We went to the butcher's, &c.
We didn't go to the chemist's because we didn't want anything there.

5. This will lead to:

When I go shopping with mother, we always go to the butcher's.
When Daddy comes with us, he always buys me an ice-cream.

and

When I went shopping with mother last week we
didn't go to the chemist's.

'Whenever' can be used as an alternative to 'when' in
this connexion (with the habitual tense). It sometimes
helps to impress the fact that 'when' or 'whenever' here
means 'every time'.

LESSON 31

Purpose (simple) with the infinitive. 'What . . .
for?' Appropriate vocabulary and verbs. Combination with Lesson 30

Sentences

1. I went to town yesterday *to buy* some shoes.
   I went to . . . yesterday *to see* Grandma.
   I went to the sweet shop *to buy* some chocolate.
   I went to the baker's *to buy* bread.
   My Auntie gave me sixpence *to go* to the pictures.

2. **Verbs used :** to get, to buy, to see, to go.

Notes

This lesson arises naturally out of the preceding one. It is
better, I find, at this stage to keep to the question form,
'What did you . . . for?' (i.e. purpose), rather than use
'Why . . .?' The children will enjoy this lesson, and of
course 'Mother Hubbard' should illustrate it. It is a very
simple introduction to the idea of purpose. Leave it as
such.

LESSON 32

Habitual tense (present indefinite), with new verbs, phrases, and adverbs, and combined with Lesson 30. More fruits and foods, trades and occupations, &c.

Habitual tense

grow	sell	want	collect	dig
deliver	guard	hire	bake	rake
control	sail	sow	cook	pick
plough	till	allow	keep	
wear	let			

Vocabulary

1. **Wild animals revised—more added**

   Leopards, ostriches, &c.

2. **Trades and occupations**

   Postman, policeman, airman, &c. (about twelve).

3. **Fruits and food from abroad**

   Oranges, bananas, tea, coffee, cocoa, &c.

4. **Combined with Lesson 16**

   A grocer keeps a $\begin{cases} \text{grocer's shop.} \\ \text{provision shop.} \end{cases}$

5. Often, sometimes, every day, every morning, &c., every other day, &c., always, never, before breakfast, after . . ., afterwards, then, nearly always.

Language

1. What do you do every day?
   What do you do every Thursday? &c.
   What does a policeman do?
   What does a butcher sell?

2. **Sentences**

   A policeman controls the traffic, &c.

3. Where do ostriches live?
   Where do bananas come from?
   Where does tea come from?
   Where do you come from, please?
   Where do you live?

Notes

This lesson is an extension of Lesson 30 on shopping. Now, however, we are going farther afield and inquiring where things come from. Here is an opportunity of fun with expeditions to shops, markets, farms (and if you are near them, docks), and pictorial maps showing where animals and plants grow. The children have already learnt about hot and cold lands; some names of countries may be added. Do not labour it but make it full of interest. Use every opportunity of widening the children's interest: films, projectors, foreign visitors, illustrations, travel folders, picture books, &c. Do not forget the contact with the parents, either personally or by letter. Many of their relatives have been abroad in the services. Encourage them to ask questions and encourage the parents to tell the children interesting items of this kind. If you can enrol the parents in this task of educating their deaf children, you have done a great thing for both parent and child.

LESSON 33

'If' in the present indefinite and future tenses only, with vocabulary of weather and adverbs. 'Happen' and 'behave'

'If' in present indefinite and future tenses only

This should have been taught with many examples incidentally,

> e.g. We shall go to the playing fields, if it is fine.
>> We shall not go to the playing fields, if it is wet.
>> If my mother gives me sixpence, I shall go to the pictures.
>> If I am a good boy, my mother will take me to . . . .

Vocabulary

1. **Weather:** fine, wet, raining, misty, clear, foggy, bright, dull.

2. **Adverbs:** carefully, carelessly, neatly, untidily, properly, badly, well.

Teach the use of the verbs 'to happen' and 'to behave' with 'if'.

Questions

> What will happen if you are a naughty boy?
> What will happen if you behave yourself this afternoon?
> What will happen if it is fine this afternoon?

Answers

> If I am a good boy, you will be pleased with me.
> If I behave myself, I shall have sixpence.
> If he behaves himself, he will . . . .

Point out the tenses. If I am . . . I shall . . . .
>> If he behaves . . . he will . . . .

Notes

This section has very little vocabulary. It provides a good opportunity of revision of Lessons 23, 26, and 32.

There is little to say about this lesson. It is but a clinching and clarification of work that should already have been done incidentally.

LESSON 34

Adverbial clause of time with future tense. Introduction of 'until' with 'to wait'

Adverbial clause of time

The adverbial clause of time with 'when' has already been introduced to the children, with various tenses. Its use is on the whole quite easy, as it is but an extension of time phrase work. The chief difficulty lies with the future tense in the principal clause, and as it is the tense children who look to the future want to use, it must be tackled.

I shall be a policeman when I grow up.

The child naturally wants to say 'I shall be a policeman when I shall grow up.'

Without bothering the children with too many rules, at the moment, it is good for them to learn by heart such useful clauses as:

When $\begin{cases} \text{I am} \\ \text{he is} \end{cases}$ grown up	I shall or I am going to.
When I grow up	I shall.
When I am ten years old	I shall.
	Daddy will.
When I am a big boy	I shall.
When Daddy comes back (if away for some time)	$\begin{cases} \text{he will.} \\ \text{I shall.} \end{cases}$

When baby is older   he will.
When I leave school   I shall.
When I finish Book I Arithmetic   I shall.

Teach them that we never use two future tenses together
with a 'when' clause, and practise much in the right way.
They enjoy this lesson, for deaf children build castles in
the air as much as children with normal hearing.

Transpose this also and practise:

I am going to be an engine-driver when . . . .
I shall have a pocket-knife when . . . .
Baby will learn to walk when . . . .
I shall have Book II Arithmetic when . . . .

Give a vocabulary of all the trades or professions they want
to be when they grow up, and of all the actions they want
to do.

Introduction of 'until'

Here is a good opportunity for teaching 'until' incidentally:

I must wait until Daddy comes back.
When Daddy comes back, he will . . ., &c.

LESSON 35

'With'. Means of doing things. Practice in
habitual tense chiefly. Appropriate verbs and
nouns

Verbs

Shoot, dig, plough, write, wipe your nose, plant, stir,
    mow, cut, cut down, eat, play, point, see, hear,
    taste, smell, measure, rule.

Vocabulary

1. Gun, spade, mower, pen, handkerchief, trowel, spoon, knife, fork, axe, ball, drum, stick, ruler, pointer, eyes, ears, nose.
2. A sportsman, a hunter, a gardener, a farmer, a woodman, a forester, a player, a bandsman, a ploughman.

Questions

What do you write with? What do you . . . with?
What does a gardener dig with?
What are you going to do with that?
Do you dig with a . . . or a . . .?

Note

Here is an opportunity for revision, using many known words and looking at them from a different angle. It is another example of the use of the habitual tense. Appeal to the child's sense of the absurd. Can you make up rhymes on the lines of: 'He combed his hair with the leg of a chair'? Bring as much fun and laughter into the classroom as you can.

LESSON 36

Cardinal numbers to 100, the date. Superlatives and the beginning of comparison. Appropriate verbs

Vocabulary

1. Cardinal numbers to 100
   First, second, &c.
2. The date. On 21st March 1953, &c., 21.3.53, &c.

3. The last, the first, the best, the worst, the tallest, the shortest, &c.
   The second best . . . next. (Superlatives only.)
4. **Verbs :** win, like, dislike, try, lose, love, hate, fail.

Language

1. Who is the first?
   " " tallest?
   Who did the best composition?
   Who won the race?
   What is the date?

2. **Sentences**

   He won the race.
   He is second.
   He wrote the best.
   He is the best of all.
3. Which lesson do you like best?
   Which animal do you like best?
   Which is the largest animal you have seen?
   " " smallest animal you have seen?
   " " prettiest animal you have seen?
4. I like . . . best.
   I like . . . the best of all.
5. Probably beginning of comparison will be needed.
   John is taller than Jane, but Gavin is the tallest of all.
6. Revise foods, lessons, and names of animals.
7. Incidental . . . . is my favourite animal.
   " " " drink.
   " " " lesson.

Note

This is an easy lesson. Revise the names of the cardinal numbers. The beginning of comparison is here, and incidentally you may find it necessary to introduce comparison between two things, '. . . is taller than . . . .' Revise the names of the months and lessons and insist on accuracy of spelling and speech. Revise also the names of animals, foods, drinks, flowers, fruits, and refresh the children's memory of these classifications.

Revision of adverbial clauses with 'when'. Past and future tenses of 'can'

'Can', 'could', 'shall be able'

The expression of ability in the past and future tenses is sometimes difficult for the deaf child and needs special teaching; especially as there is no future form of 'can' and we have to use another verb. It is unnecessary to teach the alternative form 'was able to' and 'am able to' at the moment as 'can' and 'could' are the more usual forms of speech. They will come in quite easily a little later.

Practise with things the children can do, for that is where the interest lies.

John can swim now.
He could not swim when he was a little boy.
James cannot swim yet.
He will be able to swim   when he is older.
              or   in a little while, or soon.
I can talk now.
I could not talk when I was a baby.

Vocabulary and reason

1. Add more vocabulary of things the children can do,

or of abilities they have heard about, e.g. swim the
Channel.

**2. Combine this also with reason and revise
adverbs and phrases.**

I could not do . . . because . . . .

He cannot write very well because he has a sore
finger.

I could not come to school yesterday because I was
ill.

He could not write properly because he had a blunt
pencil, &c.

LESSON 38

'How to', with more verbs and habitual tense

Verbs

1. Light a fire, make the tea, make a cake, lay a table.
2. Swim, do fractions, eat nicely, walk quietly, spell . . .,
   draw a horse, drive a car, play tennis/football, pilot
   an aeroplane. (See Lesson 12.) Milk a cow, tell the
   time, multiply by . . . divide by . . . add . . . subtract,
   do this, do that, strike a match, light the gas, ride a
   bicycle.

Questions and sentences

Do you know how to . . .?   Show me how to . . . .
Yes, I know how to . . . .   This is how to . . . .
This is the way to . . . . *or*   First you must . . . .
First I . . . .   Then . . . .
Then I . . . .   That is how to . . . .
No, I do not know how to . . . .
Please tell me how to . . . .

Speech

Here we go round the mulberry bush . . . .
This is the way we clean our shoes.
This is the way we brush our shoes.

Start simply with this and the children will enjoy it. Give first actions which the children can demonstrate.

Yes . . . I know how to . . . . This is how to . . . .

Later give the language of two or three actions. See the chapter on Composition for further comment.

LESSON 39

Habitual tense with verbs and vocabulary of natural objects. Animals and what they do.

Vocabulary of natural objects

1. Rain, sun, moon, stars, rivers, mountains, hills, valleys, the sea, land, streams, wind, earth, the world, waves, the tide, grass, flowers, trees, buds, waterfalls.
2. Shines, twinkles, flow, break, revolve, sparkle, open, grow, ebb, wane, rises, sets.

Animals and what they do

lions	roar	parrots	squawk, scream
dogs	bark, chase	geese	hiss
cats	mew, scratch, purr	cocks	crow
		hens	cluck
horses	neigh, race, trot, gallop	mice	squeak
		sheep	bleat

donkeys	bray	cows	low, give milk
birds	sing, peck	snakes	hiss, glide
ducks	quack		

Points of the compass

North, south, east, west.

Habitual tense

What does . . . do? Where does the sun set?

LESSON 40

Adverbs and adverbial phrases relating to Lesson 39. Questions—'How?' 'When?' and 'Where?'

Adverbs

1. Revision of Lesson 32 and adverbs used incidentally.
2. Addition of adverbs relating to Lesson 39.

Manner	brightly, quietly, smoothly, silently, noisily.
Time	always, never, daily.
Place	here, there.

Adverbial phrases relating to Lesson 39 and revision of others

Place

over the hills	high above the earth	down in the valley
far away	down the river	over the sea
up in the sky	up the mountain	round the world
up there	across the water	over the stream, &c.
in the west		
in the east		
in space		

Time

| for ever | at dawn | early in the morning |

for ever and   at sunset   until sunset
   ever   at sunrise   from morn till night
a month   from early morning
                         to late at night

Manner

  without a sound   with splendour
  very brightly, &c.   covered with snow

Questions

When does the sun rise?
Where does the sun rise?
Where does the sun set?
How often does the sun set?
Do you get up early in the morning?
      ,,   ,, at sunrise?
How does the moon shine? &c.

Notes on Lessons 39 and 40

Here are two lessons the children enjoy very much. Expeditions, pictures, films, models, observations will all make it live. Remember the sheer physical joy and wonder the young child experiences in nature, in sunshine, warmth, breezes, flowers. Deafness is no handicap here. Let them feel and enjoy these things while teaching them the words which describe them. Teach them through their interest in animals too, to care for them, and treat them with respect.

The understanding and appreciation of the phrases listed here and others like them will aid considerably the child's grasp of descriptions of nature in reading, and help them to picture the setting of stories.

Give the children short descriptions to illustrate in colour, e.g.

    1. A boy walked down the road when the sun was
       setting. In the west the sky was full of colour—red,

gold, and yellow. There were pink clouds above in the pale blue sky. He looked at the sunset sky and thought 'How beautiful you are!'

2. Two men were climbing up a hill; far away, over the valley, there were high mountains. In the valley a river flowed between green fields.

Do not expect or ask for reproductions in writing of similar descriptions to these. Give them for enjoyment by lip-reading and writing. Before expecting an individual child to reproduce one of these in colour try a composite class interpretation.

LESSON 41

'How much?' and 'How many?' Revision of shopping. Appropriate vocabulary

How much	did you bring? have you? do you want?	*How many*	did you bring? have you? do you want?

| a little much very much a great deal of | bread money milk water tea fruit food sand chocolate bacon sugar hair | a few many very many a great many | loaves pencils sweets books eggs cows horses seeds pennies trees stars cars, &c. |

any	some	not any
plenty of	a lot of	no

Notes

Revise and add to the names of foods, coins, vehicles, furniture. You will probably find the need for 'a pound of, a quarter of, a loaf of, a tin of, a packet of, a piece of, a slice of'. Treat it as clearly, as simply, and as concretely as you can.

Concentrate on the expressions which can be used both for amount and number, i.e. 'some', 'not any', 'plenty of', 'a lot of', 'no' ('and any', in the question form), and then give the others, 'a little', contrasted with 'a few', 'much' with 'many', 'a great deal of' with 'a great many'.

Much practice in the correct forms is the way to ensure correct usage, but clarity of teaching with diagrammatic expression is a great aid to the child in correcting himself.

Contrast: some bread　　　　two loaves of bread.
　　　　　 some chocolate　　a packet of chocolate.

Continue this with other uses of 'How much' (cost and weight),

How much did it *cost?*　　How much does . . . cost?
How much did it weigh?　　How much does it weigh?

COMPOSITION

1. *Diaries should be continued.* They should begin to be more varied and interesting. See the note on this and on paragraphing in Stage 2. Gradually three or more sentences should be included in the paragraph. The children should begin to do this naturally if your language teaching has been good. Have patience with the slower child. It will be much longer before he takes a step forward or ventures upon anything new. Encourage him but do not force him to move forward.

2. *Much fuller letters.* More real communications between parent and child by means of letters in boarding schools should now be possible. In day schools encourage the writing of letters to absent scholars or to relatives, and consult the parents about this. It is one of the best forms of written composition you can devise for the child of this age.

Letters of excuse can be begun simply, e.g. 'I could not come to school, because I was ill'.

3. *Composition on interesting people* (e.g. the postman, the policeman, the bus driver, farmer, pilot). This should be preceded (as in Lesson 32) by much conversation and lip-reading about the person concerned and dramatization of what he does. Rhythmic speech helps here very much. Do not attempt to get any expression work of this kind until there has been a wealth of impression. Play the lip-reading game I mentioned in Stage 2 first, e.g.

> What do we call a man who comes down the road every day. Sometimes he comes in a van and sometimes he walks. He knocks at the door

'rat-tat', '**rat-**tat'. He delivers letters, post-cards, and parcels.

and

What do we call a man who comes down the road every day. He comes in a van. He knocks at the door 'rat-tat', 'rat-tat'. He delivers the milk.

Then compositions such as this are comparatively easy.

The postman

> The postman delivers letters every day.
> Sometimes he walks down the road.
> Sometimes he comes in a van.
> He knocks at the doors 'rat-tat', 'rat-tat'.
> Sometimes he brings me a letter, &c.

A composition on 'The Farmer' is an easy matter after playing the game and learning the words of

Farmer come and plough your field

,,	,,	sow your corn
,,	,,	cut your hay
,,	,,	reap your corn
,,	,,	milk your cows.

Keep these compositions simple and well within the child 's capacity and you will be rewarded by the child's desire to write more compositions. Let each child keep a book in which he writes and illustrates his own. You will be pleasantly surprised to find original efforts creeping in.

4. *Continue the compositions of Stage* 2, expanding them with the new language.

5. *Where things come from*

T his is an enthralling subject to children of the end of the ju nior stage. It should form part of the talk on experiences, fi ndings, and expeditions connected with Lesson 32.

Give plenty of impressions and do not make the work on this too detailed at first. The children should have maps to fill in with illustrations, or a large class map to fill in, in the same way. A map to which you add as the knowledge is gained is much more useful than one with the knowledge ready-made for them. Give a few facts only about each article or product, e.g.

Oranges grow in warm countries (*name some*).
They come in ships over the sea to ports in England (*name some or one in particular*).
They come to the market here by train.
I went to the market.
I saw oranges.
The greengrocer buys them from the market.
I often buy oranges because I like them very much.

Milk comes from cows.
Cows live on a farm.
I went to a farm.
I saw a cowman milking the cows.
He gave me some milk to drink.
It was warm and I liked it very much.

Repeat many times and with many things for it is only when the children have a wealth of language experience to choose from that you can expect even a simple composition. A child with normal hearing has a great deal of general knowledge from which he draws to write down the facts which impress him. We often expect our deaf children to write down and remember correctly all they know. You will find that the bright child will remember almost all of the facts you have given, while the slower one will reproduce only a few well-known facts.

Numbers of these can be made into lip-reading stories and games, such as 'What am I?' changing 'oranges' to

'I'—'I grow in warm countries, &c.' Remember that the differentiating clue must be in the last sentence.

6. *Conversations*

This can be given orally and afterwards in writing. The children can illustrate by drawing and dramatizing. After a number given, expect or at least hope for some original ones, e.g.

> Last night I went to buy some sweets.
> I went into the sweet shop.
> I said 'I want some chocolate, please'.
> The shopkeeper said, 'Which packet would you like?'
> I said, 'That one, please. How much is it?'
> He said, 'Threepence, please.'
> I took the chocolate. I said, 'Thank you'.
> I came out of the shop.

These conversations on all sorts of subjects help to familiarize the children with the written form, i.e. 'said', and with inverted commas. They should learn to use them correctly.

7. *Very simple descriptions* using the new language taught, 'made of' and 'with' and the habitual tense.

That is a pen.	I have a shilling.
You write with it.	My mother gave me it.
It has a nib and a holder	It is made of silver.
The nib is made of steel.	I shall save it *or*
The holder is made of wood.	I shall buy something with it.

8. *Preparation for compositions on Lesson 38.* 'How to do it' could be *begun* in this section by lip-reading games of which I have spoken. Remember that impressions must come first.

Example: the teacher asks 'Do you know how to light a fire?'

If a child knows, let him demonstrate, and teacher and children together give the language.

First you must get some paper, sticks, and small lumps of coal.

Then $\left\{\begin{array}{l}\text{you put} \\ \text{you must put}\end{array}\right\}$ the paper *in the grate.*

Then you put the sticks *on the paper across each other.*

Then you put the small lumps of coal *on the sticks.*

Then you strike a match and put the flame *to the paper.*

That is how to light a fire.

There are only three verbs, but notice the work on phrases.

Give this and other sequences many times. Let everyone express this orally, in concert with the teacher, then in writing.

9. *Short descriptions of animals* as before adding new language and verbs as in Lesson 39.

e.g. Add—Lions live in Africa.
     They live in caves and lairs in the forest.
     They roar at night.

10. *Very short descriptions of natural objects* as in Lesson 39, following lessons, talks, and definite lip-reading games.

e.g. **The sun**

The sun shines by day.
It gives us warmth and light.
It is very very large.
It is very far away.

A river

A river is water flowing between banks.
It flows from the hills or mountains.
It flows down to the sea.
Sometimes it flows swiftly.
And sometimes it flows slowly, &c.

SPEECH

YOUR aim at this stage should be to get from your children still more clarity of speech, combined with facility. Work specially on consonants, a good attack for the initial consonants and a definite and correct ending. Be sure you have no vocalization of the unvoiced consonants. Take time at the beginning of the year to ensure that every child, however deaf, understands when he is voicing a consonant and when he is not. You will save much time and much embarrassment to the child later if you do this. You will only have to remind the child, he will correct himself. I know this is true from experience.

When teaching this let the children hold up a finger and feel the breath warm upon the hand. Let them say p, p, p and t, t, t as before, and the continuous unvoiced sounds followed by a sentence entirely without voice. Be sure there is no voice at all, even a suspicion will spoil clarity of speech. Then let the children voice the sentence. You will find that this exercise helps to give a more natural and pleasing voice as well as giving clarity of consonants.

Concentrate too on perfecting the nasal sounds; 'ng' should be no difficulty now. Work on the initial 'm' and 'n's. There should be no suspicion of 'p' or 'b' in the 'm' or of 't' or 'd' in the 'n'.

Continue phrasing. Remember that pauses are as important in phrasing as the joining of one word to another. Rivers | flow down | to the sea.

Continue the work on where the accent falls in words of more than one syllable. This can be linked up with the work on phrasing.

Point out and give some exercises on the neutral vowel—

not only in 'the' and 'a' before a word beginning with a consonant, but at the end of a word—see Lesson 30; bacon, sugar, the draper's, &c., and Lesson 32; grocer, postman, policeman, milkman, &c.

Continue intonation practice, especially of the two tunes as applied to Questions. The difference in the tunes can also be practised by giving a command (Tune I) and changing it to a request (Tune II). This is much enjoyed by the children.

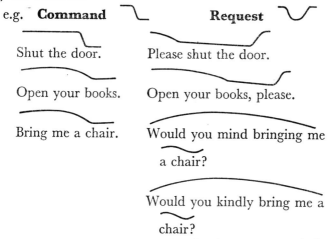

e.g. **Command**   **Request**

Shut the door.   Please shut the door.

Open your books.   Open your books, please.

Bring me a chair.   Would you mind bringing me a chair?

Would you kindly bring me a chair?

The two tunes can be referred to in rhymes too and the diagram placed over each line.

Revise, extend, and classify the work on intonation. The previous work of Stage 2 began the two tunes and the language forms which belong to these tunes. Continue this practice especially of the sentences joined by 'and', 'but', and 'while' and adverbial clause; begin the work on the intonation of these as in the Intonation Summary. Give the intonation of them as you reach this lesson in the scheme. See Appendix 2, page 377.

Keep the two tunes clearly in the children's mind and classify the work of this and Stage 2 as under:

Tune I   *Tune II*

1. **Exclamations**

   e.g. What a pity!

2. **Commands**   **Request**

   e.g. Shut the window.   Would you mind shutting

                            the window?

                            Please shut the window.

3. **An answer to a question in:**

   (a) A phrase—over the road.

   (b) Yes and No.

   (c) Yes, I do.

   (d) I don't know.

   (e) I did.

4. **A question beginning with** 'What', 'When', 'Where', 'Which', 'Why', 'Whose', 'How', &c.

   A question beginning with a verb, 'Do', 'Did', 'Does', 'Is', 'Am', 'Are', 'How', 'Has'.

   How are you?   Do you like sugar?

5. **A Statement**

It is my birthday today.

Both tunes

Tune II for the first statement and Tune I for the second.

1. **Double statements** (*a*) with 'but' and 'and' (see Lesson 26) and 'so is'.

John is tall and so is Tom.

John is tall but Jim is short.

(*b*) with 'while'.

John was playing while Jim was working.

2. (*a*) **Adverbial clause using 'when'** (see Summary of Intonation).

1. When father takes his spade to dig then robin comes along.

Adverbial clause Tune II—Principal clause Tune I

2. Robin comes along when father takes his spade to dig.

Principal clause Tune I. Adverbial clause Tune II (lower)

This contrast makes for interest and helps to clinch the apprehension of the language form.

(b) **Conditional clause**

If it is fine, I shall go out to play.

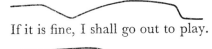

I shall go out to play if it is fine.

The same rule applies.

Rhymes and refrains

Poems with refrains are still very useful especially for the practice of particular vowels or consonants, and for voice exercises. The children still love movement, so keep up the rhythm work. Poems with repetitions are still suitable, too, and very short rhymes and jingles. Here are a selection:

1. **The postman**

> The postman's coming down the road,
> > Rat-tat, rat-tat.
> He has such a heavy load,
> > Rat-tat, rat-tat.
>
> Postman, have you one for me?
> > Rat-tat, rat-tat.
> Yes, I've one, and two, and three,
> > Rat-tat, rat-tat.

When the children have acted this and said the refrain, some might take the words of the other lines. Here is a chance to get the final 't's and the neutral vowel in 'postman' right with enjoyment (Lesson 32).

2. **The farmer**

> Farmer come and sow your seed,
> Sow your seed, sow your seed;
> Farmer come and sow your seed
> This lovely sunny morning.

Yes I'll come and sow my seed,
Sow my seed, sow my seed;
Yes I'll come and sow my seed
This lovely sunny morning.

Repeat with

> plough your fields
> hoe your swedes
> mow your hay
> reap your corn.

3. A rhyme rather similar is—**'Can you show me how the farmer'**, &c.

Can you show me how the farmer (*walking round in a ring*)

,,   ,,   ,,

,,   ,,   ,,

Sows his wheat and barley?

Yes, I'll show you how the farmer (*actions given*)

,,   ,,   ,,

,,   ,,   ,,

Sows his wheat and barley.

Now I've shown you how the farmer (*walking round in a*

,,   ,,   ,,   ,,   *ring again*)

,,   ,,   ,,   ,,

Sows his wheat and barley.

Repeat for

> reaps his wheat and barley
> brings home his wheat and barley
> rests when harvest's over.

The Game 'Oats and Beans and Barley' can be taken.

4. **The garden**

Another similar rhyme concerning a garden is enjoyed:

> This is how we dig the ground
> Dig the ground   ,,   ,,
> This is how we   ,,   ,,
> In our little garden.

Repeat for   rake the ground
                      sow the seeds
                      pull the weeds
                      pick the flowers
                      smell the flowers (Lesson 32).

5. **My friend**

> I went to call for a friend one day;
> She only lived across the way.
> She said she couldn't come out to play
> Because it was her washing day.

Refrain: *This* is the way she washed away

              ,,   ,,   ,,
              ,,   ,,   ,,
> Because it was her washing day.

Repeat first verse and then repeat refrain for

                      ironing day, sweeping day,
                      dusting day, baking day.

Last verse:

> She said she *could* come out to play
> Because it was her playing day
> *This* is the way *we* played away

              ,,   ,,   ,,
              ,,   ,,   ,,
> Because it was her playing day.

(Lessons 37 and 38.)

The actions are obvious.

Teach the children to stress 'This' and listen for a good 's'.

As much or as little of the verse can be spoken by the children as the teacher thinks fit. They will probably want to do so when they know the refrain well.

6. **'The Shepherd's Cradle Song'** is much enjoyed even by the boys. The following verse can, if desired, be used instead of the third verse:

> Sleep, baby, sleep,
> The shepherd folds his sheep,
> Sweet rest now comes to field and tree,
> And sleep my little one to thee,
> Sleep, baby, sleep.

The rocking rhythm becomes slower for the last refrain. Can be used for refrain work in the easiest stage. Most of the verse is quite easy to say. Work on a good 'ee', final 'p', and initial 's'.

7. **Ferry me across the water** (Lesson 33)

This can be used for group work with action.

8. **Here we go round the mulberry bush**

This can now be repeated. All the refrain, 'This is the way we . . .' can be said and most of the verse too (Lesson 38).

9. **Golden bridge**

> Golden bridge, golden bridge,
> Gold bridge over the water.
> Who made you? Who made you?
> The goldsmith and his daughter.
>
> All pass through, All pass through,
> Spear and rod held over you.

Two or four tall children join hands to make an archway. The rest walk round, passing through the archway at 'All pass through'. Good practice for final 'j' and 'oo'.

10. **Arches**

A marble arch for heroes
To walk in, to walk in;
A red rose arch for ladies
To talk in, to talk in.
A hempen arch for little girls
To skip in, to skip in;
An arch of stars to sleep in,
To sleep in, to sleep in. (Lesson 31)

Best used for choral speech with or without miming by
two pupils at a time. Excellent practice for final 'ch' and 'n'.

11. **Lavender's blue**

Lavender's blue,
Dilly dilly,
Lavender's green.
When I am King,
Dilly dilly,
You shall be Queen.

Lavender's blue,
Dilly dilly,
Lavender's green.
When you are King,
Dilly dilly,
I shall be Queen.
(Lesson 34.)

This can be used for group work. The actions are obvious.

12. **The merchants of London**

Hickety, Pickety, Poppety, Pet,
The merchants of London wear scarlet.
Silk on the collar, gold on the hem, (*a stately walk*)
Merrily march the merchant men.

The merchants could be preceded and followed by drum-
mers saying 'Bom, Bom, Bom, Bom'. This is a good
exercise when practising 'm's.

13. The gallant ship

Oh! three times round
Went the gallant, gallant ship.   *Walking round hold-*
Oh! three times round   *ing hands in a ring.*
Went she, went she;
Oh! three times round   *Stand still at 'ship'.*
Went the gallant, gallant ship.
Then she sank to the bottom
Of the sea, the sea, the sea,   *Appropriate action—*
Then she sank to the bottom   *hands and bodies.*
Of the sea.
'Pull her up, pull her up',
Said the little sailor boy.
'Pull her up, pull her up',
Said he, said he.   *Pulling action.*
'Pull her up, pull her up',
Said the little sailor boy;
But she sank to the bottom
Of the sea, the sea, the sea,   *As above second section,*
But she sank to the bottom   *first verse.*
Of the sea.

(Lesson 26.)

14. Please remember

Please remember the children,
    Father's gone to sea,
Mother's gone to fetch him back,
    Please remember me.

A good exercise for 'm's and 'n'.

15. I'd like to ride

'I'd like to ride in a railway train',
    Said Flo, said Flo.
'I'd like to ride in an aeroplane',
    Said Joe, said Joe.

'I'd like to ride in a motor-car
And go as I liked, so fast and far',
   Said Ted, said Ted.
'But a bumpety ride on Daddy's knee,
That's the loveliest ride for me',
   Said Golden-head, Golden-head.
                              (Lesson 26.)

This is a good exercise for 'ie'. It might be used for group
or individual work. The rhythm of the second, fourth, and
seventh lines may be a difficulty. Pause between first two
words and the second two and at the end of the line for the
silent beats, e.g. 'said Flo, said Flo'.

16. **The farmer's in his den**

1. The farmer's in his den,
   The farmer's in his den,
   Heigh ho, Heigh ho,
   The farmer's in his den.

All walk round holding hands, farmer in the middle.

2. The farmer wants a wife
3. The wife wants a child
4. The child wants a nurse
5. The nurse wants a cat
6. The cat wants a mouse
7. The mouse wants some cheese

Stand still for first two lines while the farmer chooses a wife. Move round again for 'Heigh ho', &c. (last two lines). Repeat for each verse.

8. We all dance round the cheese

All dance round—one ring goes one way and one the other.

A good spoken-language exercise on 'wants' (Lessons 26
and 41).

17. **Here we go Lubin Loo**

> Here we go Lubin Loo,
>   ,,   ,,   ,,   Light,
>   ,,   ,,   ,,   Loo,
> All on a Saturday night.

> Put your right hand in,
>   ,,   ,,   ,,   out.
> Shake your hand a little, a little,
> And turn yourself about.

Repeat first verse, then

> Put your left hand in, &c.
> Put your right foot in, &c.
> Put your left foot in, &c. (Lesson 26).

This is great fun and the children will love it.

18. **Over the brook**

> 'Over the brook to Grandmama's,
> Over the brook', said the boy.
> 'The flowers are sweet beneath my feet,
> I'll sing as I go for joy.' (Lesson 40).

This is suitable for choral work.

19. **Today**

> We had a pleasant walk today
> Over the meadows and far away,
> Along the stream, beside the mill,
> By the woodside and up the hill. (Lesson 40.)

> And if you listen to what I say
> I'll tell you what we saw today.

Both these poems illustrate phrase work. The latter opens possibilities of individuals describing 'what we saw today'.

Continue the stories with interpolations as suggested in the other section. The field is getting much wider.

20. **The cuckoo**

In April,
    Come he will.

In May,
    Sing all day.

In June,
    Change his tune.

In July,
    Prepare to fly.

In August,
    Go he must.

21. **Shopping** (Lesson 30)

Half a pound of coffee, please,
And threepence change for mother;
And have you got a paper bag
To give my little brother.

He says he wants to blow it out
And make it go off pop!
He always wants a bag to blow
When we come out to shop.

22. **Some more shopping**

A pound of tea at one and three
And a pot of raspberry jam,
Two new-laid eggs and a dozen pegs
And a pound of rashers of ham.

The story of the above is an amusing one for the children. A child (boy or girl) sets out to do the shopping as above, having made the list into a rhyme so that she remembers it. The first time she repeats it, she has it right. She goes on (here all sorts of things might happen to her, meeting a friend, seeing something of interest, &c.). After the episode she tries to remember her rhyme with a result something like this

> A pound of three at onc and tea
> And a pot of raspberry ham,
> Two new-laid pegs and a dozen eggs
> And a pound of rashers of jam.

This cannot be right and she tries again:

> A pound of tea at one and three (oh! this is right)
> And a pound of new-laid jam,
> Two raspberry eggs and a dozen pegs
> And a pot of rashers of ham.

And so on.

Children find this hilariously funny. There is some good language and speech work here too.

23. **The muffin man**

> Do you know the muffin man,
> The muffin man, the muffin man?
> Do you know the muffin man,
> That lives down Drury Lane, Oh?
> Yes, I know the muffin man, &c.
> One now knows the muffin man, &c.
> Two now know the muffin man, &c. (Lesson 31.)

This is another good exercise for 'm's and 'n's, chorus, group, and individual work.

24. **Old Mother Hubbard**

25. The following are suitable poems which can be understood by the children. The language is suitable for this stage. Choose out verses or couplet for learning by heart.

(*a*) From **'A Child's Garden of Verse'** by Robert Louis Stevenson.

    i. Bed in Summer (contrasts Lesson 26).

    ii. When I was Sick and lay Abed (Lesson 28).

    iii. The Swing (Lesson 40).

    iv. Dark Brown is the River (Lesson 40).

(*b*) From the **'Golden Staircase'. Poems for Children chosen by Louey Chisholm.**

    i. 'The Blackbird' by Herbert Wolfe (Lesson 40 and others).

      'In the Far Corner—Close by the Swings.'

    ii. 'Fly Away, Fly Away, Over the Sea' by Christina Rossetti (contrasts Lesson 26).

    iii. *'Little Girls' by Lawrence Alma Tadema (Lesson 33).

      'If no-one ever marries me' (change 'nurse says' in first verse to 'I know').

    iv. *'When Polly buys a Hat' by E. Hill (Lesson 30).

    v. 'When Mary goes walking' by Patrick R. Chalmers (Lesson 30).

    vi. 'The Robin' by Lawrence Alma Tadema (Lesson 30).

      'When father takes his spade to dig.'

    vii. 'Lady Moon' by Lord Houghton (phrases Lesson 40 and earlier).

      'Lady moon, Lady moon, where are you roving?'

    viii. *'The Fairies' by William Allingham (Lesson 40).

      'Up the airy mountain, down the rushy glen.'

ix. *'Allie' by Robert Graves (Lessons 21 and 36).

'Allie, call the birds in, the birds from the sky.'

x. *'The Gardener's Cat' by Patrick Chalmers (Lessons 26 and 29).

'The gardener's cat's called Mignonette' (1st and 2nd verses).

xi. *'Ducks' Ditty' by Kenneth Grahame (Lesson 40).

'All along the backwater, through the rushes tall.'

xii. 'Porridge' by Elizabeth Fleming (Lesson 26 and others).

'I don't like porridge, skinny and brown.'

xiii. *'The Doctor' by Rose Fyleman (Lesson 32).

'He comes with mother up the stair.'

xiv. 'Who has seen the Wind?' by Christina Rossetti (Lesson 26).

xv. 'Boats sail on the Rivers' by Christina Rossetti (Lesson 40).

'Boats sail on the rivers, and ships sail on the seas.'

xvi. *'What became of Them?' Unknown (Lesson 26).

'He was a rat, and she was a rat.'

xvii. 'There's a Cavern in the Mountain' by A. A. Milne (Lesson 40).

'Now we are Six.'

This can be used for refrain work,

Hammer, hammer, hammer,
Chatter, chatter, chatter.

* These poems are suitable to be told and read to the children as stories and dramatized. Lines and couplets

should then be learnt by the children. When the poem is read these lines and couplets can be said by the children. Selected children might dramatize. Some of those suggested in Stage 2 are still suitable.

Continue stories with interpolations as suggested in the earlier section.

Some verses of 'All things bright and beautiful' are most suitable for this age, e.g.

> The purple headed mountain,
> The river running by;
> The sunset and the morning
> That brightens up the sky.

The whole of 'Glad that I live am I' should now be learnt. At Christmas time: 'Away in a Manger', and 'Once in Royal David's City'.

The children can understand and enjoy some of the verses of the Hymn of St. Francis. They love to join in the 'Alleluias' and 'Praise Him'. Try it.

It is good to lead them through joy in beauty to praise. If you can give them a feeling of the underlying joy and goodness of God and can encourage an outward-reaching spirit in your pupils, you will have done much for their present and future poise and happiness.

LANGUAGE

READ again the summary of the work of this stage in the introduction. As you will see, the chief concern is to give the pupil the language he needs for wondering, thinking and imagining, remembering, wishing, and looking forward. This section deals with noun, adverbial, and adjectival clause usages, and lays the foundation of the complex and complicated language of books. Its aim is the stimulation of thought, and it gives the language necessary for its expression.

A SUMMARY OF THE LESSONS IN STAGE 4

of 'if'. Vocabulary of imaginative themes. The use of 'wish'. Adverbial phrases.

51. Comparison. Comparative and superlative and equality. Adjectives, weights, measures, and nouns of qualities.
52. Relative pronouns: 'who', 'which', and 'that'.
53. Adverbial clauses of time with 'when'. Habitual action in the past expressed by 'used to', and sequence by the present perfect tense.
54. Indirect speech. Question form. Appropriate verbs.
55. All known tenses revised and added to with appropriate adverbs, phrases, and clauses. Revision of telling the time.
56. More noun clauses with 'if' and 'whether'. Vocabulary of verbs.
57. 'Should', 'ought to', 'must', 'must not', right and wrong with 'to be' and 'to do'. Vocabulary of verbs and adjectives.
58. Offering or asking for help. Refusal or acquiescence and promises. Vocabulary of verbs.
59. Simple cause and effect 'and so', 'is called'. Nouns from verbs.
60. Revision of question forms and answers.

LESSON 42

Indirect speech. Commands only. Positive and negative. Vocabulary of new verbs and adjectives

Commands, with revision of verbs, and some new ones

1. **Affirmative**

e.g. John said, 'Wait a minute'.
John told me to wait a minute.

Rule when reporting a command: 'to' is used before the verb (i.e. infinitive is used).

2. **Negative**

> e.g. She said, 'Don't fidget'.
> She told me not to fidget.

Rule when reporting a negative command: 'don't' is dropped and 'not to' is used before the verb.

Verbs

> Fidget, remember, think, keep on, obey, forget, hurry up, try, give up, disobey, wait (a minute) (a little while).

Commands, with the verb 'to be' and adjectives

1. e.g. Mother said, 'Be careful'.
   > Mother told me to be careful.
2.   Mother said, 'Don't be so careless'.
   > Mother told me not to be so careless.

Adjectives

> Careful, careless, thoughtful, thoughtless, naughty, good, &c.

Notes

The use of reported speech is difficult for the children and needs to be taught very carefully and clearly. Take one step at a time and give plenty of practice in each step. Have clearly in your own mind the rules that are followed in our language and teach them with many examples. These lessons lend themselves to a great deal of dialogue and dramatic work. Make your lessons live in this way, use every opportunity of applying it, e.g. 'What did your mother say about . . .?' 'What did . . . tell you this morning?' Be alert for teaching incidental work connected with these lessons on reported speech now and throughout this section; e.g. three pupils come to the front of the class,

one gives a command, the second does it, the third says
'He told her to . . . .'

Turn to the class, 'Did . . . do it? Yes, she did. She
obeyed.' Again prime one of the children to refuse to obey
the command, 'Did he do it? No, he didn't. He dis-
obeyed', or 'He wouldn't do it'. Later try this with a negative command, e.g. 'Don't do that', and teach, 'He dis-
obeyed, he went on doing it, he kept on doing it.'

Do not press this incidental work or expect it to be
reproduced. Use these phrases yourself whenever the need
arises. It suffices if the pupils understand the teacher's use
of them at the moment.

LESSON [43

The use of common things—with appropriate
vocabulary. Revision of Lesson 35

Vocabulary

These are useful things:

pencils	money	cups	knives	settee
rubbers	tables	leather	forks	beds
pens	spoons	wood	matches	chair
string, &c.	spades	wheat	scarves, &c.	
flour	umbrella	over-	medicine	mackintoshes
hot-water		coats		
bottles				
soap	corn	coal	fire	keys

Verbs

To learn, to warm, to make, to put, to stir, to buy, to
sleep, to heat, to rest, to write, to cut, to light, to sit,
to lie, to keep—warm, to make—well, to make—
strong.

Revise and extend the lesson on 'What we do things with'

1. Father digs with a spade. We write with pencils.
2. What do we use pencils for?

　　We use pencils to write with *or* for writing.
　　　 ,, 　　,, 　　,, 　draw with *or* for drawing.
　　　 ,, 　 beds to sleep on 　　*or* for sleeping on, &c.

　　3. **Later,** What are spades used for? What is wood used for?

Notes

Here is an opportunity of revising and widening the vocabulary and of encouraging the children to use their brains.

　It can be compared with Lesson 35, 'What we do things with'. The different formation can be pointed out, e.g.

　　We write with pencils.
　　We use pencils to write with, *or*
　　We use pencils for writing.

Practice is needed in the alternatives (*a*) 'to write with' and (*b*) 'for' followed by the participle, i.e. 'for writing'.

　Here is a good opportunity for teaching the idiomatic expressions, 'to keep us warm, to make us warm or happy or strong'.

　It is good to start with the active form, 'We use . . . for . . . .' Later, and with the brighter children, '. . . is/are used . . .' can be taken.

　This is really a use of the passive voice and it can be compared with 'is made of' and 'are made of'. Much practice in 'We use . . . for . . .ing' and '. . . is used for . . . ing. A carpenter uses . . . for . . .ing. . . .s are used for . . .ing.'

　Some children will be interested in: 'Jumpers are made of wool, wool is used to make jumpers. Bread is made of flour, flour is used to make bread, &c.'

LESSON 44

'Should' and 'would like' with vocabulary of trades, professions, places, and games. Adverbial clause with 'when'

'Should' and 'would like' with infinitive

1. **To be** (I want to be a . . ., I should like to be a . . .).

   A cabinet maker, a teacher, an engineer, an artist, a missionary, &c. (about thirty).

2. **To play** (I want to play . . ., I should like to play . . .).

   More games: dodge-ball, cricket, baseball, rounders, tennis, football, skipping.

3. **To do** (I want to . . ., I should like to . . .).

   To cure, to teach, to preach, &c. (about thirty, as 1).
   N.B. to go in the Air Force, Army, Navy, &c.

4. **To go to**—to see (I want to go to . . ., I should like to travel to . . .).

   To travel to⎫
   to go to   ⎭ . . . to see the world.

   More places: the continents, the wonders of the world, hot countries, cold countries, abroad.

5. **To travel by**

   Aeroplane, air, train, car, coach.

'Should' and 'would like' with adverbial clause introduced by 'when'

1. What would you like to be when you grow up?
       ,,   ,,   ,,   do when you grow up?
   What are you going to be when you leave school?
       ,,   ,,   ,,   do when you leave school?
   What does an artist do?

2. I should like to be a . . . when I grow up.
I am going to be a . . . when I leave school.

3. **Incidental language**

I want to do . . . .　I don't want to . . . .
I should not like to . . . .　I should like to . . . .
What would you like to do this afternoon?
What would you like for dinner today?
What would you like for your birthday?
I should like to . . . this afternoon.
I should like a . . . for my birthday.

Notes

Most boys and girls love this lesson, and choosing what they would like to be. Keep clearly before them the difference between 'to be' and 'to do'. Use this lesson to widen the children's horizons and appeal to their imaginations.

There is room for much conversation, much dramatization, much interesting information about the wonders of the world, and much asking of the staff, friends, and relations what they would like to see and do. The expression 'would rather . . . than' can be brought in here. 'John would rather be a farmer than a dentist. Which would you rather be, a nurse or a teacher?'

LESSON 45

'Liking' and 'disliking' with infinitive and participle—also 'remember', 'forget', 'stop', 'start', &c. Appropriate vocabulary

Verbs with the infinitive and present participle

1. **Liking and disliking**

(*a*) like　　love
dislike　　hate　　prefer { to do.
or doing.

$$\left.\begin{matrix} (\text{not}) \text{ to mind} \\ (b) \text{ enjoy} \\ \text{to be fond of.} \end{matrix}\right\} \text{doing } \textit{only.}$$

2. Beginning and ending

(a) begin $\left.\begin{matrix} \text{to do} \\ \textit{or} \text{ doing} \end{matrix}\right.$ start (b) stop, finish $\left.\begin{matrix} \text{doing} \\ \textit{only.} \end{matrix}\right.$ keep on, go on

3. Remembering and forgetting

$\left.\begin{matrix} \text{remember} \\ \text{forget} \end{matrix}\right\} \text{to do } \textit{or} \text{ doing.}$

Vocabulary

Games, hobbies, lessons, sports

Notes

This lesson has very little completely new work. It revises, classifies, and points out, while trying to avoid pitfalls.

There are two things particularly to be borne in mind:

1. Seven of these verbs can be used with the participle only. They are: 'to enjoy', 'to be fond of', 'to mind' (usually 'not to mind'), 'to stop', 'to finish', 'to keep on', 'to go on'. Give copious examples of this, bringing in new verbs for the participle. Practise 'to enjoy' specially.

The other verbs mentioned can be used with both infinitive and participle. These need much practice too.

2. The infinitive and the participle are *not* affected by a change of tense in the principal verbs.

> e.g. I love wandering in the woods. I love to wander in the woods. I loved wandering in the woods (last autumn). I loved to wander in the woods (last holiday). I enjoy going for walks. I enjoyed going for a walk last night.

So many deaf children make a mistake here, either changing the present participle into the past tense when the sentence is in the past tense, e.g. 'I enjoyed went for a walk', or using the infinitive, e.g. 'I enjoy go for a walk.' Practice the correct form well and frequently.

LESSON 46

Indirect speech continued. Statements with vocabulary of weather conditions

Statements not involving subjective pronouns

e.g. He said, 'The sun is shining'.
    He said that the sun was shining.

or

He told me that the sun was shining.

Rule :—1. 'That' is used to join the two sentences.
         2. The verb in the statement must be changed to its corresponding past tense.

e.g. Present progressive 'is shining', becomes past progressive 'was shining'.
    Present indefinite 'sells' becomes past indefinite 'sold'.
    Present perfect 'has given' becomes past perfect 'had given'.

    'shall' becomes 'should'.
    'will'   ,,   'would'.
    'can'   ,,   'could'.

Statements involving change of one pronoun and verb

e.g. She said, '*I am* going to buy some sweets.'
    She said that *she was* going to buy some sweets.

Vocabulary : Weather, weather report, points of compass.

    Sultry, misty, windy, fine but cold, foggy, beautiful weather, fine and warm, bitterly cold, a lovely day, an east wind, &c.

    N.B. 'tells' and 'says' do not involve a change to past tense in the noun clauses.

Statements involving change of more than one pronoun and the verb

Following 'She said that she was going to buy some sweets',

    add (1) She said, 'I am going to town with my mother.' She said that she was going to town with her mother.

        (2) Mother said, 'You must wait until I come.' Mother told me that I must wait until she came.

Note

When dramatizing, a simple thing such as the position of the speaker will make for clarity, or otherwise. e.g. One speaker makes a statement to another in one part of the room, visible of course to the other children. To make assurance doubly sure he holds up the written form for all to see. The other speaker moves over to the middle of the room before reporting the speech, turns directly to the class, saying,

    'He said that he was going to the football match with his father on Saturday.'

Correlate of course with the preceding lessons:

I love reading.	He told me that he loved reading.
I should like to be a farmer.	He said that he would like to be a farmer.

Miss . . . said that she would like to go to Italy by air.

LESSON 47

Permission and compulsion with 'instead' and 'although'

Verbs

Let, allow, to, make, must, have to.

Question and answer

May I . . .? Yes, you may.

Will you let me . . .? Yes, I will let you. No, I won't let you. She would not let me.

What time do you have to go to bed? I have to go to bed at . . . .

Does your mother let you stay up late? Yes, my mother lets me.

Does your mother allow you to stay up late? No, my mother won't let me.

Yes, she allows me to stay up until 9 o'clock.

Revise 'although'

See Lesson on this in Stage 3.

My mother told me to go to bed.

I did not want to go, but she *made* me go.

Although I did not want to go, my mother made me.

I wanted to go to the pictures last night, but my mother would not let me. She made me go to bed instead.

Although I wanted to go to the pictures, my mother would not let me. She made me go to bed instead.

See *The Oxford English Readers for Africa*, Book 3, Lesson 35.

Notes

From early in their language career the children have learnt, 'May I go ...? May I have ...?' 'Will you let me?' is comparatively easy as an alternative form. 'I will let you ... ' leads to 'Mother would not let me', and to the compulsion to do something else instead with the idiomatic forms, 'I had to do .... She made me do....' instead. 'She refused to let me.'

'Although', of course, also has been taught in Stage 3 and incidentally as occasion arises, but here with dramatic incidents and stories the understanding of these words and phrases and their use should be driven home.

Remind the children of 'Bed in Summer' learnt in Stage 3:

I have to go to bed by day.

Point out

| 'let me write' | 'must go' | 'help me do, make me do,' |
| 'allow me *to* write' | 'have *to* go' | 'help me to do this', is also used. |

See Speech Work for story using these words (from *The Oxford English Readers for Africa*, Book 3).

LESSON 48

More noun clauses similar to Lesson 46: 'think', 'hope', &c. Vocabulary of verbs

Verbs

1.
think	read	see
hope	feel certain	remember
feel sure	am sure	am sorry
feel confident	know	am glad

Use these in both the present and the past tenses, pointing out the change of verb in the noun clause where the principal verb is in the past tense, as in Lesson 46.

e.g. I think that it will rain soon
    I thought that it would rain this morning, but it is fine after all.

2. Incidental

This lesson will most probably point the need for a lesson on 'wish':

I wish I could . . . .
I wish I had . . . .
I wish I were . . . .
I wish my mother would . . . .

This leads incidentally to 'If I had', 'If I were'.

Notes

Here again the pupil's horizon is widening. He is remembering, hoping, thinking, knowing. Revise the use of reported speech (statements) with the change of verb when the report is in the past tense. So when the principal verb is in the past tense the verb in the noun clause must also be in the past tense.

Point out the use of the infinitive for some of these expressions:

I hope to.	I remember.	He is sure to come.
I hoped to go.	I remembered to do it.	He is certain to come.
		I am sorry to tell you.
		I am glad to tell you.

Revise:

shall	should	shall be able to	should be able
can	could	will	would
may	might		

e.g. I think that I shall be able to swim next week.
    I thought that I should be able to swim last week but I cannot.
    I hope that my mother will let me go tomorrow.
    I hoped that my mother would let me go yesterday, but she would not.

LESSON 49

'Pardon', 'excuse', 'forgive', with present participle. Revision of 'because' (Lesson 23), and health and ailments

'Pardon', 'excuse', 'forgive', with present participle

1. Pardon me for . . . ing.   Excuse me for . . . ing. Forgive me for . . . ing.
2. Apologies and letters excusing absence.

This follows naturally from Lessons 47 and 48.

    I am sorry that I am late this morning.
    Please excuse/forgive/pardon me for being late.
    Dear . . .

        I am sorry that I was absent from school yesterday. Mother would not let me come.

           (*or* I could not come)

        because I have to stay in bed for a day or two (*or* because I have a bad cold). Please excuse me for being absent. I hope that I shall be able to come (*or* I hope to come) to school on Monday.

3. **Expressions**

absent	late	for being absent
present	early	for staying away from school
away		for being away
not present		for doing that

Revise Lesson 23 on reasons

Revise 'have to' and 'had to'. Health and ailments.

Incidentally as occasion arises 'I couldn't help it', 'He did it on purpose', or 'I didn't mean to do it', should be taught. These should be used as they are needed in apologies.

Notes

Other verbs using the participle following 'for' in the same way can be pointed out, e.g.

thank . . . for . . . ing.
scold . . . for . . . ing.
praise . . . for . . . ing.
pay . . . for . . . ing.
punished . . . for . . . ing.

This lesson calls for short stories and dramatic scenes bringing in the verbs and expressions to be practised.

LESSON 50

'If' and the subjunctive forms. Revision of simple use of 'if'. Vocabulary of imaginative themes. The use of 'wish'. Adverbial phrases

Revise simple use of 'if' with present and future tenses

What would you do if I gave you sixpence?
What would happen if . . . ?

Point out the subjunctive form

1. If I were a princess I should . . . .
   If I had a sixpence I should . . . .
   If I were rich I should . . . .

2. I wish I were . . . .
   I wish I had . . . .
   I wish I could . . . .
   I wish I might . . . .

Vocabulary

1. **Nouns**—who:

   A princess, a fairy, a fairy godmother, a witch, a wizard, a king, a queen, courtiers.

what:

   A fairy wand, three wishes, giant, a thousand pounds, a fortune, magic, a palace, a cottage.

2. **Adjectives**

   Rich, poor, afraid, wicked.

3. How would you travel to:

   The moon, Mars, the stars, fairyland, the planets?

I should travel by:

   A magic carpet, rocket-ship, space-ship, a coach, jet aeroplane.

4. **Adverbial expressions**

   Once upon a time.   Long, long ago.
   Once . . . .   Once . . . long ago and
   Ever after.   far away.
   In the future.   Many years ago.
   In a thousand years' time.
   Some day.

Notes

This lesson continues the idea of the previous lesson; wondering, hoping, and then wishing and planning what you would do if . . . . Imaginative stories come into their own here, not only the traditional fairy stories and folk-lore, but their more modern prototypes, of journeys and adventure by space- and rocket-ships in search of other worlds.

If you have taught the words likely to be encountered and if language so far has been well taught, your pupils will find real joy in these old and new stories and you will have at least started the children on the road to a love of reading.

Do not forget to teach expressions such as:

Once upon a time there was a . . . who had . . . .
They lived happily ever after.
Long, long, ago there lived . . . .
Once, long ago and far away there was . . . who lived . . . .
Some day, perhaps, men will travel in space-ships to the moon.

LESSON 51

Comparison. Comparative and superlative and equality. Adjectives, weights, measures, and nouns of qualities

Comparison of adjectives

cheap	cheaper	the cheapest	as cheap as
tall	taller	the tallest	as tall as
heavy	heavier	the heaviest	as heavy as

&c. (about fifteen more).

Nouns

length	thickness	breadth	height	cost
weight	depth	time	age	price
yards	feet	inches		
pounds	stones	ounces		
years	hours	minutes	seconds	

Revision of money, weights and measures, and abbreviations of these, e.g. lb., oz., pts. yrs.

Verbs

Weigh, cost, spend, measures, lose, have, take.

Questions

1. How heavy/tall/long/wide/deep/old is . . .?
   How much does he weigh? How much did you spend?
   How much does it cost? How many have you?
   How long did it take? How long (time) do you want?
2. What is the weight/height/length/width/depth/age . . .?
3. How many ounces/inches/yards/hours are there in . . .?
4. (a) Who is the tallest . . . in the school?
   (b) Who is taller than . . .?
5. Are you shorter or taller than . . .?
6. How much taller is . . . than . . .?
7. Which is heavier, . . . or . . .?

Sentences

1. John is taller than . . . .
2. Tom is as tall as Sidney.
3. Tom and Sidney are the same height.
4. 16 ounces = 1 pound, &c.
5. He is 2 inches taller than John.

Incidental work

Expressions used:

That is *very heavy*. He is *very thin* and *light*.

That is *too dear* for me. That book is *too tall* for this shelf.

Find *a shorter one*.

N.B. beautiful	more beautiful	most beautiful
difficult	,, difficult	,, difficult
interesting	,, interesting	,, interesting
bad	worse	worst
good (well)	better	best
little	less	least
much	more	most

Amounts and numbers

More, fewer, less.

1. I have five books. He has three books.
   I have more books than he has.
   He has fewer books than I have.
2. John weighs 6 stone. Tom weighs 5 stone.
   John weighs more than Tom. Tom weighs less than John.

Notes

Whether this lesson is dull or intensely interesting to the pupils depends so much on how it is taught. It calls for much purposeful activity and is one that the practical child loves. It must be related to the child himself. He should weigh himself and measure his height and record it in his own notebook under the appropriate headings. Boys will enjoy its references to boxing and the weights of heavy-weights, &c., girls the reference to the varying prices of clothes. Expeditions are called for, comparing prices in shops and the heights of buildings in the town or village. For general information the heights of buildings in New York will, of course, be compared with the heights of those in London. The depth of swimming pools are often marked clearly, the heights of floods also in river towns. Get the children to estimate and notice and to be accurate both in measurement and recording. Teach the children to be

correct in their spelling and to use the correct abbreviations. Neatness and clarity in recording should also be
insisted upon.

If this lesson is well taught, one bugbear of the Arithmetic lesson, 'How much . . . er is . . . than . . .?' and 'What
is the difference between the height of . . . and . . .?' should
be laid low. It can be demonstrated easily by children
standing beside the wall blackboard with their heights
clearly marked upon it. The differences can then be
measured. When this relates to themselves it can be readily
assimilated, and later can be applied to heights of buildings, and then other weights and measures. 'What is the
difference between John's height and Mary's?' can then
readily be understood.

Divide this lesson into sections and interpose other
lessons between its parts. They are put together here for
greater convenience.

N.B. Always link your new lesson with the preceding
ones, e.g. 'The princess was the most beautiful girl in the
world. The giant was as tall as a house. The *Queen Elizabeth*
is the largest liner in the world. The *United States* is the
fastest liner in the world. The *Comet* is the fastest aeroplane
in the world. The space-ship will travel faster than sound.'

LESSON 52

Relative pronouns: 'who', 'which' and 'that'

Who

Continue the incidental work of Lesson 50, i.e. 'Once
upon a time there was a prince who lived in a beautiful
palace', with 'I know a boy who was late for school this
morning.'

That is the girl who . . . .
Give that to the boy who . . . .

'Which' and 'that'

'Which' and 'that' are used instead of 'who' for things and animals.

That is the pencil which . . . .
That is the house that Jack built.
This is the kitten which climbed the tree.
Tell me the name of the animal which has black and yellow stripes.

Notes

Familiarize the children with copious examples of the use of these relative pronouns.

Keep it at this stage to the form given, i.e. with the clause coming at the end of the principal sentence.

Let the children put a relative clause at the end of sentences given by the teacher, e.g. those above.

Then, divide the class into two equal teams. Let them score marks for the team for correct clauses following the teacher's principal sentences. This is more fun done orally with marks at the end of each round. Then let each side in turn supply sentences for the other side to complete.

LESSON 53

Adverbial clauses of time with 'when'. Habitual action in the past expressed by 'used to', and sequence by the present perfect tense

Revision

1. Using past indefinite and continuous tenses

I saw three cows, when I was coming to school this morning.

2. With 'while', using two continuous tenses

Mother was making a cake while I was doing a jig-saw yesterday.

3. With the future tense and habitual tense

I shall go when he comes.

4. With two habitual tenses

When father takes his spade to dig,
Then robin comes along.

Additions

1. Expressing habitual action in the past

I used to go to another school when I was little.

2. Expressing sequence

When I have done this, I shall do that.

More verbs

For use here:

to stroll	to saunter	to garden	to do lessons
to creep	to stride	to hurry	to chase to follow

Notes

1. 'Used to'

e.g. 'I used to go to another school when I was little.'
The idea of habitual action in the past should be given as contrasted with the definite action in the past,

e.g. I *moved* from London to Birmingham when I was seven years old.
I *used to go* to another school when I was in London.
I often *used to go* to the zoo when I lived in London.

The same adverbs and adverbial phrases are applicable

for the habitual present tense as for this past habitual, e.g. 'often, every day, every week, sometimes'.

2. **Using the present perfect tense**

When I have done this, I shall do that.

This is best taught incidentally, of course, but its use can be clinched with dramatic episodes.

3. **Seize the opportunity to teach more verbs.**

Avoid the temptation of using the same verbs too often. Of course, use the known verbs when you are teaching a new principle but ally it to different, more unusual ones as often as possible.

See *The Oxford English Readers for Africa*, Book 3, Lesson 44.

Teach 'until' with the verb 'to wait'. It has already been used in phrases, e.g.

Wait till I come. I must wait until he comes home.

LESSON 54

Indirect speech. Question form. Appropriate verbs

The reported question form

Rule A. 1. If the question to be reported begins with a verb or part of a verb, 'if' or 'whether' is used as a conjunction.

2. The verb is changed into the corresponding past tense (see Lesson 46).

3. The interrogative order of the sentence is changed into the affirmative order. e.g. Miss . . . said to John, 'Do you like school?'

She asked him if he liked school, *or*
She asked him whether he liked school.

Rule B. 1. If the question to be reported begins with anything other than a verb or a part of a verb, the word already beginning the sentence is used as a conjunction.

As 2 and 3 above.

e.g. I said to the new girl, 'What is your name?'
I asked the new girl what her name was.

Verbs

Ask, reply, to question, to answer, demand, command.

Variations

A chain of speakers.

1. Ask . . . how old he is.
2. How old are you?
3. I am . . . years old.
4. What did . . . ask you?
5. . . . asked me how old I was.
6. What did . . . tell him?
7. I told him that I was . . . years old.

N.B. use 'whether' as well as 'if'.

Point out that 'asked' and 'told' are in the past tense and that this is generally used. If 'asks', 'says', or 'tells' is used then there is no change of tense in the clause.

Notes

It is now time for a further use of reported speech. There are difficulties here and they should be taken in steps. Revise the lessons on Commands and Statements and then start with the question not beginning with a verb, i.e. those under Rule B above. Four things have to be remembered:

1. Join the sentences with the first word of the question.
2. Change the question to a statement.

3. Change the statement into the corresponding past tense.

4. Change the pronoun, i.e. 'you' to 'I' or 'we'.

The easiest question under this rule with which to begin is introduced by 'Who', for there is no change of verb form in the affirmative statement nor of order of sentence.

e.g. She said, 'Who went to London with the school?'
She asked who went to London with the school.

Go on to the change of pronoun:

She said, 'Who went to London with you?'
She asked me who went to London with me.

Go on from this to the other question forms:

Where *did* you *go*? She asked me where I went.

did—go = went

What do you like? She asked me what I liked.

do like = like, change to past tense = liked.

Next take the question beginning with a verb and proceed in the same way. The easiest questions under Rule A are those beginning with 'Have', 'Has', and 'Can'. Give the pupils confidence with much practice of the easiest first.

As with the lesson on statements this should be dramatized. Let the children speak, using prepared cards, and let them act. Make the lesson concrete and enjoyable. Even when you are testing their grasp of this language form, have a concrete illustration in the form of pupils or pupils and teacher talking in front of them. Amusing illustrations of people talking after the style of comic strips can be devised.

All known tenses revised and added to, with appropriate adverbs, phrases, and clauses. Revision of telling the time

Especially 'since' with present perfect tense.

Tense	*Adverbs, phrases, and clauses*
1. Present continuous	
I am working	now.
2. Past continuous	
I was working	at 12 o'clock yesterday.
	at this time last week.
	while you were reading.
	when you came in.
	for a long time last night.
3. Future continuous	
I shall be working	at 12 o'clock tomorrow.
	at this time next week.
	when you come tomorrow.
4. (a) Habitual present	
I work	when/whenever you work.
	Every day, now and then, once a week.
	rarely, generally, usually, always.
(b) Habitual past	
I used to work	when I was . . . .
5. Past indefinite	
I worked	yesterday, last week, at dawn.
	once upon a time, a long time ago.
	in the past, when I got home last night.

6. **Future simple**

I shall work   soon, some day, next year, in the future.

I am going to work at 1 o'clock, when you come, when I have finished this.

7. **Present perfect**

I have worked   never (negative), already, for many years.

since Tuesday (not), since 1 o'clock (not).

once, more than once, yet (not).

Notes

It is well to pause and revise the use of tenses from time to time. The pupils are now beginning to use and understand more complicated language. It is advisable to see that the framework is secure and to see that they have clearly in their minds when to use the various tenses, and with what phrases to use them.

The idea of present, past, and future is fairly simple and will have been grasped long before this. Continuity in the present, past, and future is the idea underlying the continuous tenses. They have learnt to associate a recurring event with the habitual tense and have just learnt the idiomatic phrase 'used to' as expressing this idea in the past. The idea of the present perfect as a completed action without reference to a special time has already been taught. Now the expressions 'since 1 o'clock, since yesterday', can be added to the appropriate phrases. They should be used in the first case in the negative form, e.g. 'I have not seen you since last Monday. I have not been to town since Saturday. He has not moved since 11 o'clock. I have not seen Miss . . . for many years.'

The time

Give practice in the various ways of recording the time, i.e. a quarter to one = 12.45. The pupils will be interested in the 24-hour recording used abroad and for long journeys, i.e. 1 p.m. = 1300 hrs., &c.

LESSON 56

More noun clauses with 'if' and 'whether'.
Vocabulary of verbs

Verbs

wonder	wondered	am not sure	was not sure
forget	forgot	have not heard	had not heard
don't know	didn't know	am doubtful	was doubtful
doesn't know			

These follow the language principle used in Lesson 54 and follow the analogy of 'ask' in both Rules (*a*) and (*b*).

Point out that: 'I wonder if he has seen me' in the present tense becomes 'I wondered if he had seen me' in the past.

Note

See Lesson 54.

I wonder what my mother is doing now!
I think that she is shopping, but I am not sure.
I am not sure if she is shopping.
I was not sure if I knew the house.

Give plenty of practice as in Lesson 54.

LESSON 57

'Should', 'ought to', 'must', 'must not', right and wrong, with 'to be' and 'to do'. Vocabulary of verbs and adjectives

Obligation

I should help mother	I ought to help mother
she/he	she/he
we/they	we/they
you	you
I should not	I ought not to . . . .
It is right to	It is wrong to . . . .
I must	I must not . . . . It is good to . . . .

Verbs for use with the above

behave	tell (lies)	work	keep on (trying)
steal	cheat	think	try
lie	help (people)	play the game	give in
obey (my parents)		tell (the truth)	

'To be'

I should be....   It is wrong to be.... I ought to be....
I should not be....   It is right to be.... I ought not to be....

Adjectives for use with the above

lazy	kind	untruthful	true	obedient
industrious	happy	deceitful	honourable	disobedient
good	truthful	honest	right	
gentle	rough	rude	polite	

Point out contrasts and opposites and ote the prefixes 'un' and 'dis'.

Note

'Whatsoever things are true', &c.

The ideas embodied in this lesson should have been

taught throughout the school. One difficulty may be the lumping together of all 'oughts' in the pupil's mind as of equal importance, and the confusion of 'right' and 'compulsion.' Do not worry about this *at this stage*. These distinctions come only with the adult outlook. Build up as far as you can at the present.

LESSON 58

Offering or asking for help. Refusal or acquiescence and promises. Vocabulary of verbs

Offering or asking for help: refusal or acquiescence

Shall I do that for you?/   Yes, please/No, thank you
   Can I help you?
Will you help me?/   Yes, I will/No, I won't.
   Will you try hard?

Offering help: I will help you.   Mother let me help her.
Refusal: I won't do it.   Mother wouldn't let me
   help her.

Promises

I will be good.
I will help my mother.
I will try to do it.
I will remember.
I won't do it again.
Guides' and Scouts' promises—'I will try to do my duty.'

Contrast with simple future

Simple future: I shall go to town tomorrow.
Offering help: I will do that for you.

Verbs

To help, to try, to let, to refuse, to promise, to break a promise, to keep a promise.

Note

These language forms are, of course, taught incidentally with a wealth of incident. At this stage, however, it is good to point out the rules which govern their use. Clinch the correct usage with dramatic situations. Learning promises by heart is good. The expressions 'to break a promise' and 'to keep a promise' will be sure to crop up. Take the opportunity when it comes.

Give incidents for reading, such as this: 'Daddy promised to give me a pen-knife for my birthday. Yesterday it was my birthday and he gave me one. It was a beauty with three blades. Did Daddy keep his promise or break it?'

'Last night John went out to play after tea with his friends. His mother told him to come back at 7.30. John said, 'Yes, mother. I promise I will be back at 7.30.' He did not come back until 8 o'clock although he promised to be back at 7.30. When he came in he said, 'I am very sorry, Mother. I did not notice the time because I was enjoying myself so much. I am sorry. I broke my promise to you. I didn't mean to do it. I won't do it again.'

LESSON 59

Simple cause and effect: 'and so', 'is called'.
Nouns from verbs

Nouns and Verbs

1. to steal	a thief	to teach	a teacher
to lie	a liar	to write	a writer
to work	a worker	to think	a thinker

2. **With 'is called'**

He steals.	He is called a thief.
He lies.	He is called a liar.
He works in a factory.	He is called a factory worker, &c.

Simple cause and effect

Cause and effect have often been pointed out incidentally.

If you do that, this will happen.

You did that and so this happened.

It can be applied to the above also.

He lies and so he is called a liar, &c.

Take it further with:

I was hungry and so I asked my mother for something to eat.

She had no bread and so I went to the baker's to buy some.

The alternative, used in textbooks but not used much in conversation, 'therefore', should also be pointed out.

LESSON 60

Revision of question forms and answers

Who
or $\left.\begin{cases} \text{has done} \\ \text{did} \\ \text{is doing} \\ \text{will do} \\ \text{does} \end{cases}\right\}$ it?
What

When?

Where?

How?

Why?

What $\left.\begin{cases} \text{will} \ldots \\ \text{did} \ldots \\ \text{does} \ldots \end{cases}\right\}$ do?

What $\begin{cases} \text{is} \ldots \text{doing?} \\ \text{has} \ldots \text{done?} \end{cases}$

How many?

How much?

How long?

What kind of . . .?

What for?   What sort of . . .?
To whom?   What did . . . say?
Whom?   Which?
At what time?

Notes

This is an opportunity of clarifying the sentence form, and pointing out the essentials of a sentence, the subject and predicate. These need not be named, of course. It is immaterial, but the pupils should be taught to examine their own sentences for the fundamentals,

1. What/Who does/has done/did/is doing it?
2. What did . . . *do*?

They should have these and the answers to 'Whom?' 'When?' 'Where?' 'How?' 'Why?' 'What for?' clearly in mind. No time is wasted in clinching these essentials. Short passages of graded difficulty should be given to individual pupils, so that each is kept alert and also confident. Reading for comprehension is greatly helped by ensuring that this simple work is definite and sure.

Remember that this exercise is a breaking up of the sentences into words and phrases. Therefore the simpler and more concise the answer, the better. Do not confuse the issue by requiring sentences as answers here. Expect only the word or phrase which answers the question, but be sure that it is the whole phrase. In the case of 'Why?' the answer, of course, will usually be in a sentence. Revise words and phrases under headings. This work will help the average or dull child very much. Much preparation of work beforehand will be needed to ensure that the brighter ones also have suitable passages ready which are both within their comprehension and also sufficiently difficult to keep them alert and going forward.

All will enjoy cutting up a sentence into its parts, e.g. subject, verb, adverbial phrases of time, phrases of manner, adverbs, adverbial phrase of place, &c., participial phrases, &c. (have it written in script on a large sheet of paper or cardboard). Each pupil takes one part (word or phrase) and comes forward, speaking his phrase and holding up his card when the appropriate question is asked. Gradually the whole sentence is built up again, and read aloud. There are many variations of this theme. It can be used to point out that the sentence does not always begin with the subject, but often with the adverbial phrase or adverb. When the pupil holding the phrase moves up to the top of the line, it is impressed on the child's mind much more deeply than by seeing the transposition in writing or print.

COMPOSITION

1. *The full diary should gradually give place* to the recording of the chief events of the day before in a small notebook (or printed diary) used for that purpose. This should be done quite quickly and methodically.

2. *Conversations.* (*a*) The recording of conversations will help the children both in their spoken language and in their understanding of reading.

Give them examples of things that might happen in their own homes, e.g. 'This morning my mother told me to hurry up for school. She said, "If you don't hurry, you will be late." "I can't find my homework", I replied. "Where did you put it last night?" she asked. I said that I did not know. Then she looked for it and found it on the sideboard. I said, "Thank you, Mother." Then I ran to catch the bus.'

You will soon find the children producing original conversations.

(*b*) Conversational illustrations of breaking one's promise, offering help, &c., on the lines of Lesson 58.

3. *Compositions* on:

(*a*) What you would like to be when you grow up and why.

(*b*) Where you would like to go and what you would like to see on your holiday.

(*c*) What you remember about your first day at school (or your first year in school).

(*d*) Where you used to live and what you used to do when you were little.

(*e*) What you saw and thought when you were out for a walk.

4. *Descriptions of common things*, adding the use of things. Simple autobiographies of things, e.g. a pencil, a penny. This may appeal to some more than the description of things. Do not press the unimaginative child too far with this. Give examples of these things in lip-reading, guessing games, 'What am I?'

5. *Letters continued.* Letters of excuse, apology, and thanks.

6. *Imaginative stories begun.* Give free rein to the imaginative child here. Give beginnings to the stories:

'Once upon a time there was . . . who . . . .'

Give plenty of stories yourself by lip-reading, reading, and dramatization. Now some words of warning about this: Do *not* be discouraged if:

(*a*) the stories are not original but are a rehash of some they have read or lip-read,

(*b*) the language is simple and interspersed with 'then'.

Remember that deaf children lack language experience. However much practice you give them, they have less than the child with normal hearing. Do not discourage the children's efforts by thinking of a much better way of putting it yourself. If the language and the sequence are correct, give praise. When they have confidence in the simpler forms they will try out the new language forms. You must let them practise these first. Normal children begin in the same way but as they are younger at this stage nobody worries unduly. Use your own imagination and think what a big thing you are expecting of the child. It is only the child who expresses himself freely in the simpler forms who makes real progress in the more varied and complicated language forms.

When there has been a good deal of practice on the simpler forms, give separate lessons as in the language scheme, on, for instance, starting a sentence with an adverbial phrase or clause. Then in the next composition suggest that the children try to start some of their sentences in this way.

7. *Continue with the composition of Stage* 3, especially where things come from, how to do things, and descriptions of natural objects.

8. *Descriptions of a scene* and its interpretation in colour. See Lessons 39 and 40, Stage 3.

Throughout the telling of stories try to teach the children the difficult 'What is it about?' It is good to preface your stories with: 'I am going to tell you a story about (for instance) two boys, who went on a journey in a space-ship. Are you ready? Now here is the story.'

SPEECH

Now that we have reached what I should call the Inter-mediate Stage it would be well to re-examine what we are trying to do in the Speech section.

It is to select material for speech practise which will be within the children's capacity, and their understanding; which will be enjoyable, which will be suited to their age and development, and which will throw light upon, practise, and illustrate their language lessons. As we have said, the aim throughout Stage 4 should be the stimulation of thought and the imagination and the expression of thought in language. In poems, stories, and plays we have a source of stimulation ready to our hand. There should still be some rhythmic movement and, of course, dramatiza-tion. Poems should still have strong rhythmic beats, but some can be said without movement. Lines should be short or easily phraseable and all extracts for speech should be *short*.

It does not matter if the rhyme you select is hackneyed. It is not hackneyed to the child. It is something entirely new. Try to infuse a spirit of joy into all speech lessons. By this I do not mean that all poems should be cheerful ones. Remember one's own youth and how thrilling were some of the sad poems, those usually with plenty of rhythm. I remember well 'Toll for the brave! The brave, that are no more', and the fascination of the lines.

Therefore intersperse sad ones, if they are suitable in other ways, among the cheerful poems. They will throw the others into sharper relief.

Base your choice then on

1. Suitability as outlined above.
2. The language scheme.
3. The speech needs.

Here is a suggested lesson which practises some of the sounds on which all deaf children are inclined to slip up, which helps towards a natural pleasing voice, which is suitable as regards the points outlined above, which is enjoyable, and which has movement and dramatization.

This material will be so used that it practises correct speech, corrects faults in speech, and aims at ease and naturalness of expression.

Lesson on '*Madam will you walk?*' Use hearing-aids for all the children throughout the lesson.

A. Exercise. 1. **Breathing:** bending down, pretending to pick flowers, raising hand, smelling flowers, releasing breath with a sigh (open windows or out of doors).

2. **Finger held to lip. Three unvoiced plosives**

p, p, p.	par . . . arp
b . . .	bar . . . arb
k . . .	k . . . ark

Long continuous unvoiced consonants

f, f . . .	far . . . arf
s . . .	sar . . . ars
sh . . .	sh . . . arsh

3. **Nasal sounds 'm' and 'n'**

Practice humming for 'm' . . . and 'n'. . . .

mar, maw, moo, mee, moa,
nar, naw, noo, nee, no.

4. **'W' (often almost like an 'm' in some deaf children's speech)**

Practice a long oo   oo   o   ooaw

              ooo   ar   ooay

              ooo   ee

Gradually quicken to 'war, war, woo, way'.

5. **Again, final unvoiced plosives**

arp	art	ark
oop	oot	ook
eep	eet	eek
awp	awt	awk

6. *M*adam *me* ⎱ Insist on good 'm's with no hint of 't's
   *N*o *n*ot ⎰ or 'd's in them. Hang on to the 'm' and 'n'.

*w*ill *w*alk *w*ith   Clear 'w', no 'p' or 'm' in it.

wal*k* tal*k*   Correct unvoiced 'k'.

7. **The whole verse given.** (It should be ready on a chart or the blackboard.) The teacher reads it and paints the picture in words and actions.

> Mádam wíll you wálk?
> Mádam wíll you tálk?
> Mádam wíll you wálk
> And tálk wíth mé?
>
> Nó, I wíll not wálk,
> Nó, I wíll not tálk,
> Nó, I wíll not wálk
> And tálk wíth yóu.

Again give full value to the 'm's and 'n's.

B. Divide into two groups for the dialogue, boys and girls if possible. Phrase and try to get intonation.

Madam will you walk?	No, I will not walk,
,, ,, talk?	,, ,, talk,
,, ,, walk	,, ,, walk
And talk with me?	And talk with you.

Try movement with this, walking of course. The actions are obvious. Let the pupils dramatize and be emphatic, but insist on correctness. All this should not take half an hour.

Keep up the pace of the lesson, not necessarily of the speaking but of moving from one thing to another.

C. Finish with an enjoyable rhyme or two that the children already know, their choice usually. Have some humorous jingles, some poems which paint word-pictures; choose some for the beauty of the words. Give out cyclostyled copies of the poem.

Intonation

The teaching of both phrasing and intonation should be continued. Revise the two tunes and what has been learnt about them. See Stage 3: Speech.

During Stage 4 the chief language principle studied is that involving noun clauses. Study then their intonation as you reach the particular lesson in the outline. You are then practising both the mechanics of speech and language principles.

Here, speaking generally, the principal clause follows Tune II and the voice falls at the end of the noun clause when the thought is stated, e.g.

He told me that he could not do it.

He asked me if I would do it for him.

Have fun with intonation. Stories with exclamation and the repetitive question at the end of a statement. 'Do you?' 'Don't you?' 'Isn't it?' 'Is it?' are most amusing. It is a great help to naturalness of conversation to teach the shortened form of question coming as a response to a statement too. These usually follow Tune II. Exaggerate the rise and fall of the voice at this stage. It will settle down soon enough. Be very thankful if these lessons give some life and colour to the pupil's voice.

Conversational answers (questions and exclamations).

1. Response in a shortened question or an exclamation, e.g.

Statement. There is a huge dog running round the playground.

Response. Is there? Oh dear!

Statement. It is my birthday today.

Response. Is it? Many happy returns of the day.

Statement. I must go away from here.

Response. Must you? Why? What a pity!

Statement. (a) It is a glorious day today;

(b) It is a glorious day today, isn't it?

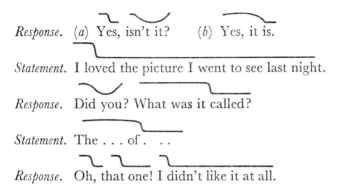

Response.   (*a*) Yes, isn't it?   (*b*) Yes, it is.

Statement.   I loved the picture I went to see last night.

Response.   Did you? What was it called?

Statement.   The . . . of . . . .

Response.   Oh, that one! I didn't like it at all.

Many more of these should be taken. Give many before you expect them given back spontaneously.

Exercises of this kind help both spoken and written language, the former in ordinary conversations and the latter in reading conversation in books.

I have placed it here with intonation work as the rise and fall of the voice is very marked, but it can be used without particular stress on it if preferred. Use them in a dramatic setting as cameo conversations.

Deaf children quite understand response to a question, but response to a statement is more difficult.

An interesting exercise for them is to present some questions and answers in direct speech and contrast the intonation of these with the report of these questions and answers in indirect speech.

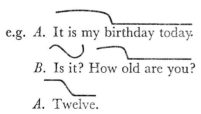

e.g. *A.* It is my birthday today.

    B. Is it? How old are you?

    A. Twelve.

B. Many happy returns of the day.

A. Thank you, I've had some lovely presents.

B. Have you? What have you had? Did you get what you wanted?

A told *B* that it was his birthday today. *B* asked *A* how old he was. *A* told *B* that he was twelve. *B* wished *A* many happy returns of the day. *A* thanked *B* and told him he had had some lovely presents. *B* asked *A* if they were what he wanted.

Give some guidance on the intonation of Lesson 56, which to some extent conforms to Tune II, i.e. 'wonder', 'not sure', 'think', 'am doubtful', 'don't know'.

I wonder if that is true.

I am doubtful if that is so.

I don't know if he will come.

I think so.

I wonder if you'd let me go with you.

I wonder if he is over there.

I wonder why she didn't speak.

I am not sure if I can go.

I think that I can go.

contrast with

I know that I can go.

I know that I can't go.

The intonation brings out the question and uncertainty in one form as contrasted with the certainty in the other.

Rhyme

It is useful to give a general idea of the intonation of the lines, i.e. if the thought is finished the voice is dropped, as in Tune I, but if the thought is unfinished it is raised, as in Tune II.

e.g. I remember, I remember

The house where I was born;

The little window where the sun

Came peeping in at morn.

The choice is getting wider now for poems of all kinds. Here are some that are suitable. There are many more.

1. **My Mother said**

> My mother said that I never should
> Play with the gipsies in the wood.
> If I did, she would say,
> 'Naughty girl to disobey.
> Disobey, Disobey,
> Naughty girl to disobey.'

The children face each other in pairs, hands ready for clapping. For the beats clap hands, between the beats clap each other's hands. It can be done sitting in desks for practice first, clapping hands and against desks (Lessons 46, 49, and 50).

2. **Where are you going to, my Pretty Maid?** (Lesson 47.)

3. **Madam will you walk?** (Lesson 58.)

4. **'The Lobster Quadrille'** from *Alice in Wonderland.*

The children will enjoy having all of this read to them, reading it themselves, and learning and saying the refrains, 'Will you, won't you', 'Would not, could not', and part of the verses as interpolation to the teacher's reading (Lesson 58).

5. **Come, follow**

> *A.* Come, follow, follow, follow,
>   Follow, follow, follow me.
> *B.* Whither shall I follow, follow, follow,
>   Whither shall I follow, follow thee?
> *A.* To the greenwood, to the greenwood,
> *A* and *B.* To the greenwood, greenwood tree.

Group work. '*A*'s move forward in one line following a

leader, beckoning. '*B*'s follow, all join hands and walk round in a ring at the last line; or the last couplet can be repeated for the walk round.

6. **'What would you like to be?'** by Paul Edmond. (Lesson 44.)

7. **Bread**

> Back of the loaf is the snowy flour
> And back of the flour the mill,
> And back of the mill, the wheat, and the shower
> And the sun, and the Father's will.   (Lesson 43.)

8. **I should like to go o'er the Rolling Sea**

The words could be learnt now of the poem 'I should like to go o'er the rolling sea', with the refrain 'Far, far, away'; see Stage 2 (Lesson 44).

9. **'I wish I lived in a Caravan'** by W. B. Rands.

All would be appreciated. One or two verses learnt (Lesson 48).

10. **'The Star.'** 'Twinkle, twinkle, little star' by Jane Taylor.

One or two verses to be learnt (Lesson 56).

11. **'Our Cat'** by Edward Abbott Parry.

> Oh, I wish that you had seen him,
> Our little pussy cat!

As before. All would be appreciated, one or two verses learnt. Refrain at end of each verse should be learnt. 'He really couldn't help it, Couldn't Smut.' (Lessons 48 and 68.)

12. **'I remember, I remember'** by Thomas Hood.

The children could learn different verses here, and

groups speak the verses in turn. They will like it all
(Lessons 48 and 53).

13. 'O Happy Wind' by W. Davies.

The whole is short. All could be learnt.

14. Wonder

> I wonder what all the stars are doing
> > Up in the sky so blue.
> I wonder if there are children in them,
> > Looking at me and you.   (Lesson 56.)

15. The Fairy-ring

> If you see a fairy-ring
> In a field of grass,
> Very lightly step around,
> Tiptoe as you pass.
> Last night fairies frolicked here
> And they're sleeping somewhere near. (Lesson 50.)

16. The Weather

> When the weather is wet,
> > We must not fret;
> When the weather is dry,
> > We must not cry;
> When the weather is cold,
> > We must not scold;
> When the weather is warm,
> > We must not storm;
> But be thankful together
> What the weather.   (Lesson 57.)

17. Monday for Health, &c.

A good rhyme by which to revise the days of the week.

18. **'January brings the Snow'** by S. Coleridge.

These couplets on the months could be learnt as each month comes round.

19. **The verse coming at the end of many round singing games** is helpful:

> Now you're married you must obey,
> You must be true in all you say;
> You must be kind, you must be good,
> And help your wife to chop the wood. (Lesson 57.)

20. **A couplet** from the children's hymn:

> Help us to do the things we should,
> To be to others kind and good. (Lesson 57.)

21. **The trees**

> The oak is called the king of trees,
> The aspen quivers in the breeze.
> The poplar grows up straight and tall,
> The pear-tree spreads along the wall.
> The sycamore gives pleasant shade,
> The willow droops in watery glade.
> The fir-tree useful timber gives,
> The beech amid the forest lives.

This can be used for group work. (Lesson 59.)

22. **The World is so Full**

> The world is so full of a number of things
> I am sure we should all be as happy as kings.

> (Lesson 57.)

23. **If All the World were Paper**

> If all the world were paper,
> And all the seas were ink,
> And all the trees were bread and cheese,
> What should we have to drink? (Lesson 50.)

24. **'If I were Lord of Tartary'** by W. de la Mare. (Lesson 50.)

25. **If All the Seas were One Sea**

> If all the seas were one sea,
> What a great sea that would be!
> If all the trees were one tree,
> What a great tree that would be!
>
> If all the axes were one axe,
> What a great axe that would be!
> If all the men were one man,
> What a great man that would be!
>
> And if the great man took the great axe,
> And cut down the great tree,
> And let it fall into the great sea,
> *What* a great splash that would be!

This can be spoken in alternate lines or alternate couplets. (Lesson 50.)

26. **This is the House that Jack built,** &c., and

27. **The story of the woman and her pig.** ('The pig wouldn't get over the stile', 'the dog wouldn't bite the pig', &c. Later 'The dog began to bite the pig', &c.)

These traditional rhymes and stories are most useful for illustrating the language taught. They are ageless.

28. **'Child's Song in Spring'** by E. Nesbit.

One or two verses
'The silver birch is a dainty lady.'

29. **'Great, Wide, Beautiful, Wonderful World'** by W. B. Rand.

30. **The story of the Arab and his camel** as told in *The Oxford English Readers for Africa*, Book 3, is excellent for

this stage. It can be used for dramatization or for a story told
by the teacher, and the children chorusing well-known parts
of it: 'Will you let me put ...?' 'Yes, you may put ...', 'It
is not big enough', 'There isn't room enough' (Lesson 47).

31. **Many of the poems listed in Stage 3** are still
suitable. Second verses can be learnt, children can exercise
choice in these.

32. **Wishes**

> I wish how I wish
> That I had a little house,
> With a mat for the cat
> And a hole for the mouse.
>
> And a clock going tick-tock
> In the corner of the room;
> And a kettle and a cupboard
> And a big birch broom.   (Lesson 48.)

33. **Summer**

> It is summer! It is summer!
> How beautiful it looks!
> There is sunshine on the old grey hills,
> And sunshine on the brooks.
> A singing bird on every bough,
> Soft perfumes on the air,
> A happy smile on each young lip,
> And gladness everywhere.

SENIOR SCHOOL STAGES

INTRODUCTION AND SUMMARY

In the detail of the work with Junior and Intermediate children, I have referred frequently to the brighter and the slower child and to their varying rates of progress. By the time the pupils reach the Senior School the gap between the two has widened considerably and this variance in attainments constitutes one of the main difficulties of the work here.

However, in dealing with the continuity of the language scheme, I have left the consideration of the more backward Senior pupil for a time, and devoted a chapter at the end of the book to this challenging problem. I am presupposing here that the Senior pupils with whom we are dealing have learnt to express themselves in the language of the first four sections of this book.

They should now realize where all the former work is leading, i.e. not only to communication with the people in their environment, which by this time should be well established, but to the acquisition of knowledge through books and the pleasure and profit of reading for enjoyment, stories, poems, plays, history, and biography. If they have been successful in reaching the standard aimed at by the end of the Intermediate Section of this book, they should be interested in words and should find the next three steps (Stages 5–7) comparatively easy.

However, the pupils have now reached or are approaching adolescence with its own difficulties and problems. Do not be disheartened if there is a temporary set-back here.

It will only be temporary, and with patience and wisdom the difficult patch will be passed and the boys and girls will progress in all subjects as before.

There is one golden rule for dealing with this age; treat the pupils as if they were adult, with kindness and courtesy though with firmness. Recognize their individuality and make them feel that they matter. Keep them moving as regards their work, but do not press them too far. The centres of interest have narrowed down again and one finds adolescent children showing a less catholic interest in all things. They show decided preferences and enthusiasms. It is a wise teacher who finds out what these are and bases the language taught on subjects which catch the interest of all in turn. It is good to turn these to good account and encourage both indoor and outdoor hobbies too. Remember to turn them to advantage in the study of language.

Some of the pupils will not want to dramatize or to take leading solo parts for a time, nor will they want to be as active in the classroom work. Recognize this and give more choral work without movement, more language and lip-reading games (call them competitions or quizzes now) where the answers are short or are written. Give plenty of practice in the known, from the different angle of calling language forms by their proper names. Give responsibilities and privileges and consult your class, asking their opinion about matters of school interest. As before, turn it to the advantage of the language taught previously or being taught now. 'What do you think about . . .? Was it fair? Why did he do it? Does anybody know anything about . . .? What ought we to do? What was his purpose in doing . . .? What use is this? Do you know why . . .? Whose duty/job/responsibility is it to do . . . this week? Have you arranged a substitute? Have you arranged the lists? Do you want me to help you? Tell me exactly what happened? What happened next? When he had done that, what happened then?'

In the early part of the work we have taught and taught and taught language. Geography, History, and Nature Study have been subordinated to this, as part of the practising ground in language.

In the senior school, English should be a subject on the time-table just as Geography, History, Arithmetic, and Science are subjects, but English should have the prior claim on time and energy. In your English lesson give the language form you are teaching its proper name as suggested, e.g. passive voice, active voice, adverbial phrase, synonyms, antonyms instead of opposites, essay instead of composition. Speech training might become Elocution. These are little things but they make a big difference to the older boys and girls.

The pupils should study a book that is suitable. Even with these older boys and girls do not make the mistake of thinking that any English book will do or of expecting them to read the normal books of their age. There are still many language forms which they do not know and they are still liable to be discouraged and confused if they are given books which are too difficult. Their work here needs grading just as carefully as before. Remember they have only learnt the foundations of complex and compound language.

I have spoken of *The Oxford English Readers for Africa* in the Intermediate work. For the seniors, Books 4–6 are excellent. The Readers are English study books with reading material. There are also reading books published to supplement the reading of the study books. These have a vocabulary and a language control and are very varied. *The Oxford English Readers for Africa*, Book 4, corresponds with the beginning of senior language and by the time the pupils have studied this book they are ready for a very good selection of stories, plays, and science and information books, all retold in simple language and with a fixed vocabulary. They have the advantage of being written for older children learning English, a very important point when dealing with seniors.

I cannot stress too much that here is where we often fail in teaching senior language. We think that the children know more language than they do and so we miss out an important step and expect them to read any book we give them. If we wish the boys and girls to love reading, we must give them plenty of reading within their capacity.

I have recommended a study book not to take the place of teaching but to be used as an aid. If you use it as such and study for yourself the suggestions in the teacher's books belonging to this series you will find them of great help. But, whatever books you use, do not use them to give the pupils something to do, without due preparation and without a purpose in your mind.

We must still continue to have a language outline and to teach language, building on the work that has been done before and correlating the speech, composition, reading, and other subjects.

Now for a summary of the work of the next three stages (Stages 5–7). As we have noticed, the actual English work is getting easier, for all the foundation work has been done. In Stage 5 there are still new forms to teach, i.e. the passive voice in all the tenses not already taken, and how these forms are used. The pupils need this form very much now, for it is used extensively in textbooks of information. The past and future perfect tenses and the past, present, and future perfect continuous tenses complete the active forms of the verb and give more exact and definite descriptions of action. Much work on phrases is necessary, present and past participial phrases and phrases of time, place, manner, degree, and kind. There is work on the use of the infinitive and the present participle. The correct phrases of time which belong to the appropriate tense are stressed. The adjectival clause using relative pronouns is gradually built up and practice in adverbial and noun clauses aid in the comprehension of more difficult language and give facility in expression. Vocabulary is widened and classified with the introduction of antonyms, synonyms, suffixes, prefixes, and collective nouns. Comparisons, contrasts, equalities and differences, and the language of arithmetical problems give practice in exact expression.

The aim is twofold; a wider understanding of language and a great precision in expression, with the understanding and use of an ever-widening vocabulary.

In the work of Stages 6 and 7 it matters less than in the other work in this book in what order you take the lessons. As the framework has already been given, the concern is now with extensions and variations of language already taught, a great widening of vocabulary, much work in phrases with idiomatic constructions, similes, and metaphorical word usages. It is concerned too with the use of those tenses already taught, especially in compound and complex sentences.

We are trying to widen the language *understanding* of our pupils, and to practice its *use*. We have therefore two aims, to help the pupils both to get pleasure and knowledge from books, and also to use in spoken and written form the ordinary language of everyday life. Reading of graded difficulty is a prime necessity. Practice in comprehension, practice in speaking and writing must be given daily. Remember nothing succeeds like success. Passages to read should not be beyond the pupils' ability to understand. That way lies the road to reading without comprehension, which in turn leads to merely looking at pictures and no reading at all.

The study of passages from textbooks, noting the phrases, clauses, and compound and complex sentences, is of great help. Throughout the language teaching we have tried to get the children to see and understand the phrase as a whole. This has gradually been expanded to seeing the clause as a whole. You will find some additional practice matter of this kind in *The Oxford English Readers for Africa*, Books 5 and 6, and their accompanying story readers.

The work is divided into:

Stage 6. The revision and extension of the passive voice, adverbial and adjectival phrases, compound sentences, conditional clauses, indirect speech, relative pronouns, adverbial clauses, noun clause, adjectival clause, participial phrases, comparison, cause, inference, conclusion, purpose, neither, nor, instead of, and the impersonal use of 'it'. Word building of nouns from adverbs or adjectives (abstract nouns), and more prefixes and suffixes are also given. Introductory phrases are also pointed out.

The aim of the work here is again twofold, i.e. the understanding of mature language and the variety and ease of its expression in both spoken and written language.

Stage 7 is mainly concerned with:

1. The study of passages from textbooks noting the clauses, phrases, compound and complex sentences.
2. The study of the previous work with special reference to the appropriate tenses involved.
3. Similes and metaphorical word usages.
4. Common idiomatic usage of words.
5. The language of forms and officialdom.

6. The widening of vocabulary in as many ways as possible.
7. The revision and extension of past work.

Its aim is simply the understanding and use of normal English.

STAGE 5

LANGUAGE

A SUMMARY of the contents of Stage 5 has already been given.

A SUMMARY OF THE LESSONS IN STAGE 5

By the side of a number of the lessons will be found the book in the series *The Oxford English Readers for Africa* and the chapter, where useful exercises on the language concerned can be found.

Lesson 61. Revision and extension of relative pronouns 'who', 'which', and 'that'. Vocabulary of 'This is the House that Jack built'. **4.** 1 and 2.

    62. Passive voice with habitual and past tenses. Vocabulary of verbs and nouns connected with citizenship, government, and general knowledge. **3.** 43.

    63. Past and future perfect tenses with revision of present perfect. **3.** 42. Appropriate phrases with 'by' and 'since'. Revision of former tenses. **4.** 4.

    64. Collective nouns and classifications. Revision of vocabulary under headings.

    65. Extension and revision of Purpose. Appropriate tenses. **4.** 10.

    66. The use of the infinitive and present participle. **4.** 7 and 8.

    67. Adjectives and adjectival phrases. Some abstract nouns. **4.** 5, 6, and 13.

    68. Comparison (comparative and superlative) of adjectives and adverbs. Revision of Lesson 51. **4.** 3.

    69. Relative pronouns revised with addition of 'whose'. Revision of possessive pronouns and apostrophe 's'. **4.** 1.

    70. Past perfect tense in adverbial clauses with 'when', 'before', 'after', 'until', leading to past participial phrase, 'having done'. **4.** 4 and 6.

71. Synonyms and antonyms and some prefixes and suffixes. **4. 2.**
72. Present, past, and future perfect continuous tenses, with revision of previous tenses and appropriate phrases. **4. 7 and 8.**
73. Relative pronouns and addition of 'whom'. **4. 1.**
74. Revision of all adverbs and adverbial phrases and clauses, with extensions.
75. Descriptions, comparison, contrasts, 'while', 'whereas', 'on the other hand'. **4. 3 and 12.**

NOTE

Be sure to use all the language forms the pupils have learnt, not only in talking to your pupils, but in the reading, stories, speech, geography, and composition lessons. In reading, speech teaching, and stories, point out new and old phrases and clauses; in the geography lessons use the passive voice, or the habitual tense. Insist on the correct use of these.

In Stage 4 the emphasis was on noun clauses of different kinds, adverbial clauses of condition, and the revision and practice of clauses of time.

Use each lesson you give, not only to teach new forms but to revise and practise the known ones. In some of the lessons which follow I have pointed out how you can do this. But this is not enough. Ask frequently, 'Do you understand how to do this? Do you know why he did that? I hope that you understand that now. Do you know where . . . is gone?' Expect answers, 'I am not sure if . . . has gone to . . . or to . . . . I think that I understand . . . . I don't know why. . . . I know where . . . lives.' Give more expressions such as 'I have no idea where . . . is, *or* why . . . did that, *or* what it means. Did . . . tell you where . . .? Can you find out whose/who . . .? . . . whether he did . . . or . . .?' From time to time gather up these expressions and give a revision lesson such as the following:

Noun clauses

Those expressing certainty or knowledge		*Those expressing doubt or lack of knowledge*	
I said	that	I asked	if
I think—thought ⎰where		I don't know	whether
I know—knew ⎱when		I cannot find out	
I heard—heard	why	I have no idea	where
I found out	how	I am not sure	when
I saw (on T.V.)	who	I am not quite sure	why
She told me	which	I haven't the slightest	
		idea	how
He informed me		I inquired	who
I read (in the paper)		I am doubtful	which
I understand		I forget	what
I am sure		I wonder	
I am quite sure			

I feel confident ⎫
I wish   ⎭ These are used only before 'that'.

Revise the rule that the tense in the noun clause is affected by the tense in the principal clause.

i.e. I know why he goes there
      I knew why he went there.

In the same way revise the adverbial clauses, giving plenty of practice. See Stages 3 and 4.

LESSON 61

Revision and extension of relative pronouns 'who', 'which', and 'that'. Vocabulary of 'This is the House that Jack built'

Revision and extension of relative pronouns 'who', 'which', and 'that'

These have been used in their simplest and easiest form in Lesson 52 and have also been encountered in reading in all their forms.

Revise: This is the man who . . . .
Once there was a boy who . . . .
Once upon a time there lived a man who . . . .

Add: A carpenter is (a man who makes tables, &c.).
A teacher is a person who . . . .
A thief is a person who . . . .
A cat is an animal which . . . .
A polar bear is an animal which . . . .
Give me the pencil that . . . .

Now show them that the sentence can be transposed:

Step 1. A man (who makes tables) is a carpenter, or is called a carpenter.
A person (who teaches) is a teacher.
A man (who works in a garden) is called a gardener.

Step 2. Give sentences to join together with 'who', 'which', or 'that'.

A. Peter has gone upstairs. *B.* He broke the window.
Teach the pupils to say:

Peter, who broke the window, has gone upstairs.

Show the children concretely by using the cards I mentioned previously that the position of the relative pronoun and its sentence must follow the antecedent: e.g. let two pupils stand in front of the class holding the sentence *A*, 'Peter (has gone upstairs)' in two pieces, but held close together to form one sentence. Two more pupils do the same with '*B*, He (broke the window)'. Another pupil chooses the card 'who' from the selection 'who', 'which', and 'that' and, dividing the two pupils holding sentence *A*, brings the two pupils holding the second sentence *B* in between them, holds over 'He' the card 'who' and the whole sentence reads: 'Peter, who broke the window, has gone upstairs.'

Vocabulary of 'This is the House that Jack built'

Pupils should learn this by heart.

bite	rat	priest	crumpled	shaven
marry	malt		forlorn	torn
kiss	maiden		tattered	shorn.

LESSON 62

Passive voice with habitual and past tenses. Vocabulary of verbs and nouns connected with citizenship, government, and general knowledge

The passive voice with two tenses only, i.e. past indefinite and habitual tenses

1. **Past tense**

    (*a*) Peter broke the window (active).
        The window was broken by Peter (passive).
    (*b*) John gave me a pencil (active).
        This pencil was given to me by John (passive).

2. Habitual Tense

(*a*) Policemen control the traffic (active).
The traffic is controlled by policemen (passive).

(*b*) We use pencils for writing and drawing.
Pencils are used for writing and drawing.

3. Point out the use of the passive voice in the habitual tense in geography and general knowledge, e.g.

Tea is grown in Ceylon.
Oranges are exported to England from South Africa.
Cotton is manufactured in Manchester.
The city is governed by councillors.
Water is supplied to all the houses.

Vocabulary

1. Verbs

govern	send	control	supply
export	import	manufacture	produce

2. Nouns

Mayor	councillor	traffic
Mayoress	police	Lord Mayor
	members of a council	

Compare Lesson 20.

We use a pencil to write with or for writing.
A pencil is used to write with or for writing.

Questions

1. By whom is the city governed?
2. By whom was the window broken?
3. To whom was the pencil given?
   By whom was the pencil given to you?
4. Where is tea grown?

5. What are pencils used for?
6. What is manufactured in . . .?

Recapitulate Lesson 32: Where things come from (Stage 3), and Lesson 43: What things are used for, transposing the active habitual tense to the passive voice. Again change narrative past tense to the passive voice.

Notes

The teaching of the passive voice presents no real difficulty as far as *understanding* is concerned. Do not expect its *use* by the pupils very quickly, except of course in answer to a direct question and in the exercise of changing the active to the passive voice.

Point out that the participle is that used in forming the present perfect tense. Practice in these is needed especially in those irregular ones which are so commonly used, e.g.

broken, done, known, sold, eaten, drunk, slept, said, sung, got, thought, made, gone.

Remember, in this and in all ensuing lessons, to keep alive in the pupil's minds question and answer in both direct and indirect speech and to ask the pupils what they think or know about the matter in hand. For instance, change the question form suggested, i.e. 'By whom is the city governed?' *to* 'Do you know how the city is governed? Do you know by whom the window was broken?' Let them answer, 'I am not sure by whom, . . . told me that it was broken by, . . . I believe that it was broken by, I think that it was broken by.'

A. The verb 'can' and 'to be able' is often very confusing when dealing with the passive voice. Give some help by tabulating in the following way:

Present (habitual) tense

Active voice	Passive voice
I can do it.	It can be done (by me).
I cannot do it.	It can't/cannot be done.
or	
I am able to do it.	It is possible for it to be done.
I am unable to do it.	It is not possible for it to be done.
I am not able to do it.	It is impossible for it to be done.
It is not possible to do it.	
It is impossible to do it.	

Future tense

I shall be able to do it.	
I shall not be able to do it.	It will (not) be possible for it to be done.
I shall be unable to do it.	
It will be possible (for me) to do it.	It will be impossible for it to be done.
It will not be possible (for me) to do it.	
It will be impossible (for me) to do it.	

Past tense

He could do it.	
He could not do it.	It could not be done.
He was able/unable to do it.	It was impossible for it to be done.
It was impossible/possible (for him) to do it.	
It was not possible (for him) to do it.	

B. 'Must' and 'have to' present some difficulty.

Present (habitual) tense

Active	Passive
I must do it.	It must be done.
I have to do it.	It has to be done.
It is necessary (for me) to do it.	It is necessary that it should be done.

Past tense

I had to do it.	It had to be done.
It was necessary (for me) to do it.	It was necessary that it should be done.

Future tense

I shall have to do it.	It will have to be done.
It will be necessary (for me) to do it.	It will be necessary that it should be done.

The future tense is included here for convenience as regards tabulation and reference. It is not necessary to teach it unless it is required.

LESSON 63

Past and future perfect tenses, with revision of present perfect. Appropriate phrases with 'by' and 'since'. Revision of former tenses

Past perfect

I had finished my breakfast by 8 o'clock yesterday.

Future perfect

I shall have finished my breakfast by 8 o'clock to-morrow.

Illustrate with many adverbial phrases of time and contrast with former tenses.

Phrases

By . . . yesterday.
By this time tomorrow. By . . . o'clock.
By . . . next week.

Present perfect

Since (date).
Not yet.

'Since' with adverbial clause

e.g. Since you were here last.
Since you came.
Since the war ended.
Since I saw you last.
Since we had a car.

Notes

These tenses have already been used in reported speech.
It remains now to show their use with appropriate phrases
and other clauses. The preposition 'by' is usually used for
both the past and the future perfect tenses: 'By this time
tomorrow, By this time yesterday, By the time you come
home tomorrow (I shall have done this), By the time he
came in last night (I had done it).'

Here is more work on the participle used in the previous
lesson on the passive voice.

Take the opportunity to revise the other tenses and their
appropriate phrases. Compare:

He did it at 5 o'clock yesterday.
He was doing it at 5 o'clock yesterday when I went in.
He had done it by 5 o'clock yesterday.
He has done it already.

He has not done it $\begin{cases} \text{since Tuesday, since you came.} \\ \text{yet.} \end{cases}$

He often does it.

He used to do it when he was a child.

He will do it tomorrow. $\Big\}$ Alternative forms.
He is going to do it tomorrow.

He will be doing it at 5 o'clock tomorrow.

He will have done it by 5.30 tomorrow.

Practice in fitting sentences to the appropriate phrases as well as phrases to the appropriate sentences. Remember to begin with these phrases as well as placing them at the end. Ask the class to complete these sentences:

By this time tomorrow . . . .

By the time you came in last night . . . .

In the past . . . .

In the future . . . .

Notice phrases in text- and reading-books and teach them. Let them keep records of phrases under appropriate headings. You will be surprised how the pupils' grasp of language and understanding of reading widens, and how gradually their own language expression becomes fuller and more accurate. Expect accuracy.

Point out also that they have learnt the passive voice form for two tenses only, the most commonly used forms, i.e. the past tense, 'It was grown'. The habitual tense, 'It is grown'. There is no need for more than this at the moment, unless it is asked for or needed.

LESSON 64

Collective nouns and classifications. Revision of vocabulary under headings

Collective nouns and classifications

1. What do we call a number of . . .?

people persons	⎧a host ⎪a crowd ⎪a multitude ⎨a company ⎪a nation ⎪a tribe ⎩a jury	sheep	a flock
		ships	⎧a fleet ⎩flotilla
		sailors	⎧a crew ⎩the navy
		soldiers	⎧army ⎩company
		airmen	⎧a squadron ⎩the air-force
cows	herd	geese	skein
savages	a horde	cricketers	⎧an eleven
boys gangsters	⎱a gang	footballers	⎩*or* a team

Scholars/pupils—a class, the whole school, a school, the lower school.

Furniture—a suite.

2. A number of, a dozen of, a score of, a heap of, &c.

A bunch of . . . .
A bouquet of . . . .
A bundle of . . . .
A faggot of . . . .
A posy of . . . .

Revise headings of vocabulary with lists

Clothing, fruit, vegetables, boys' names, animals, vehicles, buildings, advertisements, flowers, trees, trades, professions, virtues, vices, furniture, parts of body, footwear, food, drinks, birds.

An article of . . . .

A piece of . . . .

A cat is an animal.

A . . . is a vegetable, &c.

Play game 'Twenties'. (Beginning of definitions.)

Notes

This is an easy lesson and one which the boys and girls love. It is a great help both in clarifying what they already know and in widening their vocabulary. Various games can be played, including a version of 'Animal, Vegetable, and Mineral', and 'Twenties'. In the former any three headings can be taken, not necessarily those of the title, say, 'Animal, clothing, vehicle'. The pupils and teacher sit in a semicircle. One takes the teacher's place and, throwing a duster or soft ball at one of the pupils says, 'Animal' or one of the other headings. The one thrown at must catch the duster and say the name of an animal before the rest of the class has counted five. If he fails he takes the centre place.

'Twenties' is a written form of this. In the original game twenty headings are chosen and written down. Ten will suffice here. Then a letter is chosen and each player must write down an article under each heading beginning with the same letter—in a specified time, say five to ten minutes. Ten marks are given for a unique and correct name and five marks for a correct name shared by someone else.

LESSON 65

Extension and revision of purpose. Appropriate
tenses

*Extension and revision of purpose 'in order to', 'so that', 'in order
that'*

1. **Revision of purpose with the infinitive.** I went
to the shop to buy bread.

2. **New language form**

(*a*) Habitual,
    Present perfect,
    Present continuous,   so that   can
        and   in order that may
    Future tenses

    Past indefinite,   so that   could
    Past continuous, and   in order that   might
    Past perfect tenses   would

(*b*) in order to:

This can be used as an alternative to the infinitive only,
e.g.

I went to the shop to buy a new coat.
I went to the shop in order to buy a new coat.

Questions

1. What are you going to town tomorrow for?

    To
    In order to } get a new coat.

2. What are you going to this shop for?

    So that
    In order that } I may get a new coat.

3. What did you go to the shop for?

> To buy.
> In order to buy.

4. For what purpose did you go to the shop?

> So that I might buy.
> In order that I might buy.

Notes

Simple purpose with the infinitive has already been taken and should be in constant use in diaries and in class conversation, e.g. 'I went to town with Mother to buy a new coat. What did you go to the cupboard for? To fetch or to get a pencil.' 'In order to', as a substitute for 'to' is quite simple. The expansion into an adverbial clause with 'so that' and 'in order that' is not difficult either.

A similar rule as to use of the tenses is in force as for 'say, said, tell, told', i.e. the habitual present, perfect, and future tenses are followed by the present (in this case 'may, can') and the past and past perfect tenses are followed by the past (in this case 'might, could, would').

'In order that' and 'in order to' are not used generally in conversation. Point this out to the pupils. 'He went to town for the purpose of buying a new coat', is again not used in conversation. It should, however, be noted in reading. Give examples and compare (simply) purpose and reason, e.g.

I gave John some money to buy another pen because I broke his.

What did I give John the money for? ⎱ To buy an-
For what purpose did I give John the money? ⎰ other pen.
Why did I give John some money? ⎱ Because you
For what reason did I give John some ⎱ broke his
  money? ⎰ pen.

Do not lay too much stress on this. It suffices here to point out with simple illustrations and dramatic episodes that there is a difference.

Correlate with former work and ask what the pupils think, bringing in this language form, e.g.

What do you think he did that for?
I am not sure what he did it for, &c.
What was his reason?
What was his purpose?
I think he did it because . . . .
I expect he did it so that he . . . .

The use of the infinitive and the present participle

Infinitive only

1. (*a*) Purpose: infinitive *only*.

   e.g. I went to the cupboard to get a pencil.

   (*b*) Use: e.g. I used the pencil to draw with—A pencil is used to write with.

2. **After the following verbs**

try	promise	ought	help
pretend	refuse	want	have
		hope	compulsion
		(wish)	

help / have / compulsion } to do.

N.B. 'help' sometimes drops 'to'

to be able
going (future) } to do.

3. **With some adjectives** : see Lesson 48.

$$\left.\begin{array}{l}\text{to be sure}\\\text{to be certain}\\\text{to be glad}\\\text{to be sorry}\end{array}\right\}\text{to do.}$$

4.

$$\left.\begin{array}{ll}\text{tell} & \text{somebody}\\\text{ask} & \text{,,}\\\text{allow} & \text{,,}\\\text{invite} & \text{,,}\\\text{order} & \text{,,}\\\text{command} & \text{,,}\end{array}\right\}\text{to do.}$$

5.

$$\left.\begin{array}{l}\text{know}\\\text{don't know}\\\text{show somebody}\\\text{tell} \quad\text{,,}\\\text{ask} \quad\text{,,}\end{array}\right\}\left.\begin{array}{l}\text{how}\\\text{when}\\\text{where}\\\text{what}\end{array}\right\}\text{to do.}$$

6. **'To' omitted**

$$\left.\begin{array}{l}\text{make somebody}\\\text{let} \quad\quad\text{,,}\\\text{can}\\\text{must}\end{array}\right\}\text{do it; 'to' omitted.}$$

Infinitive or participle

1. **'To' omitted**

$$\left.\begin{array}{ll}\text{see} & \text{somebody}\\\text{hear} & \text{,,}\\\text{watch} & \text{,,}\end{array}\right\}\text{do } or \text{ doing; 'to' omitted.}$$

2.

$$\left.\begin{array}{ll}\text{dislike} & \text{begin}\\\text{love} & \text{start}\\\text{hate} & \text{remember}\\\text{prefer} & \text{forget}\end{array}\right\}\text{to do } or \text{ doing.}$$

Participle only

enjoy
to be fond of
(not) mind
stop   } doing *only*.
finish
keep on
go on

Notes

This is, of course, a revision lesson. It is useful at this stage to remind the pupils of these verbs and to give practice in the correct usages.

The chief points for them to remember are:

1. When the 'to' is omitted.
2. The verbs which use the participle *only*, especially enjoy. (See Lesson 45.)
3. That neither participle nor infinitive are affected by the tense of the sentence. (See Lesson 45.)

Use a wealth of incident from reading, dramatic incident, and action.

LESSON 67

Adjectives and adjectival phrases. Some abstract nouns

Adjectives

| powerful | brave | happy | kind | mischievous |
| peaceful | courageous | joyful | strong | |

Nouns

| power | bravery | happiness | kindness | mischief |
| peace | courage | joy | strength | |

Phrases

'Who' or 'what'

1.

A man	of great power.
A boy	of great courage.
A woman	of great kindness.
A man	of great goodness.
A place	{ of peace. / full of peace.
A boy	full of mischief.
A baby	full of fun.
A kitten	,, ,,
A girl	full of happiness.
A bride	full of joy.

2.

A book	{ with a green cover. / with a leather cover. / without a cover.
A bird	{ with a broken wing. / with a yellow bill. / like a crow.
A fruit	{ like an apple. / like a ball.
A book	{ like mine. / just like mine.
A frock	{ just like hers. / almost like hers.

3.

A stick	{ a foot long. / about a foot long.
A book	about an inch thick.
An island	ten miles round.
A town	five miles away.

| A pool | six feet deep. |
| A giant | ten feet tall. |

4.

| Buildings | ten stories high. |

5.

A tree	laden with apples.
A bush	covered with roses.
A house	built of brick/stone, &c.

6.

A visitor	from India.
A man	from London.
The book	on the shelf.
The book	in my car.
The hole	in the ground.
The book	near the end of the row.
The book	at the end of the row.

Notes

You will note that throughout the book stress is continually being laid on phrases. It is most important that you should teach your pupils to apprehend the whole phrase. It will facilitate their comprehension of language more than any single thing you do. The phrases under 2 will also facilitate their exactitude of expression.

1. These phrases give the pupils two ways of saying the same thing and involve the use of some abstract nouns. Taken simply in this way to start with, they should now be easy to apprehend, e.g.

    (*a*) He was a very powerful man.
           He was a man of great power.
    (*b*) This is a peaceful place.
           This is a place of peace/full of peace.

(*c*) I met a very strong man.
   He was a man of great strength.

For practice, give the adjectives and ask the pupils to make
   phrases from them.

   kind or very kind, of great kindness.
   mischievous, full of mischief, &c.

3–6. These are the phrases which help with exactitude
of expression. For the lesson have either pictures or articles
ready, a number of one kind with different qualities, e.g.
books of different sizes, with different covers; sticks of different lengths, colours, and thicknesses; boxes of different
sizes, shapes, and made of different materials. Let each
pupil choose one and describe it in one or two phrases,
e.g. 'I have chosen a book, about an inch thick, with a
blue leather cover'; again, 'I have chosen a thin book
about 10 inches long and 8 inches wide, with a cover made
of red cloth'.
   Then place the objects in different parts of the room with
different objects in juxtaposition and use all kinds of
phrases:

   Bring me the book almost like yours but with a green
      cover which is between two red books on the table
      under the window (there should be another green
      book on the table).

After some practice give lip-reading and written competitions, dividing the class into two sides, each correct reading
scoring a mark for the side. Show also that it is good to
vary one's sentences by using adjectives, phrases, and
clauses:

   I have chosen the green leather book about half an
      inch thick which was on the shelf near the door.

LESSON 68

Comparison (comparative and superlative) of adjectives and adverbs. Revision of Lesson 51

Revision and extension of Lesson 51

1. How tall is Peter?   Peter is 4 ft. 5 in.
   How tall am I?   I am 4 ft. 3 in.
   Who is taller?
   How much taller is Peter than I?

Follow on to:
   How much heavier . . .?
   How much longer . . .?
   How much wider . . .?

2. **Time**

   You began your composition at 10.30. You finished at 10.50.
   How long did it take you?
   Doris finished at 10.55.
   How long did it take her?
   How much longer did it take her than you?
   How much less time did it take you than her?

3. What is the difference between your weight and Doris's? &c.
   Are your weights the same or different?

4. What is your weight?
   Who are of the same height?
   Give me two pencils of the same length, &c.

5. Who is the fastest runner in the school?

6. What is his speed?

7. Who holds the record for (*a*) speed? (*b*) the high jump? (*c*) the long jump?

8. Who has more marks than Peter?

Vocabulary

1. Length, breadth, height, weight, depth, age, price, &c.
2. Nearly the same, of the same, not quite the same, exactly the same.
3. **Adjectives**: cheap, dear, light, heavy, old.
4. **Adverbs**

quickly	more quickly	the most quickly
slowly	more slowly	the most slowly
happily	more happily	the most happily

5. *much* taller   *a great deal* heavier
   much more quickly   *much more* slowly
   very much taller   very much more slowly
   the very smallest.

Notes

The foundations for this lesson have been laid in Lesson 51 in Stage 4. The emphasis there was on the concrete representation of 'greater' or 'less than'. The meaning of 'How much . . . er is . . . than . . .?' was demonstrated. More work on this with copious examples is necessary. Do not make the calculations difficult. Leave that to the Arithmetic lesson. Concentrate on the understanding of the language and revise by concrete examples, i.e. the weighing and measuring of each other by the pupils. A little more on sport and records is always welcomed by the pupils, especially the boys.

Do you know who holds the world record for . . .?
Try to find out who holds the world record for . . .?
. . . told me that . . . holds the world record for . . . .
I am not sure who holds the world record for. . . .
I am not sure what my weight is, but I think that it is . . . .

Comparison of adverbs

(*a*) Those in which the degree of comparison is formed by adding -er and -est, in the same way as adjectives. These have one syllable only:

fast	late
hard	far (farther, farthest)
soon	
near	

(*b*) Irregular forms

well	better	best	much	more	most
badly	worse	worst	little	less	least

(*c*) Adverbs ending in 'ly'—comparative 'more', superlative 'most'.

wisely	more wisely	most wisely
beautifully	more beautifully	most beautifully

Who can run as fast as John can?
Who can sew more neatly than Jean can? &c.

LESSON 69

Relative pronouns revised with addition of 'whose'. Revision of possessive pronouns and apostrophe 's'

Whose

1. There is the cat whose kittens are lost.
   I know the girl whose book is lost.

2. Sally, whose book is lost, has not done her homework.

Possessive pronouns and plurals revised

The girl's books	the girls' books.
Her books	their books.

Revision of 'who', 'which', and 'that'

(Lessons 61 and 52)

What is a man who . . . called?
A man who writes is called a writer.

Notes

Begin simply with the clause at the end of the principal sentence:

I know a man whose dog is lost.
I know a boy whose father is in Korea.

Point out that 'whose' is a substitute of any of the possessive pronouns. Practice substituting for all of them.

Impress on the pupils that the relative pronoun must come next to the noun to which it refers. As in Lesson 61 use action, coloured chalks, any visible means of helping the pupils to remember this. Then go on to the next stage:

Sally has not done her homework.
Her book is lost.
Sally, whose book is lost, has not done her homework.

The use of this interposed clause will only come with practice. Do not expect original sentences bringing it in at this stage. Be sure that they understand and can put two sentences together using 'whose' correctly. Notice in their original work any two sentences which could be joined together in this way and suggest this as an improvement. Be sure the understanding of its use is clear but do not dishearten the children by expecting its use at once.

LESSON 70

Past perfect tense in adverbial clauses with 'when', 'before', 'after', 'until', leading to past participial phrase, 'having done'

Present participial phrases revised, with new vocabulary

I heard a bird singing in a tree.
I met a man running down the road.
I met a boy carrying an injured dog.
I noticed a man creeping stealthily round the house.
Look at the sun shining on the water.

Past perfect tense with 'after', 'when', 'before', and 'until'

(*a*) After I had done my homework, I went out to play.
After I had had my tea, I did my homework.
After I had been to Scouts, I went to bed.

(*b*) He came in before I had finished my homework.
I asked him to wait until I had done my homework.
When/After I had done my homework, I went out to play football.

Past participial phrases

Having done my homework, I went out to play.
Having had my tea, I did my homework.

Notes

1. **The present participial phrase** should be well known by this time. Revise it with new verbs.

2. **After and before**

Be sure that the sequence of events is quite clear in the pupils' minds.

(*a*) When I got home from school last night, I read my library book.

(*b*) Then I had my tea.

(*c*) Then I did my homework.

Taking the middle sentence, show that the action of sentence (*a*) comes *before*, and of sentence (*c*) *after* it.

Express this sequence now in two complex sentences showing the relation to the middle sentence, which must come in both, though in a different tense.

> Before I had my tea (past tense), I read my library book.
>
> After I had had my tea (past perfect tense), I did my homework.

3. After much practice in this way, go on to the next stage, e.g. using present and past participial phrases.

The present participial phrase takes the place of the simple past tense and the past participial phrase, that of the past perfect tense, e.g.

Before I had ⎫
Before having ⎭ my tea, I read my library book.

After I had had ⎫
Having had ⎭ my tea, I did my homework.

LESSON 71

Synonyms and antonyms and some prefixes and suffixes

Synonyms

almost	nearly	cannot ⎫	impossible
hardly	scarcely	unable ⎭	
completely	wholly	happy	glad
		unhappy	sad
		can	⎧ possible ⎨ able

Antonyms

(Made with prefixes and suffixes)

less	careful	careless
in	direct	indirect
un	true	untrue
dis	honest	dishonest

Prefixes

in = not
direct   indirect
un = not
true   untrue
happy   unhappy

Suffixes

1. (*a*) **-er, -ar, -or**

work	worker (the person who)
bake	baker
lie	liar
sail	sailor
teach	teacher

(*b*) **-er** (comparative form for adjective)

old   older
young   younger, &c.

2. **'-y' making adjectives**

stone	stony
sun	sunny
stick	sticky
ink	inky
dirt	dirty

3. '-ly'—adverb

beautifully, happily, sweetly, carefully, carelessly, loudly, &c.

4. '-ness'—noun

sickness, happiness, sweetness, carefulness, carelessness, goodness, darkness.

5. '-less'—without

care	careless	useless
fear	fearless	cloudless
water	waterless	endless
life	lifeless	hopeless
wire	wireless	friendless

6. '-like'—like

warlike   lifelike

7. '-ful' —full

care	careful	useful
beauty	beautiful	hopeful
forget	forgetful	fearful

8. '-ion', forming nouns

subtraction	(to subtract)
election	(to elect)
action	(to act)

Notes

Here is an excellent opportunity to revise, to add to vocabulary, and to teach the pupils to notice words and their formation. It is only the beginning of a fascinating study, one which will help their understanding of what they read enormously. One word of warning; be sure that the use of these words is known, e.g. when adding '-y' to form an adjective, give examples. 'He threw a stone.' 'We went up a stony path on the hillside.' You will probably have other suffixes and prefixes suggested by the pupils. Add these to the lists, of course. Let them make lists for themselves in their own notebooks. Give them passages to read from books. As I have said, be sure that the pupils know the use of these words, but do not expect them to use them at once.

The purpose of this lesson is the widening of the pupils' vocabulary and understanding of the meaning of words. Impression comes before expression. You will see the fruits of this lesson and others like it later, perhaps not at once.

LESSON 72

Present, past, and future perfect continuous tenses, with revision of previous tenses and appropriate phrases

Present perfect continuous

Built up upon the former lessons.

> Are you still writing your composition?
> How long have you been doing it?

I have been writing my composition for twenty minutes and have not done yet.

I have been working at this sum for ten minutes and I cannot get it right.

He has been working there for many years.

You are late. What have you been doing? I have been helping Miss . . ., &c.

Past perfect continuous

I had been writing for twenty minutes when you came in.

I had been writing for twenty minutes at ten o'clock yesterday.

Future continuous

I shall have been writing for twenty minutes at this time tomorrow.

It is sufficient that the children understand the use of this tense. Facility to use it will come with practice.

Phrases

1. For twenty minutes.
   For a long time.
   Since 10 o'clock.
   For nearly half an hour.
   For many years.
   All this time.
   From . . . o'clock to . . . o'clock.

2. Revise phrases used with continuous tenses (Lesson 55).
   For twenty minutes.
   At 12 o'clock tomorrow.
   At this time yesterday.

Notes

Here are the last three tenses to teach. They are not difficult if the pupils understand the previous work and if incidental work in the classroom has been well done. 'Where have you been?' and 'What have you been doing?' to a pupil away from the classroom too long or to a pupil who brings out his work late and unfinished. 'What have you been doing all this time? It is 12 o'clock now, and you started at 11.30. What have you been doing from 11.30 to 12 o'clock?'

The idea is that of completed continuity from one set time to another. Teach 'How long . . .? What a long time you have been!' 'How long' is sometimes confusing and this lesson helps to point out the expression of length of time. Be sure that the children understand by doing a great deal of action work. For example, let one or two pupils go out of the room. The rest choose an action and do it the whole of the time until the teacher calls the others in again. Then the class stops. The incomers ask, 'What have you been doing all the time while we were out of the room?' and each answers, 'I have been . . .ing all the time, while you were out of the room.' (See *The Oxford English Readers for Africa*, Book 4, Lessons 7 and 8.)

Show that in the past and future perfect continuous tenses, two time phrases, or a time phrase and a time clause, are used to give the meaning of completion and continuity, e.g.

(shall have been doing) for twenty minutes at this time tomorrow.

(I had been . . .ing) for nearly half an hour ⎰ at 12 o'clock last night. ⎰ when the clock struck 12 last night.

(He had been living there) for many years when I first met him.

LESSON 73

Relative pronouns and addition of 'whom'

Whom as a relative pronoun

There is the girl *whom* I saw at the pictures.

Revise other relative pronouns

'who', 'which', 'that', 'whose'.

Revise pronouns

Especially objective ones.

Notes

The pupils are familiar with 'whom' in question form. Begin with some of these questions,

Whom did you see last night at the club?

     ,,   ,,   ,,   meet ,,   ,,   ,,

Point out that 'whom' is always followed by a pronoun or other noun, i.e. the subject of the new sentence.

e.g. I gave the book to the boy *whom* I met last night.
     I gave the book to the boy *who* had lost it (subject as well as relative pronoun).

Comparison of the two forms will often clarify the difficulties, again:

     The boy (*whom you* saw last night) came to see me today.
     The boy (who had lost his cricket bat) asked me about it today.

Practice

whom I	whom you	whom he	whom they
whom she	whom we	whom it	whom the boys

There is one exception to this which can be pointed out when it occurs. A sentence can contain 'who, I' in juxta-position when an interpolation, such as 'I am sure', 'I think', 'I know', comes after the relative pronoun:

e.g. I know a man who, I am sure, will help you.

Teach this as an exception to the rule when it arises.

LESSON 74

Revision of all adverbs and adverbial phrases and clauses, with extensions

Adverbial phrases

1. Time.
2. Place.
3. Manner.

Extension of adverbs

1. Time.
2. Place.
3. Manner.
4. Degree.

Transposition of adverbial phrases

To beginning of sentences, &c.

e.g. I went to the pictures *at half past six on Saturday night* with . . . .

On Saturday night at half past six I went to the pictures with . . . .

Extension of previous adverbial phrases

1. **Time:**

At what time?	How long?
at . . . o'clock	since last May

at half past . . .
at a quarter to . . .
when?
at midnight
at cock-crow
at dead of night
in the middle of
    the morning

for many a year
from morn till night
all day
for . . . hours
for ever and ever
how often?
every day
now and then
every so often
very frequently

2.   **Place:** Where?

far distant
far away
in the distance
beyond the moon
across the world
round the world

3. **Manner:** How?

in a stealthy manner
with stealth
without fear
in a harsh way
with kindness
without mercy
more quickly than I

Adverbs

Time: When?	Degree: How much?	Place: Where?	Manner: How?	Number: How often?
soon	too	here	stealthily	once
immediately	very	there	craftily	twice
yesterday	almost	everywhere	calmly	again
today	nearly	near	happily	seldom
now	rather	far	sweetly	often
late	completely		merrily	never
presently	not quite			sometimes
ago	rather			
afterwards	somewhat			
before	partially			

Notes

1. This is an extension of previous lessons and as such does not need comment. Do not forget to have as much action and dramatization in your lessons as possible.

2. Let the pupils search (*a*) for adverbial (and adjectival) phrases in their reading books, (*b*) for adverbial clauses beginning with 'when', 'until', 'before', 'after', 'where'.

3. Practice extending time phrases into sentences and revise the knowledge of the interdependence of the tense in the principal clause on that in the adverbial clause.

We went	at midnight.
We shall go	,,
We went	at dead of night.
We shall go	,, ,,
We stayed	all day.
We went	when the clock struck twelve last night.
We shall go	when the clock strikes twelve tonight.
We went	when/after all was quiet in the middle of the night.
We shall go	when/after all is quiet in the middle of the night.
We stayed	until the sun set.
We got up	before the sun rose.
We got up very early in the morning.	

4. **Practise clauses beginning with 'where'.** These have been used much incidentally. Gather them together here.

(*a*) Stand where he was standing just now.
(*b*) Stand where you can see me well.
(*c*) Sit where the light is better.
(*d*) Put your book where I can see it.
(*e*) I put it where you told me.

Give further examples and refer to 'The Chilterns' (see Speech Section).

LESSON 75

Descriptions, comparison, contrasts, 'while', 'whereas', 'on the other hand'

Comparisons and contrasts

What is the difference between . . . and . . .?
. . . is a small animal while . . . is a large one.
They are both animals but one is larger than the other.

Vocabulary to be used

while, whereas, on the other hand.

Revision of vocabulary

the same	size	colour
different	weight	shape
alike	height	
unlike		

How are . . . and . . . alike?
How are they different?
They are alike in . . . .
They are different in . . . .
They are both . . . .

Revise 'Although'

Although they are both animals they are different in size.
Although they are alike in . . . they are different in . . . .

Notes

This is again an extension of previous lessons. Hark back to differences in height, weight, &c. Let them compare two things and see in what respects they are alike and in what different, e.g. 'Here are two things',

How are they alike? They are both books.
How are they different? (In what ways?)

1. One has a blue cover while the other has a green one.
2. The blue one is thicker than the green one (or the one with a blue cover is).
3. One is an English book while the other is an Arithmetic one.
4. The green one is larger than the blue one.

Again:

Are their shapes/lengths the same or different?
What is the difference between English and Indian children?
English children have white skins, while Indian children have brown skins.
How are they similar? They both like playing, running, learning, adventuring, &c.

COMPOSITION

KEEP compositions short and clear. Insist on paragraphs. Insist on correct punctuation and neatness. Give different kinds of compositions, for some will excel in one kind and some in another:

> Narrative, Imaginative, Descriptive, Definitive, Informative.

Here are some suggestions for Stage 5.

1. *Conversations continued.*

2. *Continue this story:*

e.g. (a) One night Jack woke up when all the house was quiet. He looked out of his window and saw . . . . (What did he see and what did he do?)

 (b) A man crept stealthily down the road at midnight . . . . (Continue this.)

 (c) Once upon a time there was a poor boy who lived . . . . (Tell me about him and what he did.) (Lesson 74 and previous ones, 39 and 40, &c.)

3. *What would you do* if someone gave you . . .?
 ,, ,, ,, if you saw . . .?
 ,, ,, ,, if you found . . .? (Lesson 50.)

4. *Geographical composition.*

Give an account of a certain place: (a) what the climate is like, (b) what is grown there, (c) what is made there, (d) what is exported from there. (See Lesson 62.)

5. *Making up arithmetical problems* on money, weights and measures. (See Lesson 68.)

6. *Autobiography* of an orange, a tin of pineapple, &c.

7. *Definitions*. (See Lesson 61.)

8. *Consecutive events*

What you did when you (*a*) got home from school last night? (*b*) got to school? (*c*) went out? &c.
Tell your actions in order in three ways:

  (i) First write in short sentences:
       First I did . . . .
       Then I . . . .
       Then I . . . .
  (ii) Then rewrite it using adverbial clauses with 'after' and 'before'.
  (iii) Rewrite again using past participial phrases.

9. *Biographies* of great men and women (simply).

Notes on former reproduction of stories. Give plenty of practice before writing.

10. *Compare* (*a*) girls and boys, (*b*) a mouse and an elephant, (*c*) a robin and an eagle. (A few lines only, plenty of practice first.) (See Lesson 75.)

11. *Description* of (*a*) a sunset or sunrise, (*b*) a winter scene, (*c*) a country scene, (*d*) a town scene, &c. Describe what you saw in the park last night, describe the people you met, and what they were doing. Try to make your reader see it too; tell what the weather was like, what the park was looking like, what the people looked like.

12. *Letters:* (*a*) thanks, excuse, apology, (*b*) to a pen friend describing yourself, your school, your likes and dislikes, your home, asking questions. (Lesson 66.)

13. *Favourites:* (*a*) your hobby, why you like it, (*b*) your favourite game, book, &c. (Lesson 66.)

14. *Accounts* of (*a*) expeditions, (*b*) holidays, (*c*) school holidays.

15. *Short stories* giving cause and effect. (See Lesson 65.)

At tea-time yesterday we had no bread because the baker was late, so my mother said to me, 'Will you go to the shop for me to buy some bread?' I said, 'Yes mother'. She gave me the money.

I went to the . . . but they had no bread there, and so I went on to another shop.

There they had a small loaf and I bought it.

My mother was glad when I got home with the bread. She was surprised that . . . had no bread. She was sorry that I had to go such a long way in order that I might buy bread for our tea.

Stories such as these should be given to the children and similar ones invited. Pupils who cannot think out original stories can often think out some happenings of this kind.

STAGE 5. SPEECH

See page 324.

LANGUAGE

A SUMMARY of the contents of this stage has been given in the introduction to Senior School Stages.

A SUMMARY OF THE LESSONS IN STAGE 6

As in Stage 5 the numbers after the lessons refer to useful exercises in *The Oxford English Readers for Africa*.

'yet', 'nevertheless', 'all the same', 'even though', 'in spite of'.

87. Differences, comparisons, and contrasts. **5**. 16.
88. Extension of (*a*) cause: 'because', 'since', 'as', 'inasmuch as', 'for', 'being', with clauses and phrases; (*b*) purpose: 'so that', 'in order that', 'for the purpose of', 'lest'. **5**. 10.
89. Introductory phrases and exclamations.
90. The impersonal use of 'it' with the infinitive, with clauses and with weather vocabulary. **5**. 2.
91. Extension of 'if', 'or', 'else', 'unless', 'even if','provided that', 'whether or no', 'had he'. **5**. 4–6.
92. Extension of inference and conclusion: 'so', 'therefore', 'consequently', 'and so', 'then', 'so then', 'as a result'.
93. Extension of 'neither', 'nor', 'nor did', 'either', 'or', 'else', 'otherwise'.
94. More prefixes and suffixes: '-ment', '-ure', &c. Formation of verbs and nouns.
95. Extension of 'instead of', 'in place of', 'as a substitute for'.
96. 'So (tired) that', 'too . . . to', 'not . . . enough'. **5**. 6.

LESSON 76

Extension of the passive voice, with more tenses

Revision of tenses already taken

1. **Present indefinite.** *Active.*   Policemen control the traffic.

   Passive. The traffic is controlled by policemen.

2. **Past tense**

   Active. Peter broke the window.
   Passive. The window was broken by Peter.

The future tense

Active. I shall write a letter tomorrow.
Passive. A letter will be written by me tomorrow.

The perfect tenses

1. **Present perfect**

Active. He has done a lot of work.
Passive. A lot of work has been done by him.

2. **Past perfect**

Active. He had done all the work before I arrived.
Passive. All the work had been done before I arrived.

The continuous tenses

1. **Present continuous**

Active. They are doing a lot of work here.
Passive. A lot of work is being done here.

2. **Past continuous**

Active. John was cutting the lawn when we got there.
Passive. The lawn was being cut by John when we got
there.

N.B. The future continuous and the perfect continuous
tenses are long, involved, and somewhat clumsy in the
passive voice.

They are very rarely, if ever, used.

Questions

1. By whom will the letter be written?
2. What was being done when we got there?

3. What is being done here?
4. What had he done before I arrived?

Notes

There is little difficulty in this lesson. As I have already said, if the foundation has been well laid and the pupils understand the change to the passive voice in previous tenses, it only remains for them to practice and memorize the new forms.

Here is another opportunity at the beginning of the new Stage to revise the use of the tenses.

Your pupils are older now, but do not forget to make your lessons concrete, active, and alive, just as you tried to do when they were younger. Try to find interesting ways of emphasizing and practising what you are teaching, especially using action combined with speech.

The Oxford English Readers for Africa, Book 4, has one way, and a very good one. (Exercise at the end of Lesson 17. Speech and Action.) Use this and others.

LESSON 77

Phrases (repetitive) and revision of adjectival and adverbial phrases

Repetitive phrases

to and fro	round and round	here and there
up and down	backward and forward	arm in arm
one by one	from place to place	face to face
two at a time	little by little	back to back
step by step	there and back	

Contrast

straight there	right to the end	in a roundabout way
all round	at one step	at one bite
as one man	in concert	in one jump

Notes

This is a lesson to extend the vocabulary and understanding of common phrases. Let the pupils act the phrases—and use them in sentences.

The pupils will probably have met a number of these in their incidental work and reading.

It is well, however, to have a lesson such as this which gathers phrases of this kind together, and makes sure that they are understood. It is so easy to expect our pupils to know what has never been explained to them.

As I have said before it is most important to try to teach our children to see and apprehend the phrase as a whole. Remember that phrases are easier than words to lip-read, and the understanding of phrases clarifies both reading and lip-reading. Continue to clinch the knowledge with the question form—'How?' (adverbs and phrases of manner), 'Where?' (adverbs and phrases of place), 'When?' (time), 'How much?' (degree), 'How often?' (frequency), 'How far...?' (distance), 'How long...? (time).

Here is a good opportunity to revise the former work on phrases and on their transposition in some sentences. It is worth while to spend some time on this (it is always interesting to the pupils) if you find that your revision brings to light weaknesses in understanding here. It is so varied that there is plenty of work for both the more advanced and the weaker pupils.

LESSON 78

Extension of 'if' and use of relative pronouns. Definitions with vocabulary of nouns: people and their occupations, &c.

Definitions

The use of relative pronouns and the extension of 'if'.

1. (*a*) A man who makes tables, chairs, &c., is called a carpenter.

A woman who nurses sick people is called a nurse, &c.

See Lesson 61.

(*b*) A boy who steals is called a thief.
A girl who lies is called a liar.

See Lesson 59.

2. An athlete is a person who runs, swims, or jumps very well.

3. If I did something brave, I should be a hero.
If he ran very well, he would be an athlete.

New vocabulary

1. **Nouns**

burglar	a sport	leader
detective	coward	follower
millionaire	sportsman	idler
hero	politician	a motor mechanic
heroine	person	

2. **Verbs**

to burgle	to do something	to follow
to detect	cowardly	to lead
to work		{ to waste time
		{ to idle

to do something   to run ⎫
    very brave   to swim ⎬ very well
               to jump ⎭

to make ⎫
to repair ⎬ motor-cars
to overhaul ⎭

to play football,
   cricket, &c.
to play games well

3. **Revise and add to adjectives**

truthful	cowardly	idle
untruthful	heroic	engineering
dishonest	political	mechanical
observant	athletic	leading

4. **Point out**   **Used as adjectives indicating purpose,** e.g.

⎧ football   the football field
⎨ cricket   ,,   cricket   ,,
⎩ travel   ,,   travel agency
   mission   ,,   mission field
     and
   missionary   ,,   missionary society.

Notes

This is a revision lesson on alternate forms of definitions. It provides an opportunity, too, for revision of Lessons 50 (if with the subjunctive form), 59 (works in a factory and so is called a factory worker), and 61 (A man who makes tables and chairs is called a carpenter).

It is well, here, also to revise other uses of 'should' and 'would' Lessons 44 (should like), and 57 (I should tell the truth (ought to)).

1 and 2. Revise first Lessons 61 and 59 with all the vocabulary—adding as suggested.

    (*a*) A man who . . . is called a . . . .
    (*b*) A . . . is a person who . . . .

3. (*a*) Point out in this use of 'should' that the action comes first. If I *did* something, I should *be* a certain kind of person.

> If I *did something* brave—I should *be* a hero.
> If I *did something* cowardly—I should *be* a coward.
> If I stole, I should *be* a thief.
> If I wasted time, I should *be* an idler.

(*b*) Revise the other uses of 'should' and 'would'.

> i. I should (like to be a carpenter). (Lesson 44.)
>   He would like to do something.
> ii. If I were . . . I should. If he were . . . he would.
>   If I had . . . I should. If he had . . . he would.
> iii. Should = ought to.
>   We should try to do right ⎱ 'would' is not used here.
>   He should try to do right ⎰
> iv. 'Would' = past tense of 'will' indicating determination.
>   She wouldn't do it. ⎫
>   I   „   „   ⎬ 'should' is not used here.
>   He „   „   ⎭

Reported—future tense:

> 'I shall not go tomorrow', he said.
> He said that he wouldn't go tomorrow.
> 'I shall go tomorrow', I said.
> I said that I should go tomorrow.

There is much interest in this lesson to growing boys and girls; what they are hoping to be, what they want to do, what qualities they admire, what makes people become what they are, what great men have wanted to do—what they became.

Extension of (*a*) 'and', 'both', 'moreover', 'too', 'also', 'in addition to being', 'as well as'; (*b*) 'but', 'whereas', 'on the other hand', 'yet', 'without being'. Revision of adjectives with additions

(*a*)

He was just and merciful also.

He was a just man, he was also merciful.

He was both just and merciful.

He was just, moreover he was merciful.

He was merciful **in addition to being** just.

He was merciful **as** well as just.

(*b*)

He was just, but he was not merciful.

He was just, yet he was not merciful.

He was just, on the other hand he was not merciful.

Comparison of two people:

He was just whereas his father was merciful

He was both just and merciful,

whereas his father was just ⎰ without being merciful.
⎱ but not merciful.

Note

There is no difficulty in understanding here. Give plenty of practice in its use, especially 'in addition to' and 'without being', which are followed by a present participle, and 'whereas' which contrasts two people or things with different qualities, not two qualities only.

Revision of indirect speech and tenses involved
in noun clauses. Vocabulary of verbs

Verbs

Inquire, remark, cry, reply, answer, ejaculate, call,
exclaim, add, whisper, admit, suggest, inform,
respond, sigh, explain, announce, smile, begin,
shout, mutter.

Language

1. Special attention to tenses.

2. Revise lessons on indirect speech (Lessons 42, 46, 48,
54, 56).

Notes

The purpose of this lesson is twofold. First to help the pupils
to understand and enjoy reading stories containing conversations, and second to revise the rules of reported
speech, in order to help the pupils in its use so that their
own expression is improved.

If you will glance through any book of fiction, you will
find many words used in place of 'said', 'answered', or
'asked'. These sometimes bring in two meanings, e.g.

'How do you know that?' he smiled.

This of course means:

'How do you know that?' he asked, smiling.

We do not always realize how confusing these expressions
can be to our pupils. They need explaining and dramatizing. A full understanding of this will help both the apprehension and the enjoyment of reading. There is much
scope for dramatic episodes here.

Relative pronouns, 'by whom', 'to whom', 'of whom'. Revision of relative pronouns and of passive voice

Relative pronouns

1. Revision of former relative pronouns.

2. **By whom, to whom, of whom**
    (*a*) These have been used in question form.
    (*b*) The use of these as relative pronouns.

Passive voice

Revision of passive voice: 'By whom was it done?'

Notes

You will notice that I have suggested many steps in the teaching of relative pronouns with much practice and assimilation between.

It has been my experience that even bright pupils find, not the understanding of these, but their use, difficult; so be wary and teach one step at a time, revising the former steps as you go along.

Here are the former lessons:

1. Stage 4, Lesson 52. 'Who', 'which', and 'that', introducing the subordinate clause at the end of the principal sentence. (**4.** 1–3.)
2. Stage 5, Lesson 61. 'Who', 'which', and 'that', the subordinate clause inserted after the antecedent in the principal clause. (**5.** 1.)
3. Stage 5, Lesson 69. The former relative pronouns

revised and 'whose' added. Special revision and contrast of Steps 1 and 2, with this new pronoun. (**4.** 1.)

4. Stage 5, Lesson 73. These relative pronouns revised and 'whom' added. Again revise Steps 1–3. (**4.** 7.)

This further lesson should be regarded as one in comprehension. 'To whom', 'by whom', and 'of whom' are not very much used in conversation.

It is easier to start with the use in question form, and with it the passive voice may be revised:

By whom was it done?   It was done by him.
To whom was it given?   It was given to her.
Of whom was it said?   It was said of him.

Then change to the simplest form of this relative. 'That is . . ., the man *by whom this* house was built', '. . . the girl to whom I gave the parcel', 'That is the boy by whom the poem was said'. Emphasize that the antecedent must be followed by the relative pronouns concerned and in the case of 'whom' by the subject of the next sentence, e.g. . . . the man by whom this house . . . .' (See Lesson 73.) Then show in the same way as in Step 2 that the subordinate clause can be inserted in the principal one, e.g. 'The man *by whom this house* was built has gone away from the town'.

LESSON 82

Abstract nouns with adjectives and adverbs and new adverbial phrases using these nouns

Formation of cognate words

Adjectives	**Adverbs**	**Nouns**
happy	happily	happiness
merciful	mercifully	mercy

Nouns

goodness	truth	truthfulness	peace
love	joy	long-suffering	faith
lying	untruthfulness	dishonesty	honesty
laziness	sloth	gladness	beauty
righteousness	sweetness	industry	prosperity

Vocabulary

1. Based on extracts from books, especially the Bible and *Pilgrim's Progress*.

Cf. 'Mercy and Truth are met together.'

'Surely goodness and mercy shall follow me . . . .'

2. **Opposites** :   honesty   dishonesty
                 goodness   evil.

3. 'The fruits of the Spirit are . . . love . . . joy . . . peace.'

4. Revise suffixes, '-ness' and '-ly'.

Revise phrases and add more (Lesson 67)

Adverbial

with truth	with harshness
with joy	without mercy
with love	without fear
with happiness	in peace

Adjectival

Full of sweetness, full of joy, full of deceit.

Notes

Here is an opportunity of extending the vocabulary and understanding of your pupils, and of adding to their phrases. Give plenty of examples of the use of abstract nouns in passages such as I have mentioned but do not expect the pupils to use them at first. Our literature, both poetry and prose, abounds in examples of the use of these words couched in simple and beautiful language. If the pupils appreciate and understand, you have done much.

Point out the difference between the use of the adjectival and the adverbial phrases, e.g.

Adjectival. He was a youth full of promise.
He was a man of great kindness.
He was a man without mercy.

Adverbial. He spoke with truth.
He jumped in without fear.
He went forward in fear and trembling.

A helpful exercise, and one which prepares for Lesson 92, is to change a sentence using an adjective to one using a noun, e.g.

I am very happy.   My happiness is great.
He was very merciful.   His mercy was great, *or*
He was full of mercy.

Take this very simply. It will prepare for the more difficult change later and help in its understanding.

LESSON 83

Directions, with appropriate vocabulary of nouns, verbs, and phrases

Verbs and phrases

Verbs	**Useful words**			**Phrases**
turn		left		straight on
go		right		to the end of the road
take		down		at the cross-roads
keep	*plus*	up	*or*	past the big building
cross		first		round the corner

bear   then   across the road
form   at the end
                                over the road
                                near the . . .
                                the other side of the road
                                round the bend
                                on the left-hand side
                                to the left
                                straight on

Nouns and phrases

the traffic lights	a refuge
the traffic signals	the traffic
the sign-post	a bend
the cross-roads	the roundabout
the turning (first, second)	a level crossing
the Belisha crossing	the road junction
the zebra crossing	the corner
the pedcstrian crossing	the fork

Directions

1. To motorists or cyclists

Keep right on to the end of the road.

Then turn left.

Take the first turning to the right.

Bear left at the fork

Turn right at the cross-roads.

Fork left in half a mile.

Keep straight on.

Keep straight on till you come to the cross-roads.

2. To pedestrians

Cross by the Belisha crossing.

Cross by the zebra crossing.

Look both ways before crossing.

Cross over the road, go past that big building, and take the first turning to the left.

Notes

This lesson calls for a great deal of activity. Go out and do these things. Then dramatize, draw plans, and let the pupils give directions and trace them with arrows on blackboard or paper. The boys especially enjoy this lesson very much. Be sure that they really understand and can put this understanding into words. It will add greatly to their enjoyment in life if they fully understand maps and directions both written and oral. A study of the highway code is indicated for boys and girls interested and advanced enough. Traffic signs and signals could be studied by all.

LESSON 84

Adverbial clauses of time, using 'when', 'while', 'after', 'before', 'just before', 'just after', 'as soon as', 'as', 'until', 'whenever', and tenses concerned

Examples

1. I saw him *when* I got there.
2. He came to the house *while* I was there.
3. *After* I had had my tea, I went out.
4. I went home *before* you did.
5. He came in *just before* I left.
6. *As* he came in, I went out.
7. *As soon as* he saw me, he spoke to me.
8. I did not go out *until* my father came home.
9. *Whenever* I go out, my dog wants to come too.

Notes

The knowledge of the use of these new words and phrases gives the pupils more varied and more exact modes of expression. There is no particular difficulty. Be careful to teach the correct tenses concerned. Notice in these and other clauses mentioned before that the future tense in the principal sentence is followed by the habitual tense in the subordinate tense. This has been pointed out in earlier lessons, but it is well to emphasize it here:

e.g. I shall do it when I go in.
      I shall see him when I go home.

Never—I shall do it when I shall go in,

a mistake often made, not only by our pupils, but also by people learning English as a foreign tongue. Again with the other words:

I shall finish this before I go home.
I shall finish this just before I go home.
I shall have my tea as soon as I get home.
I shall not see him until he gets home.
I shall wait until he comes.

LESSON 85

Revision of noun clauses: 'That is why . . .', 'where', 'when', 'what', 'how'

That is why . . .

Do you know why he went to . . .?
Yes, I know why he went there. Why?
Because he wanted to see his friend.
That is why he went there.

How

Do you know how he did it?
Yes, I know how he did it. How did he do it?

He did it like this
   or by . . . ing . . . *or* with a . . . .
That is how he did it.
Who told you? He did. He told me how he did it.

'*Where*', '*when*', '*what*', '*why*'

1. That is where he went.
   That is what he did.
   That is when he went.
2. I don't understand why he did it. Do you?
   Yes, I know why he did it.
   He did it because . . . .
3. Do you know where to go? Yes, I know where to go.
   Do you know what to do?
   Do you understand what it means?

Notes

This lesson calls for a great deal of conversation and dramatization, e.g.

Teacher to A. Ask *B* where he went last night.

A to B. Where did you go last night?

B to A. I went to . . . .

Teacher to A. Did he tell you where he went last night?

A to Teacher. Yes, he did.
                He told me where he went last night.

    Again

Teacher to A. Show me how to strike a match.

Teacher to Class. What did he show me?
                He showed you how to strike a match.

    Do you know how he made that model?
    Yes, I know how he made that model.

Do you understand what I said?
Yes, I understand what you said.

This lesson is quite easy and it aims at two things, (*a*) facility in expression, and (*b*) understanding of reading. So often the deaf pupil when being asked 'Why . . .?' looks for a sentence containing 'because', 'since', 'as', 'for', &c.

Passages based on these exercises, giving various facts and ending with 'that is why' or 'that is the reason I did that', help to draw the pupils away from this tendency and direct them to examining the text for *meaning*, not for the language form, when answering questions.

This exercise also helps them to give the general answer instead of the particular:

e.g. 1. What did *A* tell you? He told me what to do.

2. What did the cyclist find out from the map? He found out which way to go.

3. What would you do if you wanted to find out how to get from *A* to *B*? I should look at a map to find out how.

LESSON 86

Revision of 'although' and 'though', with addition of 'yet', 'nevertheless', 'all the same', 'even though', 'in spite of'

The idea of concession or contrast has been developed earlier. It remains only to give the new conjunctions and point out, in various contexts, their use.

Revision of 'although' and 'though'

1. Although this book is cheap, it is a good one.
2. This book is a good one, although it is cheap.
3. Although that dog is so huge, it is very gentle.
4. That dog is very gentle, although it is huge.

Even though

Greater emphasis than 'although'.

1. Even though that dog is so huge and looks fierce, it is very gentle.
2. That dog is very gentle, even though it is so huge and looks so fierce.

Yet

Show how 'yet' can be added for emphasis.

1. Although that dog is so huge, yet it is very gentle.
   ('Yet' cannot be transposed to the beginning of the sentence.)
2. That dog is huge, yet it is very gentle.

All the same

1. That dog looks fierce and is huge; all the same, it is very gentle.
2. That dog looks fierce and is huge; it is very gentle all the same.
   ('All the same' cannot begin the two sentences.)

Nevertheless

1. That dog looks fierce and is huge; nevertheless it is very gentle.

2. That dog looks fierce and is huge, it is very gentle nevertheless.

('Nevertheless' cannot begin the sentence.)

In spite of

The only real difficulty in this lesson is with 'in spite of'; not in its understanding, but in its use. As with some of the other extensions with which we have dealt, 'in spite of' is used to introduce a participial phrase, not a sentence. Here again the sentence has to be changed into a phrase.

1. In spite of looking fierce and being huge, that dog is very gentle.
2. This book is a good one, in spite of being cheap.
3. 'In spite of that' can also be used:

> That dog looks fierce and is huge. In spite of that, it is very gentle.
>
> This book is a good one. In spite of that, it is cheap, *or*
>
> It is cheap in spite of that.

4. In spite of being cheap, this book is a good one.

Give practice in this. It is a great help in understanding and later, after much practice, in variety of expression.

Let the pupils try to write a similar sentence to the one given in as many different ways as possible.

Note

'Yet', 'nevertheless', and 'all the same' cannot be used to usher in the sentence.

'All the same' and 'nevertheless' may go to the end of the whole sentence.

LESSON 87

Differences, comparisons, and contrasts

Vocabulary

1.   **Nouns involved**   **Verbs**

taste	size	direction	differ (from each other
character	beauty	distance	in)
appearance	wealth	shape	resemble (each other
height	depth	speed	in)
weight	colour	rate	
age	heat	amount	

2. **Phrases and sentences**

They are different in (character, colour).

They are quite different in (character, colour).

They are very different in (character, colour).

They are alike in (character, colour).

They are of equal (thickness).

They are alike.

They are just alike.

This is . . . whereas that is . . . .

One is . . . while the other is . . . .

. . . is not so large as . . . .

. . .er than . . . .

. . . better than . . . .

. . . is the same as . . . .

. . . just the same as . . . .

. . . both . . . .

It is like (a rose), &c.

Similar to . . . .

They have $\begin{cases} \text{the same (height).} \\ \text{equal (heights).} \end{cases}$

3. **Adjectives and adverbs** needed, revised and added to.

Questions

How do . . . differ from each other?
How do . . . resemble each other?

Notes

This lesson takes comparing and contrasting a step further, revises and adds to abstract and general nouns, revises adjectives and adverbs concerned, and gives useful phrases for use in descriptions.

Do not, as a result of this lesson, expect profound and accurate assessments of differences and similarities, but if the pupils can put into words one or two broad and essential comparisons and can understand written descriptions of people and things giving more minute differences, be content. Do not try to run before you can walk and so dishearten the children.

LESSON 88

Extension of (*a*) cause: 'because', 'since', 'as', 'inasmuch as', 'for', 'being', with clauses and phrases; (*b*) purpose: 'so that', 'in order that', 'for the purpose of', 'lest'

Extension of cause

'Because', 'since', 'for', 'as', 'inasmuch as' ('being', 'having', &c.).

1. I could not come to school because I was ill.
2.   ,,   ,,   ,,   ,, as I was ill.
3.   ,,   ,,   ,,   ,, for I was ill.
4. As I was ill, I could not come to school.
5. Inasmuch as I was ill, I could not come to school.
6. Since I was ill, I could not come to school.

7. Being ill, I could not come to school.
8. As I had no mackintosh, my mother would not let me go out in the rain.
9. Having no mackintosh, my mother would not let me go out in the rain.

7 and 9. The participle 'being' or 'having', &c., cannot be used as a conjunction. It is used only in a phrase. All the others usher in adverbial clauses.

5. 'Inasmuch as' is not, of course, used in conversation.

Note

This is an easy lesson. Encourage the pupils to get more variety into their language forms by using the alternatives they are now studying.

The causal phrases with the participle are more difficult. It is sufficient here to understand their use and to spot them in their reading.

Purpose

Revise Lesson 65.

Add work on 'lest', for comprehension rather than use ('lest' = 'so that . . . not').

1. I fed the famished animal to save its life.
   He fed the famished animal (so that it should *not*) die.
   He fed the famished animal (lest it should) die.
2. The old man walked with a stick (lest he should) stumble.
   The old man walked with a stick (so that he should not) stumble.
3. The guide tied the rope round the climber (lest he should) slip.
   The guide tied the rope round the climber (so that he should not) slip.

4. Hold the child's hand (lest he should) run on to the road.

Hold the child's hand (so that he should not) run on to the road.

Introductory phrases and exclamations

Introductory phrases

Of course, As a matter of fact, In fact, As a rule, As a general rule, For instance, In the first place, Roughly speaking, For example, To begin with, Well, Personally, Let us think for a moment . . ., By the way . . ., Let us suppose . . ., Suppose you are . . . .

Exclamations and ejaculations

How delightful! Good gracious! I *am* surprised! 'How kind you are! Really! Did you really? Well, well! What a pity! What a shame! What a noise! 'What a to-do! What a fuss! What lovely weather! 'How happy he was! What a nuisance! What fun! 'Oh dear! What a long time you've been! How nice! How horrible! What a grand idea!

Notes

Here is another lesson which should help first the comprehension of reading and of lip-reading and which should bring a good deal of fun and laughter into the classroom. To the deaf child, these extraneous and sometimes superfluous phrases deflect the attention from the main sentence and add to the difficulty of understanding. There is a marked improvement in comprehension when these are explained, the pupil is aware of them, and they take their rightful place.

With this lesson could be taken a revision and gathering together of exclamations previously taught or encountered. It is a great help to naturalness of conversation if a deaf child understands and knows how to use exclamations. Devise interesting ways of practising these, e.g. with intonation in the speech lesson. Another way the pupils enjoy is to tell a story in which they interpolate exclamations. The first time it is told the children could suggest appropriate exclamations.

Intonation and speech practice could here be interwoven.

Much good work, with enjoyment, would be the result.

Written conversations could be asked for, using as many exclamations as possible. The best could be acted.

LESSON 90

The impersonal use of 'it' with the infinitive, with clauses, and with weather vocabulary

With the weather

It is raining. It is windy, &c.

With the infinitive

It is possible to do	*or* to be.
It is easy to do	,, ,,
It is difficult to do	,, ,,
It is wrong to do	,, ,,
It is right to do	,, ,,
It is necessary to do	,, ,,
It is unnecessary to do	,, ,,

It is impossible to do   *or* to be
It is most difficult to do   ,,   ,,
It is difficult for him to do   ,,   ,,
It is easy for you to do   ,,   ,,
It is impossible for . . . to do   ,,   ,,
It is necessary for you to do   ,,   ,,
It is unnecessary for you to do   ,,   ,,
It is hard for a young child to do   ,,   ,,
It is easier for me to do . . . than . . . .
        ,,   ,,   to be . . .   ,, ...
It is harder for me to do . . .   ,, ...
        ,,   ,,   to be . . .   ,, ...
It is more difficult to do . . .   ,, ...
        ,,   ,,   to be . . .   ,, ...

With clauses

It is certain that . . . .
It is uncertain whether/if . . . .
It is not decided whether . . . .
It has not been decided yet, whether . . . .
It is true that . . . .
It is untrue that . . . .
It is false that . . . .

Notes

1. The impersonal use of 'it' has been taught very early when noting the weather, e.g. 'It is windy', 'It is wet', 'It is raining', 'It is fine', &c.

2. The use of 'it' with the infinitive has also been met in reading. It is good to gather these examples together and to ensure at the same time that the idea of what is possible, impossible, necessary, right, wrong, difficult, or easy should be quite clear. At the same time the construction, 'difficult for *me* to do . . .', should be taught.

3. The extension to the clause with the ideas of certainty, uncertainty, decision or indecision, truth or falsehood, is quite easily and naturally made.

LESSON 91

Extension of 'if', 'or', 'else', 'unless', 'even if', 'provided that', 'whether or no', 'had he'

Revision

1. **A probable happening**

If he comes, I shall ask him a question.
If it rains, we shall not go to the playing field.

2. **Very doubtful**

If he came, I should ask him . . . .
If I were a king, I should . . . .
If he should come . . ., I should . . . .
Should he come . . ., I should . . . .

A thing which did not happen

If he had come, I should have asked him (but he did not);

and the alternative form:

Had he come, I should have seen him.

Point out (this is taken more fully in Lesson 93).

He did not come, or I should have seen him.
    ,,   ,,   ,,   else I should have seen him.

Note

This is an opportunity to revise 'if', with special attention to the tenses.

1. If he comes (habitual tense), I *shall* ask him (future). (Simple conditional—'He will probably come'.)

If I am ready . . ., I shall go with him.
If it stops raining . . ., we shall go out.

2. If he came (past), I *should* ask him;

and the alternative:

If he should come, I should ask him,

and

Should he come, I should ask him.
If he *were* here, I should be happy.

The implication here is that it is very doubtful if he comes.

3. If he *had come* (past perfect tense), I *should have* asked him;

and the alternative:

Had he come . . ., I *should have* asked him.
If only he had come . . . .

The implication here is that he did not come though he might have done so.

Go on from this to the statement:

He did not come, or I should have seen him.
He did not come, else I should have seen him.
I should have seen him, if he had come.

'If I were' and 'if he were' under 2 should be pointed out, and noted in reading. In all other cases the subjunctive form is tending to die out and there is no need to teach it to the pupils.

Have clearly in your own mind the underlying ideas governing the use of the three forms in 1–3 above.

1. Something that will probably happen, simple conditional.
Habitual tense followed by future.

2. Something which is very doubtful. Past tense and subjunctive.
3. Something which might have happened but did not. Past perfect tense (had done) and subjunctive perfect tense (should have done). Then give and expect many examples of its use.

Unless

This is easily grasped if the meaning and use of 'if' is understood.

If he comes, I shall go to the pictures.
If he does not come, I shall not go to the pictures.
Unless he comes, I shall not go to the pictures.

I think it is easier if the main clause is put first:

I shall go, if he comes.

I shall not go, $\begin{cases} \textit{if} \text{ he does } \textit{not} \text{ come.} \\ \text{unless he comes.} \end{cases}$

Provided that

A substitute for 'if':—

I shall go provided that he comes.

LESSON 92

Extension of inference and conclusion—'so', 'therefore', 'consequently', 'and so', 'then', 'so then', 'as a result'

Inference and conclusions

'So', 'therefore', 'consequently', 'and so', 'as a result', 'then', 'so then', 'hence', 'accordingly'.

I was hungry, and so I asked for something to eat.
,, ,, therefore I asked for something to eat.
,, ,, consequently I asked for something to eat.

If you don't behave, then you won't go out.

She didn't, so then she was not allowed to go out.

He was disobedient, therefore he was punished.

,,   ,,   ,,   and, as a result, he was punished.

There was very little rain, accordingly the crops were poor.

There was very little rain, therefore the crops were poor.

There was very little rain, hence the crops were poor.

There was very little rain, consequently the crops were poor.

As a result of the small rainfall, the crops were poor.

There was very little rain. As a result of this, the crops were poor.

Use of conjunctions

The difficulty here is not so much in understanding, as in the different usages of these conjunctions. The idea of cause (Why?), of purpose (What for?), and of effect (and so), have already been taken and should all be revised here.

Comparing and contrasting these ideas will help to get the use and construction firmly fixed.

1. Those used when answering the questions 'Why?' or 'What was the cause?' The result stated first and the reason or cause given, e.g.

He came to school late—Why?—because he had
                                        overslept.
                              since
                              as
                              for
                              having overslept

2. Now show with reference to, 'and so', 'so', that the statement of the cause can be put first, and what happened because of it, or the result, second.

He overslept, and so he was late for school.

,, ,, ,, as a result he was late for school.

,, ,, hence he was late for school.

,, ,, consequently he was late for school.

Give the question form:

What was the result of (his oversleeping)?

The result of (his oversleeping) was that he was late

or

He was disobedient. What happened? What was the result?

3. Revise 'What . . . for?'

For what purpose did he . . .?

He went to town. What was his purpose?

His purpose was—to buy a suit (infinitive).

For what purpose did he go?—For the purpose of buying a suit.

In order to buy a suit.

In order that he might buy a suit.

So that he might buy a suit.

4. Care must be taken in the correct sentence form for answering the question:—

Reason

(*a*) Why did he do it?

He did it because

,, ,, for

,, ,, as

,, ,, since

,, ,, inasmuch as

,, ,, being ill

,, ,, having a cold

,, ,, someone having told him to do so

{ (i) he was ill.
(ii) he had a cold.
(iii) someone told him to do so.

The last one is somewhat difficult, but should be pointed out for comprehension.

(b) What was/his reason for/doing it?
              /the cause of his/doing it?
       and

His reason was *that* he was . . . .
The cause was *that* . . . .

Never His reason was because . . . .
       The cause was because . . . .

Purpose

(a) For what purpose is he going to do it?
    ,,   ,,   ,,   did he do it?
He is going to . . . .
He did it to . . . .
   ,,   ,, in order to . . . .
   ,,   ,, so that he . . . .
   ,,   ,, in order that he . . . .
   ,,   ,, for the purpose of . . .ing.

(b) What was his purpose in doing it?

He did it to/so that, &c.
His purpose was to/that he . . . .

Never His purpose was in order to/so that/in order that/for the purpose of.

Result

The chief difficulty here is the form the question takes. Statements giving results are made, as above. However, to put the question form we have either (a) to repeat the statement and follow it by 'What happened?' or 'What was the result?' or (b) to change 'He overslept' into 'his oversleeping' and to put the question, 'What was the result of his oversleeping?'

The answer to the question can, of course, be simply the sentence, 'He was late for school', and is usually used in conversation. 'The result was that he was late' can also be used and should be pointed out in reading.

It is better to begin by method (*a*) above and gradually, during the year, as the occasion arises, point out how 'the result of' must be followed by a noun, e.g. You cannot say 'the result of he overslept was', but 'the result of his over-sleeping was', *not* 'the result of he was disobedient was', but 'the result of his disobedience was'. Give plenty of practice in the change as below. The pupils will find it interesting and it will add to the vocabulary.

There was very little rain.	The small rainfall.
There was a great deal of rain.	The heavy rainfall.
The child was naughty.	The child's naughtiness.
She was ill.	Her illness.
I was hungry.	My hunger.
I was thirsty.	My thirst.
He behaved in a very cruel way.	His cruel behaviour.
He hesitated to speak.	His hesitation to speak, &c.

Then put these into sentences showing consequences and expect the correct question and answer from the pupils.

> e.g. There was very little rain, therefore the crops were poor.
>
> What was the result of the small rainfall?
>
> i. The crops were poor.
> ii. The result of the small rainfall was that the crops were poor.
> iii. The result was that the crops were poor.

LESSON 93

Extension of 'neither', 'nor', 'nor did', 'either', 'or', 'else', 'otherwise'

Note

As with other lessons in this Stage the work is not new but the simpler forms already known need clarifying, amplifying, and practising. Alternative and similar forms need teaching.

'*Neither*', '*nor*'

Give examples of 'neither' and 'nor' followed by a reversion of the sentence, e.g.

He *has no* pen, neither has he a pencil.
She *was not* kind, nor was she good.
He *could not* play games, *nor could* he walk far.
She *did not* smile, *nor did* she speak.

'*Anything else*', '*anyone else*', '*someone else*', '*somebody else*'

He wanted neither that nor anything else.
He did not want to go with me nor with anyone else.
He wanted a book or something else for a present for his mother.
She wanted me or someone else to go with her to the dentist.

'*or*', '*else*', '*otherwise*'

Make haste or you will be late.
   ,,   ,,   otherwise you will be late.
   ,,   ,,   else you will be late.
   ,,   ,,   or else you will be late (see Lesson 91).

LESSON 94

More prefixes and suffixes: '-ment', '-ure', &c.
Formation of verbs and nouns

Verbs

to govern	to close	to utilize	to appear	to silence
		to unite	to resemble	to present
				to absent oneself
				to differ

Forming nouns from verbs

-ment	**-ure**	**-ty**	**-ance**	**-ence**
government	closure	utility	appearance	silence
		unity	resemblance	presence
				absence
				difference

Suffixes

Verbs—{ to make lengthen darken lessen sharpen
         { -en   soften   harden shorten

Prefixes

en = in	**ex = out**	**im = not**	**re = again**
enlighten	exit	impossible	return
entrance	examination	imperfect	redo
	expect	impersonal	relight
	except	inaccurate	rewrite
	extend	incorrect	

Notes

This is to remind you of useful prefixes and suffixes. The lesson can be used both as revision and to add to the existing vocabulary. It is not necessary to take the lesson as a whole. Much good work can be done in an odd ten minutes fairly frequently. Taken in this way the pupils find it interesting and stimulating. Revise other prefixes and suffixes in the same way and add others not included here as you come across them.

In other lessons give examples of their use and point them out in reading. Give time to assimilate before expecting their free use in compositions. In any case do not encourage the use of long words if a simple one will do equally well. The important things are (a) to give the pupils understanding of these words, and (b) to give them more exact expression. Therefore encourage the use of the longer word if it fulfils condition (b).

LESSON 95

Extension of 'instead of' 'in place of', 'as a substitute for'

The simpler uses of 'instead of'

These have been taken previously, i.e.

1. John came instead of his father to help us.
   We had a History lesson instead of a Geography one:

'in place of' and 'as a substitute for' are quite easily used here.

2. I wanted to go out but I had to go to bed instead:

'in place of' and 'as a substitute for' are not used here.

'Instead of' used with the participle

Instead of learning lessons, we played games, *or*
We played games instead of learning lessons.
Instead of going to school, he had to go to work.

The formation here needs definite teaching. The mistake so often and so logically made is,

We played games instead of learnt lessons.

Give copious examples both orally and in writing and point out its occurrence in reading.

LESSON 96

'So (tired) that', 'too . . . to', 'not . . . enough'

A

So cold that	too . . . . to, not old enough to.
,, tired that	*too young* to . . . .
,, happy that	*not old enough* to . . . .
,, quietly that	
,, badly that	
,, suddenly that	

1. I am so tired that I must go to bed.
2. I am so happy that I want to sing.
3. The little boy was so naughty that his mother sent him to bed.
4. He walked so quietly that I did not hear him.
5. He did his work so badly that he had to do it all again.
6. He opened the door so suddenly that he made me jump.

B

I am too tired to move.
I am too happy to be cross.

This work is too bad to mark.
I am too cold to write.

C

He is too young to go to an 'A' film.
He is not old enough to go . . . .
This work is not good enough to mark.
I am not warm enough to write.
He is too short to reach the shelf.
He is not tall enough . . . .

Notes

These language forms deal with cause and effect.

A. In the first examples, 'the effect of', for example, 'his walking so quietly is that I did not hear him'. Always teach this with the adverb or adjective placed between the 'so' and 'that', to avoid confusion with 'so that' signifying purpose. If there is any confusion, show the different use of the two forms side by side.

B and *C.* The same idea of cause and effect are here. They are best taught as phrases in opposition. 'He is not old enough to go. He is too young to go.' They have probably been met incidentally with reference to the cinema, to leaving school, &c. When you are sure that these forms and that of *A* are really apprehended, you might try expanding *B* and *C* into *A*, which exercise will clarify and pinpoint the difference.

e.g. He is too young *to go* to an 'A' film alone.
He is so young that *he cannot go* to an 'A' film alone.
This work is too bad for me to mark.
This work is so bad that *I cannot mark* it.
I am too cold to write.
I am so cold that *I cannot write.*

He is too short to reach the shelf.
He is so short that *he cannot* reach the shelf.

Do not attempt the converse, i.e. *A* into *B* and *C*, yet.
Lesson 88 (1) could be combined with this:

It is difficult for him to do that.

(*a*) It is too difficult for him to do.
It is not easy enough for him to do.
(*b*) It is too difficult for me.

Expand to 'so difficult that'.

(*a*) It is so difficult that he cannot do it.
(*b*) It is so difficult that I cannot do it.

Point out that 'for *me* to do' becomes 'that *I* cannot do it'.
and that 'for *him* to do' becomes 'that *he* cannot do it'.

COMPOSITION

SEE notes at the beginning of Stage 5.

1. All those listed under Stage 5 are most suitable. Give much practice in 2, 8, 9, and 10.

2. Writing conversations with the new verbs and expressions as indicated in Lesson 80.

3. Giving directions as to how to reach a certain place (Lesson 83).

4. Comparisons and contrasts of two things, a development of Stage 5: Composition 10 (Lesson 87).

5. Short stories with exclamations and introductory phrases (Lesson 89).

Any new work must be preceded by practice. Though the pupils are gaining in language experience it must be remembered that new language forms are, in the main, really new to them. Even if you have given some familiarity with the form earlier, they still lack practice in its use. They must practise understanding and recognizing its use before you can expect easy reproduction by them.

STAGE 6: SPEECH

See page 324.

LANGUAGE

B Y the time the pupils have reached Stage 7 a good English textbook should certainly be used, preceded by *The Oxford English Readers for Africa*, Book 6. I have thought it well, however, to remind you of various studies which should be taken and which you should make it your business to include if they are not already provided for. At the same time, I have pointed out how the previous work can be revised at the same time.

The work on idiomatic usages is specially important. These are the remaining stumbling blocks to reading with understanding and to normal expression. Read again a summary of the aims and contents of this stage in the introduction to Senior School Stages.

A SUMMARY OF THE LESSONS IN STAGE 7

Lesson 97. Study of passages noting clauses and phrases. Revise all kinds of phrases and adverbial clauses.

    98. Similes, traditional and original. Revise comparisons and adverbial clauses of comparison and contrast.

    99. The use of the definite and indefinite articles. Adjectival phrases and clauses.

    100. Proverbs, mottoes, abbreviations, and sayings. Revise exclamations and introductory phrases.

    101. Colloquialisms and current sayings. Revise indirect speech and interdependence of tenses.

    102. 'To make' with various meanings and idiomatic expressions. Revise conjunctions, inference—cause and purpose.

    103. The idiomatic use of 'do' and 'does'. Revise adverbial clauses, passive voice.

104. Common idiomatic usages of various verbs:
     to keep, to look, to have, to catch, to turn, to get, to take.
105. Miscellaneous idiomatic expressions. Revise all conditional clauses.
106. The language of forms and officialdom. Ways of saying the same thing.
107. Vocabulary building by reading, classification and allied and contrasted words, affixes, word building, and use of dictionary.
108. Suggested subjects for vocabulary and phrase building.

LESSON 97

Study of passages noting clauses and phrases. Revise all kinds of phrases and adverbial clauses

Study of passages

More work with all kinds of phrases and clauses and the transposition thereof.

Revise with much practice phrases, placing them before or after subject or predicate.

Passages and poems should be studied with this in mind.

Revision

1. Revision of phrases of all kinds.
2. The difference between phrases and clauses.
3. Revision particularly of adverbial phrases and clauses of time, place, manner, number, and degree.

Notes

This study of passages from books with reference to the structure of the sentences should go on throughout the period, a little at a time. Point out how writers get variety:

(*a*) by varying the lengths of the sentences,

(*b*) by varying the position of the clauses and phrases.

The pupils are growing up, but they will still enjoy concrete manipulation of a complex sentence in the way I have described in other Lessons and Stages. Give the correct name of the phrase or part of speech, e.g. adverbial phrase of time, participial phrase, &c., adverb.

For instance, let them divide this complex sentence into phrases and clauses, letting the appropriate number of pupils take one each.

On looking out of his window, one moonlight night when all was still, John saw a man creeping furtively along the dark side of the road, just opposite his house.

participial phrase	adverbial phrase of time
On looking out of his window	one moonlight night

adverbial clause of time	subject	verb predicate
when all was still	John	saw

object	participial phrase
a man	creeping furtively

adverbial phrase of place	adverbial phrase of place
along the dark side of the road	just opposite his house.

Let the pupils try how many ways this could be rearranged.

They will find that the two participial phrases are more fixed than the phrases and clauses of time.

The participial phrases must be on the same side of the predicate as the nouns which they describe.

Similes, traditional and original. Revise comparisons and adverbial clauses of comparison and contrast

Similes

as white as snow/milk	as soft as silk
as sweet as sugar/syrup	as pretty as a picture
as happy as a sandboy/king	as brown as a berry
as black as ink/coal	as blue as the sky
as green as grass	as good as gold
as nice as pie	as blind as a bat
as red as a beetroot/rose	as cold as ice
as quick as lightning	as quiet as a mouse
as deaf as a post	as hot as fire
as like as two pins/two peas in a pod	as fair as a lily

Revision

1. **Revise 'is like a' and 'is just like a'.**

e.g. He stood like a rock against all aggressors.
    The boy squirmed like an eel.

2. **Revise comparatives and superlatives.**

    The loveliest girl in the world.
    The greatest sailor the world has ever known.

Point out that these similes can be found in the comparative form.

whiter than snow	happier than a king
finer than silk	greener than grass
softer than silk	fairer than a lily

Notes

This is an interesting lesson, but do not use it to teach only the traditional similes. Give and try to get original ones. They will mean much more to the pupils.

The poems I have suggested in this section and in the past ones, and many more, will contain similes, e.g.:

> Clouds like sheep, Steal o'er the deep grey skies.
> 'The Chilterns', Rupert Brooke.

> I wandered lonely as a cloud, *and*

> Continuous as the stars that shine,
> And twinkle on the milky way.
> 'Daffodils', W. Wordsworth.

> No time to see, in broad daylight,
> Streams full of stars like skies at night.
> 'Leisure', W. H. Davies.

It is but a step from this to personification:

> April, April, Laugh thy girlish laughter.
> Sir W. Watson.

> Slowly, silently, now the moon
> Walks the night in her silver shoon.
> 'Silver', W. de la Mare.

> The trees are Indian princes,
> But soon they'll turn to ghosts.
> 'Robin Redbreast', William Allingham.

> The silver birch is a dainty lady;
> She wears a satin gown.
> 'Child's Song in Spring', E. Nesbit.

> Wide are the meadows of night
> And daisies are shining there
> 'Wanderers', W. de la Mare.

From the Bible are many arresting similes:

> He leadeth me beside the still waters.
>
> My cup runneth over.
>
> The shadow of a great rock in a weary land.
>
> Thy word is a lamp unto my feet,
> And a light unto my path.

Now that the pupils have material and experience on which to draw, they will find this an exciting and interesting lesson.

LESSON 99

The use of the definite and indefinite articles. Adjectival phrases and clauses

Lesson scheme

1. Some rules for the use of 'a' and 'the'.
2. Phrases in which the article is omitted.
3. Revision of number and amount:
     some, any, hardly, any, very many, a great deal, a huge amount.
4. Incidental revision of abstract nouns and adjectival phrases and clauses.

Notes

This lesson is a gathering together of work that has surely been done throughout the school. The correct use of 'a' and 'the' is difficult for deaf children and all the help possible should be given to them. We can give some rules:

1. **When we generalize we use the indefinite article** ('a' or 'an').

   (*a*) 'I saw a man walking down the road.'
   (*b*) 'Bring me a chair, please' (if there are several chairs in the room).

(c) 'Put it on a table in the classroom' (when there are several tables and any one of them will do).

(d) 'Choose an apple from the dish' (when there are several apples to choose from).

2. **When we tell something particular** about a man, in other words point out which one we mean, we use 'the'.

We could *follow* the sentence under (a) above by saying: 'I saw a man walking down the road.'

(a) 'The man stopped and asked me the way to the Town Hall.'

i.e. 'This man of whom I have spoken, who was walking down the road, stopped and asked me the way.'

(Revise here relative pronouns.)

(b) 'Bring me the chair, please' (if there is only one chair in the room).

or 'Bring me the chair which is at the back of the room.'

(c) 'Put it on the table under the window.'

Give many examples:

She is a teacher at my school.
She is the teacher of my class.
She is the head teacher of my school.
He is a pupil at my school.
He is the captain of my school.
She is the girls' captain.
She is a member of my class.
He is the prefect of my class.
He is a school prefect (one of a number).

3. **The definite article is used:**

(a) Before the *names* of rivers, e.g. 'A river flows through London.' 'The River Thames flows through London.' 'The Thames flows through London.'

(b) Before the names of mountain ranges, e.g. 'The Alps are beautiful mountains in Switzerland.'

(c) Before the names of groups of islands, e.g. 'I have been to the Hebrides.'

4. No article is used before other proper names, including other geographical names.

5. No article is used before an abstract noun.

Mercy and Peace are met together (Lesson 82).

6. (a) No article is used before a material noun.
Revise numbers and quantities.

I am very fond of milk. Sugar comes from Jamaica. Rice is grown in India.

Cotton is manufactured in Manchester. What beautiful silk!

(b) **Exception:** when we particularize a special bowl of sugar or packet of rice or piece of silk.

'Pass the sugar, please'—means the bowl of sugar which is on the table.

'Pass the milk, please' (the jug of milk).

'Bring me the rice from the cupboard' (the packet of rice).

'Where did you buy the silk for your dress?'

7. No article is used in a number of phrases:

at ease	by day	in fact	to school
at dinner	by night	in trouble	to dinner
at home	by tram	in debt	catch fire
at school	by plane	in hand	leave school
at church	by name	in heaven	leave work

at work	by land	in bed	keep house
at sea	by water	in time	for love
at play	by air	to church	on fire
at sunrise	take breath	to sea	on earth
set sail			on board

Proverbs, mottoes, abbreviations, and sayings.
Revise exclamations and introductory phrases

Proverbs

A stitch in time saves nine.
There's many a slip 'twixt cup and lip.
Don't count your chickens before they're hatched.
Many hands make light work.
Too many cooks spoil the broth.
A bird in the hand is worth two in the bush.
It's a long lane that has no turning.
You can take a horse to the water, but you can't make
    him drink.
It's a rolling stone that gathers no moss.
Look before you leap.
Penny wise—pound foolish.
Take care of the pence and the pounds will take care
    of themselves.
Many toys make tiresome boys.
Satan finds some mischief still for idle hands to do.
Jack of all trades, master of none.

Mottoes

Forward!
Play up! play up! and play the man!
I serve.
Towards the stars.

Abbreviations

So many of these are used nowadays it is not necessary to list them, but the pupils should know the most usual.

Notes

1. **Proverbs.** Many of these call for illustration by way of stories, dramatization, series of drawings, &c. They can be most interesting to the pupils but the meaning must be clear. Give several stories or dramatic interludes for one proverb. First the concrete illustration of the particular, and then an application to a different set of circumstances:

e.g. Too many cooks spoil the broth—

an illustration or dramatization drawn from the kitchen first and then an illustration of some other work spoilt by too many people meddling.

Note, too, such expressions drawn from these proverbs as:

He is a rolling stone, He is a Jack of all trades, That is penny wise, pound foolish.

Suggest that the pupils ask other people, their home people and other staff, if they know any more proverbs, after work on a number of proverbs in the way I have described.

2. **Mottoes.** School and town mottoes will be the starting-point for work on this.

3. **Abbreviations.** The pupils usually enjoy this and collect many of them. Revision work on exclamations and introductory phrases works in well here. Teach the pupils the *normal* exclamations of the average school boy or girl of this age.

LESSON 101

Colloquialisms and current sayings. Revise indirect speech and interdependence of tenses

Colloquialisms and current sayings

If you are teaching the boys and girls to understand conversation which goes on around them, you must teach them current sayings, some slang, and colloquialisms. Some of these eventually find a place in our literature, and are very vivid and arresting. As they vary from year to year, it would be useless to list them here.

Remember to teach the *normal* current sayings—such as, 'You're telling me', which is one of the sayings at the moment of writing. Many of these are exclamations and the lesson would naturally revise some of these and follows naturally on from the last lesson. It is a good opportunity too to revise contractions, 'I'd', 'I've', 'I'm', 'you're', 'she's', &c.

Reported speech

While talking of conversation it is good to revise the reported speech. Be careful, however, here. Do not let the pupils try to change the current saying by rule into reported speech. Either let them give the saying in direct speech or translate it into its meaning: e.g. 'You're telling me!' should be either reported: 'He said "You're telling me"' or 'He said that I was telling him something he knew already.' This might be expected of the super-intelligent child.

Notes

The whole lesson calls for dramatic representation. It is amusing for the pupils to write conversations to be acted by the pupils, bringing in as many current sayings as possible! It should be linked up with the previous lesson, as many colloquialisms are exclamations.

It is good to give the pupils some guidance as to *when* slang is permissible. A difficult problem!

LESSON 102

'To make' with various meanings and idiomatic expressions. Revise conjunctions, inference— cause and purpose

The verb 'to make'

1. **With its most usual meaning**—to build or construct, to fashion or form.

> To make a dress, to make a model yacht, to make a cake.

2. **Meaning to cause** (*a*) **'to be'**, (*b*) **'to do'**

    (*a*) With adjectives.

    > To make (him) happy, to make (him) glad, to make . . . sad.

    (*b*) With verbs.

    > To make . . . tremble. To make (the kettle) boil.
    > To make . . . shiver. To make . . . smile.
    > To make . . . stop.

3. **Meaning 'to force to',** an extension of 2.

    > To make me do it. ('My mother makes me go to bed early.')

4. **In idiomatic phrases** (general ideas as above, 1 and 2).

To make arrangements.		To make haste.	
,,	an attempt.	,,	a blot.
,,	a profit/a loss.	,,	a noise.
,,	progress.	,,	room for.
,,	fun of.	,,	a discovery.
,,	a difference to.	,,	a promise.
,,	something clear to somebody.	,,	peace with.
		,,	a mistake.
,,	something plain to somebody.	,,	a face.

5. **Idiomatic phrases**

(*a*) To make out.

I can't make it out (understand).
I can't make out what you are saying.
I can't make out the meaning of this, &c.

(*b*) To make for (to aim at).

Make for the goal.
Make for that tree.

(*c*) To make after.

He made after the escaping thief as quickly as possible.

(*d*) To make away with (to take away).

The dishonest cashier made away with his employer's money.
The housewife turned out the attic and made away with all the rubbish.

(*e*) To make up (to fabricate).

1. She often makes up tales to tell us.
   She often makes up parcels of many little things to bring us.

2. Passive Voice. The parcels are made up of a number of little things. Great Britain is made up of England, Scotland, Wales, and N. Ireland ('consists of' could be brought in here).

(*f*) To make believe (to pretend).

(*g*) To make up for.

He gave the little girl a pencil to make up for the loss of her own.

(*h*) To make *something* of.

I think we shall be able to make a writer of him.

Revision

Ways of expressing cause and effect.

Notes

It is suggested that this lesson should be a gathering together and a clarifying of work already done.

The pupils should keep notebooks and jot down the headings with those already known listed under them.

It is surprising how many will be contributed when different members of the class give one or two each.

Don't forget dramatic stories and series of drawings as illustrations of these expressions.

Suggested revision here is of the various ways of expressing cause and effect.

LESSON 103

The idiomatic use of 'do' and 'does'. Revise adverbial clauses, passive voice

'Do' and 'does', 'doing', 'did'

1. **Used as a verb:** I am doing it now.

2. **Used as a part of a verb** to express a negative:
He does not like it.

3. **Used in asking questions**

Did you like it?

4. **Used for emphasis**

(*a*) In a statement.   I do wish you would be quiet.
(*b*) In a request.   Do let us go, please.
                          Do let me do that.

5. **Used in answering questions**—

Do you often go there? Yes, I do.

6. **Used instead of repeating a verb**

He likes dancing and so do I (like dancing).
He likes going to concerts, but I don't (like going to
   concerts).

7. **Used in colloquial conversation**

I love gardening, don't you?
I don't like swimming, do you?

N.B. Affirmative statement—negative question.
        Negative statement—affirmative question.

Revision

Adverbial clauses, passive voice.

Notes

The most difficult use for deaf children is the use of 'do'
as a verb (meaning perform), not so much that it is difficult in itself, but they do find difficulty in knowing when
to use it.

In colloquial everyday English it is used a great deal

and this should have been taught incidentally throughout the child's school life. Even if one deprecates its universal use instead of verbs deaf children should realize its universality as an aid to their lip-reading and reading. Can we give them any guides as to when it is used?

1. **In recounting or asking about work that has been performed**

> Have you done your history homework? *instead of*
>   Have you learnt your history?
>   Have you written your history essay?
> Have you done your work? *instead of* Have you finished your work?
> Have you done the dining-room? *instead of* Have you mopped and dusted the dining-room?
> I've done my history but not my geography homework.
> I've done the mopping but not the dusting.

Teachers should be careful not to use the verb 'to finish' too frequently. It has its place when asking directly if a child has come to the end of its work, but it is not used generally in this recounting of performances.

It will be noted that the special verb for which 'do' stands is indicated by its object.

2. **Instead of 'to fasten' buttons**

> Do up your buttons, undo your buttons, undo the knot—*instead of* untie or unfasten the knot.
> Go and do your hair.

3. **With 'can'**

> I can't do this.
> I can't undo this.
> I can do many things, but I can't do that.

4. Used in idioms with an abstract noun instead of using the verb.

e.g. to do wrong   do good (to)
     ,,   harm (to)   do right
     ,,   damage   do (my) utmost to help
     ,,   more harm   do little good
     ,,   a favour to
     ,,   without some-
            thing

This lesson calls for a great deal of conversation, both spoken and written.

As in previous lessons, devise yourself and get the pupils to devise dramatic situations, conversations, or stories, which can be acted. Use specially the 'do you' or 'don't you' at the end of a statement. Bring in exclamations and colloquial sayings. A great deal of fun and laughter can be had here, no normal colloquialism barred for the time being! Judgement and choice will follow.

As a change, revise the passive voice, especially its use of 'was done', 'has been done', 'had been done', and 'to be done'.

LESSON 104

Common idiomatic usages of various verbs

To keep

1. **With an adjective**	2. **With a participle**	3. **With a noun**
to keep clean	to keep moving	to keep (an object)
warm	burning	a promise
healthy	going	
busy	closed	
quiet	open	
	shut	
	polished	

4. **With preposi-tions and adverbs**	5. **Idiomatic expressions**	6. **Connected nouns**
to keep in	to keep body and	a keeper
on	soul together	a time-keeper
under	to keep one's	a housekeeper
away	countenance	a keepsake
from (harm)		

To look

1. **With preposi-tions and adverbs**	2. **Other uses**	3. **Connected nouns**
to look at	to look like	a looker-on
straight at	alike	a looking-glass
for	just alike	a look-out
round		
after (to care for)		
on		
up (to search for)		
around		
through		
out of		
down on		

To have

('Have' is also used, of course, as an auxiliary verb.)

1. Active—to have to do—to be compelled to—I have to go to bed by day.

   Passive—to have to be done (It had to be done at once).

2. To have a try.   To have a good view of.

     ,,   a go.   ,,   charge of.

To have nothing to do   To have some fun with.
          with.   ,,   a word with.
    ,,   little to do with.   ,,   a game with.
    ,,   no use for.

3. To have . . . on (to wear).

4. To have got (colloquial but universal).

5. To have—meaning to outwit. He had me. I was had. This is a colloquial but correct meaning of the verb 'to have'.

To catch

to catch cold.   to catch fire.
       measles, &c.   it (a scolding)
       hold of.   sight of
       a bus, &c.

To turn

1. **With prepositions and adverbs**		2. **With adjectives**
to turn back	to turn on	to turn pale
up	off	red
round	upside down	black
out	inside out	
into	over	

To get

1. **With prepositions**	2. **With adjectives**
to get up	to get wet
off	better
on	hotter
over	

3. **Nouns**   4. **To have got**

a get-up   (*see 'To have' above*)
What a get-up!

To take

1. **Idioms**

to take advantage of   to take turns with
   hold of   turns at
   pains over   a photograph
   place   a step
   care of   after
   trouble with   notice of/no notice of

2. **Connected noun**

a take-off

Notes

Here, as in previous lessons of this kind, anecdotes, dramatic interludes, tableaux, mime, and illustrations (picture and drawing) should all be used to make these lessons real. They can be quite simple and short, e.g. 'to keep moving' could be illustrated by drawing or tableaux of an incipient traffic jam and the action and instructions of a policeman to 'keep moving'. These dramatic interludes continue, at a level enjoyed by the senior pupils, the language games of the earlier lessons. Use them in this and in Lesson 105. As I have suggested in Lesson 102, keep notebooks containing these idiomatic expressions and add to them and revise from time to time.

LESSON 105

Miscellaneous idiomatic expressions. Revise all
conditional clauses

More idiomatic expressions

1. **To put** on   to put away   to put an end to
   off   down (crush)   trust in
   in for   back   faith in

To put up with   to put out   to put to death
        up (build)   to sea
        up for
            election

To put two and two together.

Nouns. A putting-green.

2. **To fix** up a date, &c.   3. **To deal** with.
        him up with clothes.

4. **To give** in to.   5. **To stand** up to/for.
        up.   it.
        way to.   firm or fast.
                           on his dignity.

6. **To be fed** up with.

7. **To hold** a meeting.   to keep hold of.
        fast.   to get.
        on to   to catch.
        out.

Revision

All conditional clauses.

LESSON 106

The language of forms and officialdom. Ways of saying the same thing

This is a necessary part of the pupils' education in this era of a multiplicity of forms.

Get as many actual forms duplicated as possible and teach the pupils to fill them in. We must remember that one incomprehensible word may obscure the whole meaning of a sentence. Directions for filling up may still more obscure the matter. Here are some suggestions as to forms, &c.

1. Application forms for posts.
2. National Savings forms.
3. Post Office savings forms.
4. Municipal bank book.
5. Income-tax returns.
6. Pay sheets.
7. Applications for passports.
8. Applications for visas.
9. Cheque books.
10. Pensions forms.
11. Application for a driving licence.

Notes

1. Teach the new words; (*a*) verbs, (*b*) nouns and phrases, before presenting the forms. Choose the easiest first. Do not be discouraged. Many people with normal hearing and a good education make mistakes in these or find them difficult. Prepare your children as far as possible for a form-filling world.

2. **Practice in the sending of wires.** The language used in telegrams is a different matter. It is a good exercise in condensation and in choosing the salient point.

3. The drawing up of advertisements is another good exercise in choosing the salient points.

4. Answering advertisements and applications for posts should also be taken.

LESSON 107

Vocabulary building by reading, classification and allied and contrasted words, affixes, word building, and use of dictionary

We have come to the end of building our language framework, but we still need (*a*) a widening of vocabulary, (*b*) practice and understanding of more idiomatic and metaphorical phrases, (c) practice in the more complex sentence structure.

A good English book written for normal children will give you all these.

A teacher of the deaf must always be on the look-out for ways of widening the vocabulary understanding of his pupils. Here are some ways of doing this.

1. Reading.
2. The use of a dictionary.
3. Continue the work on affixes.
4. Continue the work on word building, e.g. 'merciful, mercifully, mercy, merciless, mercilessly'.
5. Gather together vocabulary synonyms and antonyms into centres of interest, e.g.

Buildings

Many of these words will not be new to the children but others will.

(a) **Allied and contrasted verbs**

(i) to build　　to erect　　to decorate　　to lay bricks
　to put up　　to plan　　to make　　　to fit up
　to construct to paint　　to distemper

(ii) to damage　　to destroy　　to demolish
　to alter　　to pull down　to take down

(b) **Nouns**

(i) People concerned in building.

builder	mason	carpenter	housepainter
plumber	joiner	electrician	decorator
brickmaker	architect	gas-fitter	bricklayer

(ii) kinds of buildings.

building	tenement	flat	villa	skyscraper
erection	dwelling (house) (place)	apartment	château	block of offices
construction	bungalow	house	chalet	block of flats
residence	cottage	shed	castle	cabin
mansion	hovel	hut	ranch-house	log-cabin
palace	cattle-shed	stable	outhouse	outbuilding
school	college	university	hospital	clinic
pigsty	barn	garage	shop	office
cinema	theatre	music-hall	church	chapel
cathedral	abbey			

(iii) Contrasts

damage   demolitions   ruin/s   alterations

(iv) Things used in building

bricks   stone   concrete   steel
mortar   wood   logs

(c) **Words used in buying or renting a house**

(i) main services   modern conveniences
   a house agent   (mod. con.)
   an auction   a house agency
   a sale   hire purchase
   a building society   a mortgage

(ii) Verbs.

to let	to sell	to auction	to buy
to purchase	to rent	to live	to dwell
to reside	to mortgage		

(d) **Correlation with geography and history**

1. The evolution of the modern dwelling.
2. Famous buildings of the past and present.

Notes

Search out reading material where these words are used. Bring them in again and again in all your work. Remember the need of a deaf person for much practice.

There is a fund of material here for information given in lip-reading and writing by teacher and pupil of visits to London, to New York; what the buildings are there, what they are like; a visit to a house agency, going over a new house, your dream house, how to buy a house; what the buildings are like in your own town, what old buildings there are, what they are built of, &c. Advertisements and descriptions of houses should be read. Some information about famous buildings of the present day or long ago in various countries of the world could be given.

See that the new words acquired by the children are not only understood, but *used*.

LESSON 108

Suggested subjects for vocabulary and phrase building

Centres of interest

These can be used in the way suggested in the previous lesson.

1. The country.
2. The town or city.
3. Holidays.
4. Traffic.
5. Parliament.
6. Animals (*a*) at home.
   (*b*) abroad.
7. Birds.
8. Bridges.
9. Communications.
10. Rivers—canals—lakes.
11. Insects.
12. Trade.
13. Local government.
14. Business.
15. The United Nations.

16. Manufacture.

  (16a) Local manufacture.

17. Vehicles.

18. The Press.

19. Health.

20. Hospitals and clinics.

21. The Commonwealth.

22. Libraries and books.

23. Parks and gardens.

24. The cinema.

25. The Post Office.

26. The wireless.

27. A journey through space.

28. Choice of occupation.

29. The employment exchange.

30. The City of London.

31. Hobbies.

32. Games and sport.

33. The sea—ships and fishing.

34. Famous men, pictures, books.

35. Scouts, Guides.

36. Visitors and visiting.

37. Words used in a day in the life of:

  (a) a doctor or nurse;

  (b) teacher;

  (c) other occupations.

38. The army, navy, or air force

COMPOSITION

As before, with the addition of:

1. *Anecdotes and dramatic interludes*, illustrating the use of idioms and of proverbs.
2. *Compositions based on centres of interest* including trades and professions and what the pupils hope to become.
3. *Writing descriptions* using similes.
4. *Short stories* bringing in exclamations and colloquial language.
5. *Telegrams and advertisements* (drawing up).
6. *Letters of application.* Answering advertisements.
7. *Biographies* of great men or women—see Centres of interest.

The imaginative boy or girl will be able to invent new anecdotes, but the teacher should accept a report or slightly different version of those given in class. Not all boys and girls of this age are imaginative. Do not try to force it. If the pupil has understood and reports in good English, that is sufficient and a full mead of praise should be given.

SPEECH

THOUGH in one respect (as regards language comprehension) the choice of speech practice is becoming wider, in other ways it is narrowing; for the pupils are approaching or have reached adolescence and special care is needed. Poems and selections should never be childish. Appreciation of selection should be designated Literature, and their practice Elocution; stories should come under Scripture, History, or Literature.

If stories or poems are about children, they should be written from the point of view of the adult, with whom the pupil can identify himself. For instance, 'Sweet and low' and Brahms's 'Lullaby' are suitable for senior girls as the speaker is identified with the mother.

Give beauty of thought and word in poems and extracts, and fun and laughter in sea chanties and the refrains found in student song books. The stories of some of the ballads are suitable. Keep the extracts learnt short. Dramatize the ballads and use group choral work for the psalms and selections from the Bible and for some poems. Divide into heavy and lighter voices when the passage calls for it. All these things add interest to the speaking.

Revise phrase work; it is most important here, although the bulk of the work should have been done earlier. Revise all the intonation work done previously as you revise the language form (see Intonation Summary). Add work on adjectival clauses and study the intonation of the poems and prose passages spoken.

Give some of the variations due to stress and emphasis. Stress chiefly the two main tunes, but show the slighter variations within them. Do not over-emphasize this, but make it an amusing and interesting thing. Use hearing-aids, of course, and encourage the very deaf. If they can get any difference at all, it will make for a natural quality in the voice, and you are aiming at this, rather than at exact reproduction. Do not let the severely deaf pupils feel any sense of failure in this. It would be better not to take this at all if the pupils feel that they cannot succeed. Show how the tune of the sentence varies with (*a*) the position and the intervention of phrases, and (*b*) the emphasis required.

e.g. A man engaged a negro servant.

Once upon a time, a man engaged a negro servant.

Once upon a time a man engaged a negro servant, not

a white one.

Once upon a time, when few people had met negroes,

a man engaged a negro servant.

I went to see my friend after supper last night.

After supper last night I went to see my friend.

When? After supper. I went after supper.

Who went? I went. I went to see my friend.

Whose friend? My friend. I went to see my friend.

Which night? Last night. I went last night.

I thought she didn't like you! Oh yes, she does. She is

my friend.

Exercises such as this are very interesting if you treat the work lightly and happily. Notice that the emphasis changes the shortened question form into Tune II instead of Tune I.

Expect more from those who hear more and so distribute the appreciation that all are happy and at the same time working hard.

You will notice that a good deal of the speech work is given as chorus work. I have found that for practice this has several advantages.

1. It gives confidence to the diffident child.
2. The volume of sound enables pupils with any hearing at all to get an idea of sound.
3. As with choral singing each member of the chorus can add something to what can be a pleasing and polished whole. It is a great uplift to deaf children to feel that they can produce something which is pleasing for others to listen to.

Naturally choral work is only part of the whole work on speech. The teacher should hear every child speak individually also. Each lesson should be a skilful blending together of both choral and individual speech. When a particular sound is being revised or a particular word taught, each child should be heard in turn. When a poem is being learnt the class can be divided into groups for each line or couplet, and then into individuals. Keep this part of the work moving. If you have done your work well, a pupil will need only to have a mistake pointed out. Do not stop for lengthy corrections. Skill is needed in teaching here; skill in keeping the interest high; in obtaining correct speech at the same time; in listening to individuals while the children are speaking altogether or in groups, and in spotting a mistake. In the advanced stages work towards self-criticism by the pupils, e.g.

> Somebody vocalized a 't' in that line. Who was it? *or* Somebody's 's' was not correct.

> Say it correctly. Right. Now be careful, everyone. You can do it correctly, can't you? Once more, that is splendid, everybody correct. Is everybody sure about each word? Are there any difficulties? If so, please tell me now. I think this word . . . and this word are difficult. Are you all sure about them? Let us say them together. Now singly, quickly.

Remember that your aim in the Speech section is the practice of spoken language. It follows that the mechanics of speech must be correct. Never practice incorrect speech. Use these poems and passages to practice correct speech and let the beauty of the words or the aptness of the phrase inspire the pupils to do the very best they can.

Keep up the breathing, consonant and voice exercises, especially lipping, to which I have referred before. Call the consonants consonants, the vowels vowels. Give the correct description, e.g. voiced consonants, unvoiced consonants. Refer to them in this way. Use the poems for work on a particular sound as you see the need. For instance, what could be better for the advanced pupils for practising 's' or 'l' than the poem 'Silver'?

> Slowly, silently, now the moon,
> Walks the night in her silver shoon, &c.

' s' has a contrast in the second line, i.e. 'sh'; 'l' has a contrast too in both lines, i.e. 'n'. You will find that these contrasts clarify and pin-point the difference between sounds that are often confused.

In the second or third year in the senior school an elocution book should be used. It helps the pupils very much to feel that their speech exercises are also needed and used by pupils with normal hearing.

Speech material

In the following pages I have included poems and prose extracts suitable for senior children. You will find the simpler poems which should appeal to the pupils learning Stage 5 placed first, after them come the prose passages and the hymns which could be used for a common assembly, some of the student and Scout songs with good choruses which can be used for all, and at the end the more difficult or the more mature poems.

I have not touched on the value of singing in the speech sections. It is so much a matter of amount and type of hearing. However, I am convinced of the value of (*a*) all children with any perception of pitch having choral singing of hymns and songs especially those with choruses. In my experience this singing has a wonderfully normalizing effect on the speaking voice although it may not produce good singing; (*b*) All children having the same hymns and songs as choral speech, even if only the chorus is learnt. The effect on the speech and voice I have spoken of in dealing with choral speech. The effect of having the same songs and hymns as their normal brothers and sisters (apart from the effect of the words themselves) helps so much towards a normal and happy outlook on life.

In assembly both (*a*) and (*b*) can be combined in corporate worship. I have found the effect of this to be far-reaching.

I have not ventured to do more than suggest some of the passages from the Bible and some of the hymns which I have used myself. The same applies to the student songs. There is a wealth of traditional songs and choruses to tap here.

1. Ariel's song from *The Tempest* is most suitable, 'Where the bee sucks'.
2. 'Under the greenwood tree', from *As You Like It*.
3. 'Over hill, over dale', from *A Midsummer Night's Dream*.
   Part of this down to 'the fairy queen' is suitable.
4. 'I wandered lonely as a cloud', William Wordsworth.
5. 'The Forsaken Merman', Matthew Arnold.
6. 'Spring goeth all in white', Robert Bridges.
7. 'Robin Redbreast' (*Goodbye, goodbye to Summer*), William Allingham.
8. '*The Brook*', Tennyson.
9. 'Overheard on a Salt Marsh.'
   Good for group work (boys in one group, girls in the other).

10. 'Sweet and low', Tennyson.
    See note at beginning of this section.

11. **Mont Blanc,** unknown.

    Mont Blanc is the monarch of mountains;
    They crowned him long ago
    In a mantle of light and a robe of cloud
    And a diadem of snow.

12. **Day and Night,** Lady Lindsey.

> Said Day to Night
>   'I bring God's light,
> What gift have you?'
>   Night said, 'The dew'.
>
> 'I give bright hours',
>   Quoth Day, 'and flowers',
> Said Night, 'More blest,
>   I bring sweet rest'.

13. I will give you the keys of heaven.

>   ,,   ,,   ,,   ,,

Refrain I

Madam will you walk, Madam will you talk,
   ,,   ,,   ,,   ,,   and talk with me.
Though you give me the keys of heaven,

>   ,,   ,,   ,,   ,,   ,,

Refrain II

No I will not walk, yet I will not talk,
   ,,   ,,   ,,   and talk with you.
I will give you a new silk gown.
To make you fine when you go to town.

Refrain I

Though you give me a new silk gown,

Refrain II

I will give you a coach and six,
Six black horses as black as pitch.

Refrain I

Though you give me a coach and six,

Refrain II

I will give you the keys of my heart,
And we will be married till death us do part.

Refrain I

If you will give me the keys of your heart,
Then we'll be married till death us do part.
Yes then I will walk,
Oh yes I will talk,
Oh yes I will walk and talk with you.

14. The world is very old, The world is very old,
  But every year,   But every Spring
  It groweth young again It groweth new again
  When buds appear.   And sweet birds sing.

             Unknown.

15. When shadows from the East are long,
   Then larks go up for morning song;
   When shadows are not seen at all,
   Then green leaves into silence fall;
   When shadows from the West grow long,
   Then blackbirds meet for Evensong.

             Unknown.

16. The roses in the moonlight
   Are sleeping long ago,
   And all the slender lilies
   Sway lightly to and fro;
   And as the gentle breeze goes by
   The waving poplars sigh,
   Lullaby, sleep my baby,
   Sleep, my baby, sleep.

17. **Autumn**

   You wonder why I look so sad,
   When all around is gay,
   I mourn in crimson and in gold,
   For summer goes away.

> But see, the precious fruits I bring
> Which only autumn can,
> Without me then you could not live,
> For food I bring to man.
>
> > Unknown.

18. 'The Wood of Flowers', James Stephens.

19. 'Leisure', W. H. Davies.

20. 'February', Dorothy Una Ratcliffe.

> Today I saw the catkins blow,
> Although the fields were white with snow.

21. 'A Memory', William Allingham.

> Four ducks on a pond.

22. 'Blow, bugle, blow', Tennyson.

> The splendour falls on castle walls.

23. 'The Pied Piper', Robert Browning.
    (Extracts for learning by heart.)

24. > Speed bonny boat like a bird on the wing
    > Onward! the sailors cry.
    > Carry the lad that is born to be King
    > Over the sea to Skye.

25. > The tide in the river,
    > The tide in the river,
    > The tide in the river runs deep.
    > I saw a shiver
    > Pass over the river
    > When the tide turned in its sleep.

26. **Suitable student songs with good choruses:**

'Clementine.'
'Poor Old Joe.'
'Here's a health unto.'
'O dear what can the matter be.'

'There's a tavern in the town.'
'John Peel'.
'O who will o'er the downs with me.'
'London's burning.'
'Three blind mice.'
'Upidee, Upidee' (Excelsior).

27. **Passages from the Bible.**

Rejoice in the Lord alway, and again I say Rejoice.
Whatsoever things are true, &c. Phil. iv. 4–8, all or
  part.
Surely goodness and mercy shall follow me all the days
  of my life. And I will dwell in the house of the Lord
  for ever. Psalm xxiii.
The Beatitudes.
And now abideth faith, hope, charity, these three, but
  the greatest of these is charity. 1 Cor. xiii. 13.
Inasmuch as ye have done it unto one of the least of these
  my brethren, ye have done it unto me. Matt. xxv. 40.
Psalms xxiii, xxiv, cxxi, cl.
Part of Psalm cxxxvi.

28. **Hymns**

I know not where His islands lift
I know not what the future hath.
} The first lines of two verses of a poem —'The Eternal Goodness', by Whittier.

'The country faith', Norman Gale.
God be in my head.
All people that on earth do dwell.
All creatures of our God and King.
Let us with a gladsome mind,
    Praise the Lord for He is kind.

Morning has broken,
   Like the first morning.
The summer days are come again.
New every morning is the love.
Rise up O men of God.
The King of love my Shepherd is.
The God of love my Shepherd is.

29. **Ballads**

'Lord Allen's Daughter', Thomas Campbell.
'The Ballad of Summer Water', William Watson.
'Earl Haldan's Daughter', Charles Kingsley.
'Get up and bar the door', 'King John and the Abbot of Canterbury'.
'The Wraggle Taggle Gypsies.' 'The twelve days of Christmas.'
'Green grow the rushes Oh!' *Robin Hood Ballads*.
Other traditional ballads to be found in collections.

30. **Sea Chanties.** These are very useful.

31.   These are these, and those are those,
      Now we have all come hither:
    But these are those, and those are these,
      As soon as we go thither.

32. Bertha sews with thin thread and Martha sews with thick;
Bertha sews a thin silk shirt while Martha sews a tick.
So Bertha sews with thin thread while Martha sews with thick;
For Bertha sews a thin silk shirt and Martha sews a tick.

33. 'When you walk in a field', James Stephens.

34. 'Full fathom five thy father lies', Shakespeare.

35. 'Tired Tim', Walter de la Mare.

36. 'High o'er the lonely hills', Jan Struther.

    Black turns to grey.

    The first two verses of this are suitable for choral speech.

37. Oh, for a book and a shady nook,
    Either in door or out;
    With the green leaves whispering overhead,
    Or the street cries all about.
    Where I may read, all at my ease,
    Both of the new and old;
    For a jolly good book, whereon to look,
    Is better to me than gold.

38. My Grandfather's clock was too high for the shelf
    So it stood ninety years on the floor.
    It was taller by half than the old man himself
    Though it weighed not a pennyweight more.
    It was bought on the morn
    Of the day that he was born
    And was always his treasure and pride;
    But it stopped short,
    Never to go again
    When the old man died.

39. Drift down, drift down from the skies
    Little white snow-flakes falling fast,
    Like sleep that falls on tired eyes
    To bring us peace at last.
    Drift down, drift down from the skies
    Little white snow-flakes falling fast.

40. **Holiday Fellowship verse**

    Friend when you stray or sit and take your ease
    On moor or fell, or under spreading trees,

Pray leave no traces of your wayside meal,
No paper bag or scattered orange peel,
Or daily journal littered on the grass;
Others may view it with distaste and pass.
Let no one say and say it to your shame
That all was beauty here until you came.

41. **Hymn of St. Francis**

Blessed indeed are we in that our brother the sun brings
us the day and brings us the light, yea, fair is he and
shines with a very great splendour.

Blessed are we in our sister the moon and the stars which
are set so clear and lovely in the sky.

Blessed are we in our brother the wind, and the calm
and the cloud and the air which upholdeth life in all
creatures.

42. 'How sweet the moonlight sleeps upon this bank!'
(6 lines) From *The Merchant of Venice*.

43. 'Blow, blow, thou winter wind.' *As You Like It*.

44. 'There is a wind where the rose was.'
Four lines from 'The Chilterns', Rupert Brooke.

45. **The Names of Lovely Things** by A. Stevenson Nicol

At times, the wish hath come to me to write
Only unordered names of lovely things.
White misty snows under the moonrays white,
Rich rhododendron blossoms in green springs,
Grey lichened rocks whereto the wallflower clings
Warm lights from cottage windows in blue eves,
Red fruited sprays on which the redbreast sings,
September suns on yellow harvest sheaves,
Black bramble berries among crimson leaves,
Stocks that fill all the darkness with delight,

Hoar-frost upon the web the spider weaves.
White pinioned birds in lofty, lonely flight.
When written thoughts but weary me, or tease me,
Such sweet unordered names have power to please me.

Books used

For Your Delight. London: The Poetry Bookshop.
The Golden Staircase. Nelson.
The Bible. A.V.
Songs of Praise. Oxford University Press.

THE BACKWARD SENIOR PUPIL

INTRODUCTION

THE PROBLEM

As I have said earlier in this book, the problem of the backward deaf pupil is a challenging one; it is indeed one of the most urgent and challenging problems of our work.

There is a very great disparity between the attainments of our most advanced pupils and those of our poorest—a much greater disparity than that which exists between the best and worst in the normal schools. This disparity may, of course, be due to lack of intelligence—but it is not always so. In fact there are a number of pupils with normal practical intelligence (not super-intelligent children, for they have the urge and will learn in almost any circumstances) whose attainments in spoken and written language are very poor. Nor are these backward children necessarily the ones with the greatest degree of deafness, although the amount of deafness is, of course, a contributory factor.

It is with a view to *preventing* backwardness in deaf children that I have laid such emphasis in this book on *practice* of the language taught in as many ways as possible so that children of different types, to whom different aspects appeal, will have equal chances. I have also laid emphasis, for this same reason, on group work, on going over the basic work with the slower child, and on preventing the feeling of failure from arising.

So much for prevention which is always better than cure. However, the problem with which we have to deal is that of the pupil who is already backward in attainments. If we have junior pupils who are showing signs of backwardness and whose intelligence is average, then the methods advocated here may help to keep them moving steadily forward, so that, although they may not reach the level of the more intelligent child, yet they will have sufficient spoken and written language to understand, to be in communication with, and to be adjusted to their environment.

It is, however, in the senior school that the gap between the attainments of the pupils is so much in evidence and where the problem becomes acute. This section constitutes an attempt to examine this problem and suggest ways of helping these pupils.

THE ATTRIBUTES OF THE BACKWARD DEAF PUPIL: CAUSES OF BACKWARDNESS

A. First let us examine these children who are backward. What are they like?

1. Their attainments are poor, i.e. their language is meagre, they may have words only, or a very few simple sentences.

2. They may have jumbled, confused language.

3. They are often lacking in confidence. They are diffident and afraid to attempt language.

4. They may be indifferent and bored, especially the adolescent.

B. Let us try to find out *why* these boys and girls are backward, for that may help us to help them. May I take an illustration?

Think of our teaching of language as a structure or building. What is requisite in a good building?

1. An architect's plan which all must follow.

2. The foundations must be well and truly laid.

3. The structure on the foundations must be built up brick by brick and story by story.

4. The framework must be firm—if some of it is faulty or just not there, the whole building is liable to come crashing down, and the ground floor is also destroyed or damaged.

5. The work of building must go on steadily, i.e. it is no good digging the foundations if only a few rows of bricks are laid. It will be a long time before your house keeps out the wet and cold.

6. It must have four walls. It is no good building up one side only, the next story cannot rest on one wall!

7. A good building must have good material.

8. There must be time to build, and the workman must get on with the job.

9. There should not only be a good architect, but a good master builder and good workmen.

C. Now let us think of these backward boys and girls with this illustration in mind, taking these requisites point by point.

1. They may have been the victims of no architect's plan, no cohesion in teaching.
This leads to confusion and so to diffidence.

2. The teaching of the foundations may have been faulty.
This leads to confusion, paucity of attainments, and lack of confidence.

3 and 4. They may have gaps in knowledge due either to (1 above) or to absence and change of school, i.e. the structure or the framework are faulty.
This leads to confusion and lack of confidence.

5. They may have been taught the foundations only and so have very little language structure in which to express their thoughts.

This leads in a good or average intelligence to boredom and indifference.

6. They may have been taught well in the classroom but have had no help outside either in school or home, i.e. one of the walls is missing.

This leads to paucity of language and diffidence.

7. They may be mentally slow with poor memories and understanding—in other words the material is not good.

This means poor attainments and confusion.

8. The children may have started very late to school and so it is very difficult to get a good language structure in the time available.

9. It may be the teaching which is at fault.

I think we should ask ourselves very seriously a few questions.

Have we been good master builders, good workmen? Have we taught language to the best of our ability, with thought, inspiration, and knowledge? Do we discipline ourselves to fit into the scheme? Do we trouble about the children who are *not* in class; do we help them to express themselves and take trouble to understand them out of school?

Do we really *teach* language?

Is it our fault that some of these children are backward and have so poor a language attainment?

Is our teaching so dull and uninteresting that the children are indifferent and bored with the whole proceeding?

Have we realized the magnitude of the task? Do we realize what difficulties the children have? Have we tried to simplify and help the children understand and overcome their difficulties?

It all comes back to the teachers, both individually and as a team.

It is my firm opinion that the number of backward children with poor language ability could be considerably reduced in our schools by good co-ordinated and systematic teaching. However, let us turn to the problems of those who are with us now. How can we help them?

Let me say here that the suggestions I am about to make refer to:

(a) The child of good intelligence who has fallen by the way because of one of the factors mentioned above, and

(b) The child of average or slightly below average intelligence who needs to assimilate any new work longer and so progresses more slowly than the brighter child and who has failed to make good.

The pupil of really poor intelligence will benefit from these suggestions, but will soon start to drop behind again and to hold up the work with the normal backward child. Such a pupil should be sent to a school or a class for backward deaf children of poor intelligence for his own sake, for he should not be allowed to fail again; and for the sake of the others whose progress is slowed up by such a pupil. My remarks, therefore, apply more particularly to the pupils who fall into the categories (a) or (b) above.

What have we to cure?

1. Lack of attainments (a) paucity.
                        (b) confusion.

2. Diffidence. Lack of confidence.

3. Indifference (lack of interest), and boredom (especially at adolescence).

The lack of attainments, the confusion and the diffidence, the lack of confidence, mean that we must go back to the simple structures, *but* the indifference, the lack of interest, and boredom mean that we must be very careful *how* we go back, and that is where the skill of it comes in.

1. These backward boys and girls should be in a class or group of their own. They must *not* be measured against the brighter and more fortunate children. When you judge a backward child, judge him by his former achievement. If he is moving on (no matter how far he is behind the other children) then give the praise and *encouragement* due.

2. Find something in which the backward child is interested and start from there.

3. Make the language so simple to start with that he *must* succeed. Nothing succeeds like success.

4. When you are making the *language* simple, be sure that the *vocabulary* is fitted to the age and interests of the pupil. Certainly revise the language scheme but do not appear to do so.

5. Inspire them to *work*. They'll enjoy it if they begin to succeed. Insist on accuracy, train their memories.

6. Simpler lessons need not be duller lessons. The more ways you can think of for presenting the same things to these children, the better. Make your work concrete, active, and diverse.

7. Encourage and encourage and encourage and keep them moving. A word on marking may not be out of place here. So many teachers love to see blue pencil or red ink slashed all over a child's work. They give as many marks

to a child who has hardly attempted anything as to one who has made an honest effort and made mistakes. No wonder the pupils get discouraged and won't try. Especially with these backward children, be most careful about this. Point out to the pupil how much is *right* as well as the mistake. It is well to award marks for making the attempt at a sentence, more for the correct answer, deducting marks for the mistakes. Do not mark the whole sentence wrong for one mistake, but give so many marks out of the whole.

For dictation or lip-reading I find it good to give a certain number of marks, say twenty-five, and deduct one for each mistake. It is a small thing, just a matter of emphasis (on the right answer rather than on the wrong), but it makes a big difference.

What I said as regards treating the seniors as seniors is of great importance with the children who feel they have failed. They must also feel that there is no difference in treatment and regard between them and the brighter children.

They also should have English lessons and Geography, History, and Science lessons, but with this difference: the subjects should be based on the language scheme. I will come back to this in a moment.

It is most important that these children should have their first feeling of failure wiped out, and their self-confidence returned to them. It is the first step in a move forward. Then work them and keep them moving.

You will see from all this that what I said earlier is most necessary here. You must know the language outline. You must know the simple language and how it is built upon to produce the complex language. You must be able to spot where each child has gone off the rails (if he were ever on them) and be able to rectify his mistakes. You must make him feel that the simple language which you are helping him to know is not childish language, and that it will aid him to obtain knowledge about the things in which he is interested, and you must inspire him to put forth effort to learn and to remember and to go forward.

LANGUAGE AND COMPOSITION

BEFORE discussing detail of teaching backward deaf pupils let us consider what should be our aim with these children.

1. To give confidence and poise, and a desire to learn.
2. To help the pupils to express themselves in clear simple language.
3. To help them understand everyday language.
4. To give them the ability to ask questions and to find out for themselves.
5. To widen their interests and their thoughts.

Now for more detail. Perhaps you have decided that the pupil has some foundation language although he is confused. Then where should we start?

I think on the whole it should be where we started with the Stage 3 work with excursions into the former work of Stage 2. Among the work I enumerated on the habitual tense there should be something to capture the interest. It may be how to do things, what you would do things with, where things come from, how you play a game, what people do, who is best at certain games, &c.

But remember, when you have found that interest, your job is to teach language through it.

It is a good idea for each pupil to keep a scrap-book of his special interest, *but* he must be able to say and write the names of all the things he has in his book and to tell something about them. He will usually learn the names and find something to write about the pictures if his doing so is made a condition of putting them in the book.

Here are some suggestions as to scrap-books; beside them you will see the stage and number of the lesson which they help to revise.

1. Places. Stage 2: 13.
2. Cities. Stage 2: 13.

3. Football. Stage 2: 13.
4. Stamps (places). Stage 2: 13.
5. Our own city
    (town or village). Stage 2: 13.
6. London. Stage 2: 13.
7. Clothes—materials. Stage 2: 15.
    and where they come from. Stage 3: 32.

8. Games ⎫
9. Sports ⎭ Stage 2: 16 and 17
10. Buildings. Stage 2: 12 and 21
11. Aeroplanes. Stage 2: 21   ⎬ and Stage 3.
12. Engines. Stage 2: 21
13. Cars. Stage 2: 21
14. Vehicles. Stage 2: 21 ⎭
15. The weather book. Stages 2: 23 and 3: 33.
16. Health and ailments book. Stage 2: 23.
17. Pets. Stage 2: 24 and 18.
18. Times and seasons
    (everyday happenings). Stage 3: 29.

19. Shops. Stage 3: 30.
20. Railways. ⎫
21. Ships and their routes. ⎬ Stage 3: 32.
22. Air lines. ⎭
23. Food
    (where things come from). Stage 3: 32.

24. Country scenes. ⎫
25. Photographs. ⎪
26. Trees. ⎪ Stages 3: 39 and 2: 13, 18
27. Flowers. ⎬ (animals and birds).
28. Natural objects. ⎨ and 3: 32
29. Fruits. ⎪ (fruits).
30. Animals. ⎪
31. Birds. ⎭

32. People and what
    they do.
33. Trades and pro-
    fessions.
} Stage 3: 32 and Stage 4.

34. How to do things. Stage 3: 38.

35. Useful things and what we do with them. Stage 3: 35.

If you turn back to Stage 2, Lesson 13, you will see that the language used in the geography book (Centre of Interest: Places) is based on the perfect tense. (. . . has been to . . . .) and the past tense:

> He went there on (date). He did . . . . He saw . . . .
>   It is . . . there.
> He went there with . . . .
> He went there by . . . .

This is excellent practice for backward seniors. And it is not necessary only to have places to which they themselves have been, but those in which they are interested for one reason or another.

On this simple book could be based much suitable language work and revision, e.g.

> Days of the week, months, dates, time expressions (last year—last week—month). All under the heading 'When?'
> With whom did you go? Names of people.
> How did you go? By train, &c. List of names of vehicles.
> Names of places—place phrases. Where? To—, there.
> Work on the past tense—future tense (a place to which someone is going for a holiday): perfect tense—have been, have seen.

It is a good idea with backward children (bearing in mind their diffidence and lack of confidence) to start these scrap-books as communal efforts, as in Lesson 13. Then, as others are started, the pupil or two pupils specially interested should be put in charge of the particular scrap-book. The others can make contributions but their standard should be set and their fitness for inclusion decided by the pupils in charge. This makes for a high standard, for children are much harder on each other than adults are on children.

This is one of the easiest centres of interest with which to begin. Football teams (3) (also a camouflage for places) is quite easy too. Gradually add items of interest, such as what is made at each place; what buildings it has, old and new; its position (north of England, &c.); whether it has a river, &c. These things can be built up by degrees. Scrap-books on cities (2), Stamps (4), London (6), and Our own town (5), can be started in the same way.

Give plenty of practice in the simple sentences first. Let the pupils feel confidence in themselves—and then the progress will quicken.

Clothes (7) and what things are made of—make an interesting and simple scrap-book. The girls and some boys will enjoy it very much. This will revise materials, clothes, and colours (Lessons 15 and 10). Games (8) and Sports (9) will revise 'can' and 'can't' (Lessons 16 and 17). Buildings (10) will revise Lesson 21 (parts of things).

Take the opportunity to revise the correct spelling of parts of the room and furniture. It can be done by teaching the drawing of the plan of a house, discussing where the windows, doors, and fireplaces, &c., should go; and, if a room, placing all the articles of furniture in it. What an opportunity of revising adverbial phrases, e.g. 'between the window and the fire-place (or radiator)', 'in the corner near the door'.

Aeroplanes (11), Engines (12), Cars (13), Vehicles (14)

could all be treated in the same way. A health book and weather book (15 and 16) revise Lesson 23 and a pets book (17), Lesson 24. All these revise Stage 2.

Shops (19), Trees (26), Flowers (27), Natural objects (28) (rivers, mountains, lakes), Fruits (29), Animals (30), Birds (31), People and what they do (32), How to do things (34), and Useful things and what we do with them (35), all revise and practice Stage 3 as well as Stage 2.

Lesson 39 in Stage 3 is very important. On it much interesting information can be built up and a widening of the horizon and much lasting enjoyment can be given these limited boys and girls.

Lesson 38 'How to' is the foundation of the science lesson. In both these lessons, and the other centres of interest, expeditions to see, paint, and draw the natural objects or to make diagrams and plans should be taken. Some will enjoy the one thing and some the other.

If you find that you must revise even simpler work, e.g. 'to have', 'to be', and 'to like', try to think of a way to do this which will not make a senior feel he is doing the same work as the very young children.

For instance—the contents of a boy's pocket, and of a girl's handbag will make the starting-ground for work on 'has', 'have', and 'is'.

e.g. What John has in his   What Jane has in her hand-
      pocket.   bag.
   He has . . . and . . . . She has . . . and . . . .
   He has . . . also, &c. She has . . . also, &c.

Each pupil writes and learns the contents of his/her own pocket or bag—and then the contents of one another's. In this way they are using both 'have' and 'has' and you are learning what interests the pupils. Be sure that they really learn this vocabulary and then you can go on to the colours and qualities of these objects and to find out where they got them and what they will do with them. The parts of cars, aeroplanes, tractors, bicycles, &c. give practice in this same work, and they can start a scrapbook of some of these things using this very limited language. Colours and qualities belonging to those objects bring in 'to be'.

'To like' can be revised by talks about the menu of one's favourite dinner, each pupil giving his own choice. This can then be applied to sport—games-lessons.

It is the same work as is done in the junior school—the same care is needed in teaching accurately and expecting accuracy, but the approach is different. It tries to find out and to use the interests of adolescents in all their work.

Do a good deal of diary work, but do not let it appear as the daily news of the junior school. Have a book which looks like a diary; show them books in the library which are diaries; let them write entries in the same way as in these books; *not* 'today is . . .' but the date, the news. These diaries can be used when they write letters (and letters are their easiest composition at this stage).

The pupils should first of all be allowed to copy from their diaries for these letters but later should be encouraged to study them for five minutes and then write without further recourse to them.

Gradually a pattern of letter-writing should be built up:

1. Greetings and inquiries.
2. News (diaries), (*a*) past, (*b*) present, (*c*) future.
3. Answering questions in last letter.
4. Future, (*a*) what he will do, (*b*) what he hopes.
5. Messages and farewell.

Encourage the parents to *answer* these letters and to tell news in simple language.

The backward child usually knows much more than he thinks he knows. Confidence is what is needed. When once he realizes that from simple beginnings such as daily news a flow of language can result, a big hurdle has been jumped and he will tackle other composition more hopefully and successfully. Remember that your aim in teaching composition is to help him to express himself, *not* for the composition's sake but for his own sake.

I am not suggesting that the language work should be limited to diaries and to work on centres of interest. On the contrary, much work on the language principles must be done when you have found what the pupil really knows, and in what he is interested. Start there—give confidence and go on to expect work from the pupil.

So often the backward child has acquired lazy mental habits. These habits must be broken, but it will be difficult for the pupil to concentrate for long at first. Vary the lessons—act them—mime them—give speech with actions —dictation—writing—drawing interpretations—anything to impress the language taught. Study Stages 1–3 and adapt the games to the age of the pupils and use them.

Clinch your language teaching with the questions form. Be sure that the pupils are clear as to the answers to 'Who?' 'What?' 'Where?' 'When?' 'How?' 'Why?' 'What . . . for?' 'Who . . .?' 'What . . . did . . . do?' 'What will . . . do?' 'What . . . doing?' Insist on phrases in answer to the question 'Where?' and 'When?' (where necessary of course) and of words only in other cases.

Aim at clarity all the time.

Dramatize and make concrete and active their work on questions. Do this in as many different ways as you can.

Here is one way:

Have the key word of the question forms on separate cards:

WHO? WHAT DID . . . DO? WITH WHOM? WHEN?
HOW? WHAT . . . FOR? AT WHAT TIME?

Break up the sentence concerned into parts and write
them on large cards or boards. Do this as a class exercise
together first, placing the question card with the appropriate part of the sentence.

e.g. Sentence broken up into its parts:

GEORGE WENT TO TOWN WITH HIS MOTHER BY BUS
AT 9 O'CLOCK YESTERDAY TO BUY A NEW SUIT

Then mix up and give out one part to each pupil (these
constitute the sentence team). Give out the question cards
to the remaining pupils (the question team). One of these
takes the card WHO? and stands forward saying 'Who?'
and in answer the one holding GEORGE comes forward
holding up his card and says, 'George'. This is repeated
with all the cards until the whole sentence is built up. Each
pupil in the sentence team then moves forward one pace,
in turn saying the word or phrase on his card to make up
the whole sentence.

Mix up the question cards again and let the members
of the question team pick out one each at random and fire
them at the sentence team.

This makes for quickness of lip-reading and answering
clearly by speech and writing. I know of no better exercise
for straightening out muddled language.

It is rather fun to build a sentence up with the class in
this way—taking the essential subject and predicate first

WHO   DID
JOHN   WALKED

Then   adding   'Where?'   'With   whom?'   'How?'
'When?' 'At what time?' 'Why?'

No time is wasted in getting this clear. So many

backward pupils are confused. Get them to understand these things clearly and to answer the questions exactly in the appropriate word or phrase and they will—provided they have a reasonable amount of intelligence—go on apace.

When much work has been done with the key words of the question only, give the full questions but still insist on the word or phrase only as answer. When all the questions have been answered, say 'Now tell me about John', and let the pupils write the full sentence.

Go back to the key word only again if you find the pupils are not sure. When the pupils really *know* the answers in any given sentence to these questions, you will find that they are also expressing themselves more clearly and are understanding better. Give them confidence in their understanding of the simple language structure. As in all their work, confidence and surety is needed here.

Use these question forms in your daily dealings with the pupils as often as possible. '*Who* did that? *Why* did he do it? *Where* is . . .? *What* has he gone for? *Who* has he gone with? or *With whom* has he gone? Has he gone (to . . .)? Here he comes *Where* have you been?' &c.

On your time-table will be Geography. Base it on your language scheme in Stages 2 and 3. You have both physical geography and products, animals, and peoples of the world to choose from. Make your work concrete, interesting, varied, pictorial, real, and simple. Above all, make it clear.

On your time-table should be Science. It should again be concrete, interesting, *real*. For example, the work on electricity might include 'How to mend an electric iron'. Give the names of the parts, &c., and the verbs involved. Give the boys and girls language to explain it.

First you unscrew . . . .

Then . . . .
Then . . . .
Give them the verbs and the names and expect them
to memorize them.

You will often find that by teaching a new tense you are
helped very much to revise the former tenses. You will be
using chiefly the past, future, and perfect tenses in diaries
and the habitual tense in information—Geography and
Science.

Insist on the correct tense in the correct place with the
appropriate adverbs or adverbial phrases of time. Give
much practice in these.

Teach many phrases: 'Show me the boy with a blue
suit', &c.

If you have taught the backward seniors so well that
they have a good grasp of Stages 2 and 3, then go on to
Stage 4.

If again they have now very little time left at school, then
in Stage 4 there are several lessons which are of special
importance and upon which you should concentrate.

Here they are:

Lessons 42 and 46. Indirect Speech—Commands and
Statements.

Lesson 43. The use of common things.

Lesson 44. 'Should like to be', with trades and professions. This is very important.

Lesson 49. Pardon—excuse, forgive.

Lesson 51. Part of this—especially the practical part and
their own weights and heights.

Lesson 57. 'Should', 'ought to', 'must', right and wrong.
Combine Lessons 43 and 44:

e.g. What a gardener does. What he uses.
What a carpenter does. What he uses.

Correlate your speech, lip-reading, dictation, composition, and subjects all to this one end—the teaching of clear simple language, but remember to get fun and laughter there. Dramatize, mime, play games, anything to *teach* language and destroy the bugbear of failure and boredom.

SPEECH

So often those pupils who are backward in language are also backward in speech; perhaps because, having little to say, they have had little practice; or, and this is usually the case, the bugbear of failure has haunted them, giving them diffidence, lack of confidence, and despair, cloaked under a guise of not caring. As in language, success in some simple thing must be aimed at first. We must create the desire to speak and the ability to speak, and at the same time give them the language with which to speak.

Do *not* allow the speech lessons to be one more thing in which the pupils fail, nor allow it to be the same kind of lesson as those given to young children. Let them have a notebook for speech and elocution and begin by dividing the sounds up into consonants and vowels, and teach these names. Let them feel they are learning something new—something more grown up than the lessons given to young children. Give diagrams if you find they help. Teach lipping—speech without voice. Then take lessons after the pattern of that given in Stage 4, Speech, on 'Madam will you walk'. In fact this is quite a good one to start with—or to come very near to the beginning. Rectify one fault at a time.

Do *not* take any notice of the other incorrect sounds. If the pupil gives the sound taught correctly, ignore the other faults in the word, phrase, sentence, or refrain given, and give full marks. Show real appreciation and pleasure at the effort made. Practice this and then go on to another difficulty. Then you can expect two correct sounds. Do not let any slip back. Keep on bringing in the former correction until at last you have only to point to the sound wrongly produced for the pupil to correct himself.

Let me illustrate with 'Madam will you walk'.

Concentrate first on 't' and 'k', the unvoiced plosives, and when you have these sounds correct, let the pupils join in with you on the last word of both verses, 'walk—talk—walk'.

Take some work on the sound 'w' and when these are all correct, i.e. 't', 'k', 'w', take the part of the lesson on 'm' and 'n'. Nearly all your troubles will then be over. You will have catered for most of the words in this poem.

When you know that the pupils *can* produce the sounds correctly in these words let them practice with movement, taking parts.

I have found the slower pupils enjoy all this very much. Of course, they take very much longer to master the poem.

One of the difficulties here is to find simple enough and yet adult enough rhymes. The pupils are often only at the one-word or phrase stage, and certainly only at the repetitive rhyme stage.

Here are some rhymes and refrains which are suitable.

Let us see if they can help us in our correction and practice of correct sounds.

Sounds for special practice

1. A couplet from the 'Ballad of
     Scmmer Water'   'p'
   Deep asleep, deep asleep,   'ee'
   Deep asleep it lies.

2. Put the car in the car park,   'p' and 'k'
   Don't park over there.   'ar' and 'oa'

3. Madam will you walk   'm'⎫   't'   'k'
   Madam will you walk   ⎬   'w'
   Madam will you walk   ⎪
     and talk with me?   'n'⎭   't'   'k'
   No, I will not walk,   'n'   't'   'k'
   No, I will not talk,
   No, I will not walk,   'w'
     and talk with you.   'aw'

4. One man went to mow,   'w'   'm'   'n'
   Went to mow a meadow.   'e'   'a'
   One man and his dog
   Went to mow a meadow.

    (Repeat with 'Two men', 'Three
      men', &c.)

5. Where are you going to, my
     pretty maid?   'w'   'm'
   Where are you going to, my
     pretty maid?   'ie'   'ai'

6. 'Come back, come back',   'm'   'k'
   He cried in grief,
   'Across this stormy water.'   's'   's'   'w'

7. See the robbers passing by,   's'   'ee'   'ie'
   Passing by, passing by;
   See the robbers passing by,   'ng'
   My fair lady.

8. Men may come,   'm'   'n'
   And men may go,
   But I go on
   For ever.   'f'

9. Remember, remember,   'm–b' 'n'
   The fifth of November.   'f–th'

10. Bang the gong,
    Bang the gong,   'ng'
    Ring the bell,
    Ding, dong.

11. Hark, now I hear them,   'h'   'ng'
    Ding, dong, bell.

12. 'Lady Moon' (one stanza).   'm'   'n'   'oo'

13. Cockles and mussels,   'c'   'l'
    Alive, alive oh,   'ie'   'oh'
    Alive, alive oh,
    Alive, alive oh;
    Cockles and mussels,
    Alive, alive oh.

14. Revision of the days (more difficult).

Could be taken in two groups, *A* and *B*. *A* say the names of the days—*B* 'for health', &c.

> Monday for wealth,
> Tuesday for health,
> Wednesday the best day of all.
> Thursday for crosses,
> Friday for losses,
> Saturday, no luck at all.

15. Another verse from the 'Ballad of Semmer Water'.

> And many a fathom, many
>   a fathom,   'm'   'n'   'ng'
> Many a fathom below,   'oa'
> In a king's tower and a
>   queen's bower,   'ow'
> The fishes come and go.

16. Full fathom five thy father lies,   'f'   'l'
    Of his bones are coral made.   'n'   'm'

17. I remember, I remember,   'm'   'm–b'
    The house where I was born;   'n'
    The little window where the
       sun   'w'   'wh'
    Came peeping in at morn.   'ng'   'n'

18. **September**

Golden in the garden,   'g'   'n'
Golden in the glen;
Golden, golden, golden,
September's here again

Golden in the tree tops,
Golden in the sky;
Golden, golden, golden
September's going by.

19. Dark brown is the river,   'n'
Golden is the sand;
It flows along for ever,
With trees on either hand.

20. Lavender's blue, dilly
dilly.   'l'   'ee'   See Stage 3, Speech.

21. Come follow, follow,
follow.   'f'   'l'   See Stage 4, Speech.

22. Back of the loaf.   'l'   'ower'   See Stage 4, Speech.

23. O Happy Wind.   various   See Stage 4, Speech.
(Probably part only.)

24. The Weather.   'w', 'm', 'st', 'e'. See Stage 4, Speech.

25. Sweet and low.   'w', 'ee', 'oa', 's'. See Stage 5, Speech.
(Part of this only—perhaps the first four lines.)

Refrains from sea chanties and traditional songs such as are found in students' song-books are suitable.

'Under the spreading chestnut tree' as sung by Scouts with appropriate actions is very suitable. These all provide some fun and laughter.

Do not forget hymns and carols with refrains and prayers with responses.

Part of Psalms xxiii, xxiv, cxxxvi ('For His mercy endureth for ever').

Couplets and verses as the pupils progress, from the senior poems, e.g.

> Slowly silently now the moon
> Walks the night in her silver shoon.

Stories with responses and exclamations are very suitable for backward seniors, helping to wake them up, teaching them to be on the alert to use their speech quickly and accurately. There could be stories of expeditions— minor catastrophes and unexpected pleasures in the school, and traditional and historical stories, but *not* imaginative stories.

Teach schoolboy and schoolgirl normal exclamations. Nothing childish or beneath the dignity of an adolescent.

As you teach and revise language, use the phrases, question forms, exclamations, and words in your intonation and speech work in the form of rhymes, games, and stories as above.

The reading suitable for backward seniors is limited and should be built up from these stories, their scrap-books, and diaries.

For Intonation see Stages 1 and 2, and

for Phrasing see Stages 1–3.

Note particularly the unaccented 'the' and 'a' bringing in the neutral vowel:

a meadow,

the car park.

Point out the neutral vowel when it occurs,

e.g. madam, father, postman, grocer, &c.

See Speech notes for Stage 3.

APPENDIX I

SOME COMMON FAULTS OF SPEECH AND THEIR CORRECTION

In this last section I am gathering together some of the common faults found in the speech of deaf children and suggesting methods of correcting them. These are often, though not always, faults found in the speech of the backward deaf, so they are included in the work with these pupils. Of course, this is not always the case, and it is well to teach all the children the best and easiest way to produce sounds—that is to speak well.

Difficult, laboured, incorrect speech is a great drawback to the bright child and a means of retardation to the slower child. These things *can* be corrected, and deaf children *can* speak easily and intelligibly if we teach them how to do so.

Before any corrections can be done, it is necessary that the teacher should have the ability to diagnose what is wrong. It is not enough to realize that a certain sound is produced wrongly, the teacher must know also exactly what is wrong with it. He must know how it is being produced, and how this production differs from the correct production. This is the first step. When you have diagnosed the fault, comes the problem of correcting it.

If we could put ourselves in our pupil's place sometimes and, by stopping up our ears and trying to copy a new sound in a foreign language, could realize in some slight degree how difficult it is to copy a sound from sight only; how seeing one's own mouth in a mirror helps; how feeling the breath helps; how even a small amount of hearing helps, we should be most concerned to utilize all these things.

The principles governing speech teaching and especially speech correction should then be:

First. Let the pupil see (a) the teacher's mouth.
(b) his own mouth.

Second. Let the pupil feel the expulsion of breath—its amount and duration.

Third. Let the pupil hear all he can.

On these few principles hang all our skill in speech teaching. Of course, there is more to be said than the mere statement of principle.

First—the pupil must see

But

1. The position must be right.

It must be easy and natural. There must be no straining and no throwing the head back to look up at the teacher. There should be not too close a position, especially with young children.

2. The light must be good and from the right quarter (never in the pupil's eyes).

3. The mirror must be large enough to see easily.

Second—the pupil must feel

But the problem is where and how.

1. He should feel the outgoing breath—at all stages in speech training. This cannot be *seen* and the pupil should constantly be reminded that the *sounds of speech* are made by many and various modifications of the *breath*.

2. Vibration should be felt when all else fails—on the chin—on the side of the face—on the chest—but *not* on the throat.

Third—the child should hear as much as possible

Hearing-aids should be used for every child.

By using these principles, provided that you can diagnose not only which sound is incorrect but what is wrong with that sound, and provided of course that there is no physical defect of the organ of speech, you can correct all the faults of speech.

SOME COMMON FAULTS OF SPEECH

Consonants

1. Clicked 't' and 'd', 'k' and 'g'.
2. Vocalization of unvoiced consonants.
3. Sound interposed between two consonants.
4. 'Wh' or shape of mouth with no sound for 'w'.
5. 'r' for 'sh' or 'sh' for 'r'.
6. Too great effort—grimaces, &c.
7. Consonants indeterminate. Not clear cut.
8. Breathy 'l'.
9. 'm' before 'b', 'n' before 'd', 'ng' before 'g'—or in other words 'mboat' for 'boat', 'ndon't' for don't, 'nggoat' for 'goat'.
10. Nasalizing 'b', 'd', and 'g'; e.g. 'moat' for 'boat', 'non't' for 'don't'.
    'b' or 'mb' for 'm', e.g. 'mbuther' or 'buther' for 'mother', 'ndose' or 'dose' for 'nose'.
11. 'm' or indeterminate consonant for 'w'.
12. A vowel sound or a 'g' or an 'n' for 'ng'.
13. 'sh' for 's' or faulty unclear 's'.
14. Faulty 'ch'.

Vowels

1. Not clearly differentiated, e.g. 'ah' for 'ie'.
2. Indeterminate vowels.
3. Neutral vowel interposed between vowel and consonant, 'ooerp' for 'oop'.
4. Neutral vowel interposed anywhere in the sentence.
5. 'a' or something near it for 'e'.
6. 'ee' not clear.

Voice

1. Forced, unpleasing sound.
2. Breathy voice.
3. Nasal voice.

Here are some specific things to have right before you tackle the incorrect sounds.

1. Be sure that the principles outlined at the beginning of this Appendix are right.

(*a*) The pupils are in a good position for seeing you and themselves (older children have small mirrors each, young ones a large one), and that the light is good.

(*b*) The pupils all have hearing-aids, which are fitted to them and in order.

(*c*) The pupils have either apparatus for feeling the breath, such as ribbons on a frame, or are ready and alert to feel the breath on their fingers.

2. Be confident and let the pupils feel your confidence. Your attitude (even when confronted with very poor speech) should be that the pupils' speech is not very good, but that you can and will help them to speak correctly.

3. Be encouraging. Give full measure of encouragement to any effort. Praise that which is correct.

4. Tackle one thing at a time. When the pupil has learnt to say one of his faults correctly, listen for that sound in his speech. If he remembers it correctly, praise him. Do not notice his other faults except to say '—— was very good. We will tackle —— next.'

Again, when you have taken two sounds say, 'Both of those sounds are now correct. You have not many more faults now. All these sounds are already correct (pointing them out). You are making very good progress. I think we will tackle —— next week or would you like to tackle —— or —— next week?' In this way there is encouragement, and yet a looking forward to something better—both important. The pupil feels confident in his ability to tackle what lies ahead.

5. If you are teaching seniors, explain with diagrams, give technical terms (consonants, vowels, &c.). Make it appear a different subject from that taught in the junior school.

Now for particular exercises.

A. Breathing

Take breathing exercises but do *not* place hands on chest and breathe in and out to numbers. That way tension lies, a state conducive to bad rather than good speech.

Useful breathing exercises are:

1. Stooping to pick a flower—standing up—smelling it (a long breath), expelling the breath through half-opened mouth.
2. Yawning and sighing.
3. Feeling the breath sounds on the raised forefinger.

(*a*) Continuous f	. . . .	as long as possible.
	th	as long as possible.
	s	as long as possible.
	sh	as long as possible.
	h	as long as possible.
(*b*) Plosives	p p p p p p p p	as many as possible.
	t t t t t t t t	as many as possible.
	k k k k k k k k	as many as possible.
	ch ch ch ch ch ch	as many as possible.

The accent on all these is in the breath expulsions. A long in-drawing of breath will follow without tension on the part of the pupil.

B. Explanation of the part played by the emission of breath in speech

All speech (vowels and consonants) can be felt on the raised forefinger as breath coming away from the mouth and nose. (Concentrate on the mouth here.)

With raised forefinger feel various sentences, e.g.

'Go to the car park.'
'Deep asleep, deep asleep,
Deep asleep it lies.'

The pupils should feel the forefinger becoming warm. They should note that there is less breath when vowels are being spoken. They should also note the plosives and fricative consonants.

C. Practising speaking without voice

Teach the pupils to say these sentences without voice but giving full value to the consonants. The forefinger should be raised.

This is a very important exercise. So many deaf children are not absolutely sure when they are using voice and when they are not. The hearing-aids should help. If not, they must feel the difference in vibration in the teacher's chest or face and then in their own. It is well worth while to practice the pupils well in this, for failure to apprehend this has caused many of the faults of speech and much unintelligibility in speech.

When they really understand and can use voice or not at will (there must be no suspicion of voice at all when you ask for no voice) and when they have understood and performed correctly the first two exercises, you can correct many of the faults in the list at the beginning of this chapter.

D. Tongue and lip exercises

Teach these as a little light relief. Let them watch you and copy all the things you do with your mouth and tongue as quickly as possible. Do not belabour it. Treat it lightly. Emphasis is on the lips and tongue all the time. Some examples:

> pa–pa–pa–pa
> ta–ta–ta–ta
> f f f f f f f
> th th th th
> s s s s s s s
> oa–oa–oa–oa
> ee–ee–ee–ee
> oi–oi–oi–oi
> ie–ie–ie–ie
> ai–ai–ai–ai
> you–you–you
> wee–wee–wee
> woe–woe–woe
> la–la–la–la

loo–loo–loo
lee–lee–lee
lai–lai–lai
pla–pla–pla
plee–plee–plee
flow–flow–flow
flair-flair–flair
pitter–patter–pitter–patter
pree–pree–pree–pree, &c., &c.

Tongue rapidly from corner to corner of the lips—up and down in mouth—round and round. Emphasize the use made of the mouth, the lips, and the tongue in speech. Take the pupils' attention off the throat.

These four exercises should help to correct the first eight of the common faults listed under Consonants, the first four under Vowels, and the first two under Voice.

Let us take a look at them one at a time.

Consonants (1–8)

1. Clicked 't' and 'd', 'k' and 'g'.

Let the pupils feel the expulsions of breath in the correct production of 't', 'd', 'k', or 'g' and try to make the same expulsion themselves. You cannot click the sounds and expel the breath at the same time.

2. Vocalization of unvoiced consonants.
3. Sound interposed between two consonants.

When the pupils have practised and really apprehend Exercise C, it is a simple matter to point out that 'p', 't', 'k', 'ch', 'f', 'h', 's', 'sh', 'th' are all unvoiced consonants and to practice them accordingly both alone and in words. It is easy, too, to point out that there is no voice between, for instance, 's' and 'p' in 'spoon'—the voice begins after the 'p' has been produced, 'S poon'. Isolate the 's' from 'poon' for further clarity.

4. 'wh' or shape of mouth with no sound for 'w'.
5. 'r' for 'sh' or 'sh' for 'r'.

Let the pupils feel the breath expulsion in 'wh' which should not be present in 'w' except for the slight amount felt in any voice sound. Remind them that 'w' is voiced and, with the use of a mirror for correct shape, you have the correct sound.

'r' is voiced and 'sh' is not, although the shape of the mouth is practically the same. The mirror will show the difference of tongue position.

6. Too great effort—grimaces—too much pressure.

7. Consonants indeterminate—not clear cut.

Although these two faults seem to be quite opposite to each other, they are cured in much the same way.

The loosening up of the muscles by means of the tongue and lip exercises, will both do away with some of the tension evidenced by the too great effort, and will give more flexibility to the child whose consonants are not strong enough.

In both cases practice of Exercises *A* and *B* and the concentration on feeling the expulsion of air will cure these faults.

Individual work with the mirror with the teacher alone will help the pupil who makes too much effort.

8. Breathy 'l'.

Feeling on the side of the mouth—seeing the position of the tongue in the mirror, and the knowledge that 'l' is a voiced sound and that the pupil is expelling too much breath will cure this.

Vowels (1–4)

1. Not clearly differentiated, e.g. 'ah' for 'ie'.

2. Indeterminate vowels.

These can be improved by the use of the tongue and lip exercises (Exercise *D*) and by the use of a mirror.

3. Neutral vowel interposed between vowel and consonant.

4. Neutral vowel interposed anywhere in sentence.

Exercise *C*—practising speaking without voice—pointing out where voice occurs and where it does not will cure these. Show the pupils that in 'oop', for instance:

(*a*) 'oo' is voiced and 'p' is not,
(*b*) that there is no other vowel between 'oo' and 'p'.
Separate the sounds 'oo' . . . 'p', *not* 'oo -er-p'.
Practice this until you get 'oop'.

In the same way show the pupils exactly where they have been interposing a vowel sound in the sentence. Concentrate on where the voice does come and on clear consonants.

The cure of these two faults is not easy if their use has been of long duration, but it can be done by this method.

Voice (1, 2)

1. Forced unpleasing sound.

2. Breathy voice.

Good control of the breath helps to correct breathy voice. A greater awareness of the difference between voiced and unvoiced sounds is a great help too.

(*a*) For fault 1 give much practice in feeling the breath on the finger—and in speaking sentences such as are given in Exercise *B*.

(*b*) For specific exercise give

f f f f	(a long 'f') far–fee–far–foo
th th th th	than–thee–thar–thoo
s s s s	sar–see–sar–soo
sh sh sh sh	shar–shee–shar–shoo.

These exercises bring the sound forward in the mouth and help to soften harshness.

Again Exercise *C* will help here considerably. The whole aim is to alter the emphasis from the throat to the mouth cavity, the tongue, and the lips. To continue our list of exercises:

E. Nasal exercises

Good nasal resonance for the nasal consonants 'm', 'n', and 'ng' is a most important factor of good speech.

Let the pupils feel here and listen if possible. Handkerchief drill should proceed any nasal exercises.

1. Let them hold the forefinger horizontally under the nostrils (do *not* allow them to touch the side of the nose) while saying 'm'. If the sound is being made correctly, the finger will become warm.

2. Give humming exercises with 'm' followed by 'n'.

3. 'ng' is not so easy to produce as an isolated sound—and to hold it.

Start from 'bang' and hold on to the 'ng'. Use mirrors here, of course, to show the position of the tongue, and hearing-aids. Hold the finger in front of the mouth for 'ba' and change its position to the horizontal one quickly for 'ng'.

4. Repeat this exercise with 'ar-ng', 'ar ng', 'ar ng'.

Be sure that the breath change is noted and correctly produced. Do not go on with the exercise until it is understood. Go back again and again to humming with 'm' and 'n'.

Now to apply all these to the faults concerned.

Under Consonants (9–12)

i.e. 9. 'm' before 'b', 'n' before 'd', 'ng' before 'g' or 'm' before 'b'.

'mboat' or 'moat' for 'boat', 'ndon't' or 'non't' for 'don't', 'nggoat' for goat.

10. 'b' or 'bm' for 'm', e.g. 'mbuther' or 'buther' for 'mother'; 'hamber' or 'habber' for 'hammer'.

'd' or 'dn' for 'n', e.g. 'doa' or 'ndoa' for 'no'.

11. 'm' or indeterminate vowel for 'w'.

12. A vowel sound, a 'g' or an 'n' for 'ng'.

Under Voice (3)

3. Nasal voice.

All these faults spring from poor nasal resonance and from failing to understand the essential difference between nasal sounds and those produced in the mouth.

Taking the last first (nasal voice), good nasal and mouth resonance must be aimed at. A nasal voice is caused by the uvula being in a half-way position so that the breath escapes through both openings giving good resonance to neither.

Give the breathing and voice exercises (*A*, *B*, and *C*) and the nasal exercises (*E*), especially 4 'ar', 'ng', 'ar ng'.

The exercise I have suggested for a harsh, unpleasing voice (*b*) will help very much.

For faults 9 and 10

(*a*) Use the mirrors—there may be too much pressure on the lips in 'm' and the tongue in 'd'.

(*b*) Give practice in humming.

(*c*) Give practice in 'm' and 'n' finally—not initially.

   e.g. arm arm arm am am am
      oom oom oom oon oon oon

(*d*) Gradually join these together—smoothly 'armarmarm', &c.

(*e*) Feel this all the time with finger raised to nostril.

(*f*) Practice 'bar bar bar   arb arb arb arb   barbarbar', &c.

(*g*) Demonstrate—see, hear, and feel these in juxtaposition.

   armarmarmarmarm
   arbarbarbarbarb

(*h*) Practice in words and emphasize the smoothness of *M*other (make the 'm' rather long).

   moon–me–my. My mother said.
   My mother made me go to bed.

It is good to bring the contrast of the 'b' in 'bed' in the practice here.

Fault 11 ('m' or other sound for 'w')

After these exercises fault 11 is easily cured. Demonstrate the position of the mouth and that it is a vowel and not a nasal sound. Let them see in the mirror—feel where the breath is and hear it if possible.

Clinch it with:

   'One man went to mow—went to mow a meadow'
                 also
   'Madam will you walk, Madam will you talk'.

Fault 12. Various sounds for 'ng'

This has been dealt with under the heading of the exercises—however, to summarize:

(*a*) Be sure the pupil has a good 'm' or 'n'.

(*b*) Show in the mirror the position of the tongue for 'ng'.

(*c*) Show that it is a nasal sound (feeling the breath through the nose).

(*d*) Start with 'bang'. It is easier for the tongue to place itself in the 'ng' position after the vowel 'a'.

(*e*) Practice on this vowel preceding 'ng', i.e.

　　dang bang rang bang sang bang tang dang, &c.

(*f*) Practice other open sounds (not 'ing'):

　　　　bang the gong　　dang dong
　　　　She sang a song.

(*g*) Introduce 'ing' gradually:

Ding dong	Ring the bell
Dang dong	Ding dong
Bang the gong	Don't be long
Dang dong	Ding dong

(*h*) After much practice introduce the participle with 'ing' following an explosive consonant, e.g.

　　writing　reading　hopping　walking　pumping.

(*i*) 'Swimming', 'coming', 'running', &c., and especially 'singing' and 'banging' should be introduced when you are sure that the pupil can produce the sound at will.

The remaining faults cannot be grouped together. They are:

Under Consonants (13–14)

13. 'sh' for 's' or a faulty, unclear 's'.

The direction taken by the breath is incorrect here. It is escaping through the teeth at the sides of the mouth and not in a thin stream at the front. Awareness of breath and feeling this by the pupil help him to correct it.

(*a*) Let the pupil feel the breath both correctly and incorrectly produced.

(*b*) Let him see the position of the tongue in the mirror.

(*c*) Give the exercise 'th–s　th–s　th–s　th–s'.
This helps to bring the tongue and the breath to the correct position.

(*d*) Give the exercise 'a thin sound—a thinner sound'.

'the sea—the sea—the see-saw'.

(*e*) Practice 'sh' and emphasize the difference:

'she saw the see-saw'.

14. A faulty 'ch'—often almost like 'sh'.

If the pupil has a 'ch' of this kind, try showing him that the sound can be made by putting the mouth and tongue in position for 'sh' and then trying to say 't' at the same time. This is reversing the usual procedure ('t-sh') to 'sh-t'.

Take time for this and show that the tongue curls slightly and presses forward from the 'sh' position and that both the sounds are then said together.

Give diagrams for older pupils and use mirrors and breath indicators.

Under Vowels (5–6)

5. 'a' or something near it for 'e'.

'e' (as in 'pen') is one of the most difficult vowel sounds for deaf children to say correctly.

The mirror—diagrams—seeing the correct position—joining it always to a final consonant—hearing as much as possible are aids in its correction. The chief reasons for wrong production are:

(*a*) Mouth open too widely.

(*b*) Tongue not enough raised.

(*c*) Too slow a production.

The consonants I have found most helpful to link with the sound are 'n', 't', 'd', 'k', 'g', 's', 'r', 'sh', and 'l'.

You will notice that they involve movement of the tongue and so help the pupil to take up another tongue position.

Practise

ten den gen pen net met red neg ned nell
shen ken ren sen nesh neck ness len.

For too slow a production let the pupils clap for each word,

gradually quickening. Follow then with other consonants either
initially or finally:

> Ben—lend pen send fen, &c.
>
> Fetch a pen from the shelf.
>
> Lend me a pen please.
>
> Ten men went to mend a fence on Wednesday.
>
> Ten men went to mow a meadow.

6. 'ee' not clear: 'ee' is another of these difficult vowel sounds
for deaf children.

(a) Be sure that the tongue position is correct. Give diagrams
—use mirrors.

(b) Use hearing if at all possible.

(c) Let the pupil feel the jawline and just under the jaw at
the sides.

(d) Try 'g g g g g g ee g ee gee', feeling at the same time.

(e) Try 'z z z z ee ee zee zee'.

(f) These are the two most likely consonants to help the
pupil to feel the sound.

(g) I have known 'yee' and 'th-thee' to help but 'gee-gee'
has been most successful.

We have come to the end of the common faults I have
enumerated. You may meet others. Most of them can be
eliminated by following the exercises I have suggested and by
a use of seeing, feeling, and hearing as much as possible. I hope
that this chapter will help you to get good clear speech from
your pupils.

APPENDIX 2

INTONATION (SUMMARY)

THERE are some simple rules of English intonation that can be taught with advantage to deaf children. By the simple rules I mean the rules which the sentence as a whole follows, ignoring for the time being the other factors which modify these rules, e.g. emphasis.

There are two main tunes to teach the children.

Tune I which starts high or rises very quickly after an unaccented syllable and falls at the end

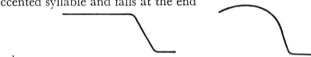

and

Tune II which starts high, falls, and rises at the end.

A child with any perception of hearing can be taught these two tunes, and the main language forms which belong to each group. Here they are:

Tune I

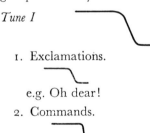

1. Exclamations.

e.g. Oh dear!

2. Commands.

e.g. Come here!

3. An answer to a question in:

(a) A phrase.

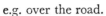

e.g. over the road.

(*b*) Yes or No.

e.g. Yes, No.

(*c*) Yes, I have, &c.

(*d*) I don't know.

(*e*) I did. He has two. It is blue. There are five.

4. A question beginning with 'What, Who, Where, Why, Which, Whose, How', &c. (*not* a verb or part of a verb):

e.g. What is your name?

5. A simple statement.

e.g. I went to the park last night.

Tune II

1. Requests.

e.g. Please come here.

Do you mind opening the door?

2. Questions beginning with a verb or part of a verb.

e.g. Are you sure? Do you like sugar?

3. Shortened question. Used as a response, or at the end of statements.

e.g. Is it?   Are you?   Have you?   Will you?

Both tunes

Tune II for the first statement and Tune I for the second.

1. Double statements

  (*a*) With 'but' and 'and':

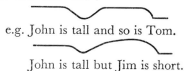

     e.g. John is tall and so is Tom.

     John is tall but Jim is short.

  (*b*) With 'while':

     e.g. John was playing while Jim was working.

In complex sentences the procedure is varied.

  1. Sentences containing noun clauses follow the same rule as in compound sentences, for the thought expressed by the principal clause is not finished, e.g.

  (*a*) I told him that I could not come.

  (*b*) He asked me if I knew where she lived.

  2. Sentences containing adverbial clauses (time, place, manner) and conditional clauses.

At the end of the principal sentence the voice is dropped (Tune I) whether this sentence introduces the complex sentence or not, e.g.

  (*a*) When father takes his spade to dig, then Robin comes along.

  (*b*) Robin comes along when father takes his spade to dig.

  Note: When the adverbial clause introduces the complex sentence it is much higher in pitch than when it ends it.

3. Sentences containing adjectival clauses.

Speaking generally the voice is dropped at the end of the complex sentence, i.e. Tune I comes at the end.

Peter is the boy who broke the window.

Tune II is used for the first sentence and/or for the interpolated sentence.

A man who makes tables and chairs is called a carpenter.

PRINTED IN GREAT BRITAIN
AT THE UNIVERSITY PRESS, OXFORD
BY CHARLES BATEY, PRINTER TO THE UNIVERSITY